The Dawn of Redemption

What the Books of Ruth and Yonah

Teach about Alienation, Despair and Return

THE DAWN OF REDEMPTION

WHAT THE BOOKS OF RUTH AND YONAH
TEACH ABOUT ALIENATION, DESPAIR AND RETURN

BY RABBI DR. MEIR LEVIN

URIM PUBLICATIONS

Jerusalem • New York

The Dawn of Redemption: What the Books of Ruth and Yonah Teach
About Alienation, Despair and Return
By Meir Levin
Copyright © 2009 by Meir Levin

Printed in Israel. First Edition.
ISBN-13: 978-965-524-022-1
Urim Publications
P.O. Box 52287, Jerusalem 91521 Israel

Lambda Publishers Inc.
527 Empire Blvd., Brooklyn, New York 11225 U.S.A.
Tel: 718-972-5449 Fax: 718-972-6307, mh@ejudaica.com

www.UrimPublications.com

DEDICATIONS

❧ ❧

❧ ❧

לזכרון עולם
משפחותינו האניג מעיר מונקאטש
שנספו על קידוש השם בשנות הזעם

רב ישראל דוב בן ר' שלום יוסף
י' מרחשון תשי"ה

חיה בת ר' דוד
ג' סיון תשי"ד

צבי אריה בן ר' ישראל דוב
יעקב בן ציון בן ר' ישראל דוב
שלום יוסף בן ר' ישראל דוב
ג' סיון תשי"ד

הי"ד ת.נ.צ.ב.ה.

☙ ❧

לזכרון עולם
משפחותינו Frankfurt מעיר ראצפערט
שנספו על קידוש השם בשנות הזעם

רב יוסף מרדכי בן ר' משה
פרימעט בת ר' קלונימוס אריה
קלומינוס אריה בן ר' יוסף מרדכי
אשר אנשיל בן ר' יוסף מרדכי
אפרים בן ר' יוסף מרדכי
פנחס אלימלך בן ר' יוסף מרדכי
שאול ישעיה בן ר' יוסף מרדכי
חיים אליהו בן ר' יוסף מרדכי
שמואל צבי בן ר' יוסף מרדכי
בילה בת ר' יוסף מרדכי

כ"ג אייר ת.נ.צ.ב.ה.

৯৯ ৯৯

זכרון עולם לנשמת

מרת יהודית זוסמן ע"ה
בת ר' ישראל דוב הי"ד

אשת חיל עקרת ביתה
אוד מוצל מאש

יראת ה' אוצרה,
אמונה פשוטה מעוזה
היטיבה לזולתה בהצנע,
צדקה וחסד הרבתה
ותיקה בשמירת המצוות,
ורדפה שלום כל ימיה
דרכיה סללה בכיבוד התורה
והחזקת לומדיה
יסוריה בשנות הזעם
קבלה בהכנעה ובדומיה
תמכה וחזקה צאצאיה
להתרוממם במעלות התורה

נלב"ע ביום כ"ו תמוז תשס"ז

৯৯ ৯৯

CONTENTS

YONAH

APPROBATIONS OF THE AUTHOR'S PREVIOUS WORKS:

Reading your manuscript gave me great pleasure. It clarifies basic and fundamental aspects of Judaism. You actually covered many *yesodei ha-das* which greatly help those who are searching for the truth....

May it be His will that you accomplish your goal to bring merit to many with this endeavor.

Rabbi Shmuel Kaminetsky, Shlita, Dean
Talmudic Yeshiva of Philadelphia

■ ■ ■ ■

Meir Levin has produced a work amazing in its fullness and depth of scholarship. He penetrates to the very roots of the subject while displaying a familiarity with all that has been said about this topic for the last thousand years....

My wish for the author is that he witness the fulfillment of the prayer of King David, "And may the pleasantness of Hashem be upon us: And the work of our hands be established for us; indeed, the work of our hands be His establishment."

Rabbi Yechiel Perr, Rosh Yeshiva
Derech Ayson Rabbinical Seminary.

■ ■ ■ ■

I bless him that he should be successful in all his pursuits, continue to honor the name of Heaven both in his Torah and his work, from Fear of Heaven....

Rabbi Mordechai Willig, Rosh Yeshiva and Rosh Kollel
Rabbi Isaac Elchanan Theological Seminary

I am pleased to speak in praise of this very worthy individual, Rabbi Meir Levin, whom I have known for a very long time… and he is a great scholar and descends in clarity to the depth of Torah teachings and he has the ability to transmit words of Torah in an organized and clear manner….

Rabbi Isroel Simcha Shorr, Rosh Yeshiva
Ohr Somayach, Monsey

■ ■ ■ ■

I can underscore that which all who know R. Meyer Levin are aware of. He is an odom ne'eman, a trustworthy person of absolute integrity. A man who undertakes his holy work with great trepidation and yiras shamayim, whose motives are purely le-hagdil Torah u-le-ha'adirah…. R. Meyer personifies that which the gemara in Masechet Temurah so cherishes, those who we confer upon them the title Ish Eshkolos, ish she-hakol bo. A man of versatility who is learned enough and talented enough to excel in many different areas, R. Meyer has earned the title profoundly. Combined with his humble posture and soft-spoken manner he is indeed someone who is eminently qualified to undertake a project of this sort.

Rabbi Moshe Faskowitz, Rosh Yeshiva
Yeshiva Madreigas ha-Adam

■ ■ ■ ■

These rabbanim have not reviewed and are not commenting on the current work, The Dawn of Redemption: What the Books of Ruth and Yonah Teach about Alienation, Despair and Return.

FOREWORD

THE MATERIAL PRESENTED in this book first appeared in serialized form on Torah.org. The thoughtful exposition of moral, psychological and devotional issues about topics that we all consider as we seek meaning and understanding of ourselves and our Creator attracted much comment and discussion among the thousands of readers who followed it week by week.

I am delighted that Rabbi Levin undertook the task of re-editing and publishing his writings in order to bring them to an even wider audience in print. I am also humbled that he requested a few words of introduction from me when his published works have already won a great deal of approbation from leading Torah scholars.

Rabbi Yakov Menken, Torah.org

PREFACE

WE ARE IN TROUBLE. Modernity has brought alienation, a sense of absurdity and feelings of despair to contemporary humanity. Yet it is not only that human beings feel alone in a meaningless world. Bereft of faith in a Higher Being, they also struggle with disorientation in the social sphere. People do not know where to belong. What does it mean to be member of a family, a people or a civilization if we are here by chance, if no specific purpose brought us to this point, to these people, to this belief system, to this culture and sense of values? Nothing matters or makes sense. Meaninglessness corrodes heritage as mercilessly as it corrupts religion.

Modern people often think that ancient teachings do not address their concerns since, as they believe, these teachings stem from assumptions and experiences that are far removed from their own. Could Biblical characters, living in a homogenous community of faith, secure in the value of their clan, tribe, society and ruler possibly understand the mindset of the modern, twenty–first-century human being? Certainly, we reason, the Bible has nothing to tell us about belonging, common purpose, society, family and tradition.

However, nothing can be farther from the truth. Tanach, an eternal work with a Divine message, has something to say to all audiences and to all times. It may be surprising to some to learn that these existentialist issues occupied the Prophets, who thought and wrote a great deal about them. As is the case with all sacred writings, belonging or not belonging, tribal loyalty vs. a universalist ethic, the burdens of family traditions vs. individual freedom, the demands of God vs. personal autonomy – are all amply reflected in the Torah. However, these subjects are not discussed as philosophical matters. Although they may take the form of a story or a poetic reflection, a nuanced detail within a narrative or an indirect turn of phrase, nevertheless they exist, they are prominent, they speak to us and they are backed by the authority of Holy Writ. However, they require interpretation, a listening ear and an understanding heart. Among the Biblical books, two in particular contain a great deal of such material. They are the books of Ruth and Jonah.

This work is an interpretation of what these two Biblical books say about these topics. I focus on each book separately without attempting to reconcile them, for their messages are not spoken in the same form. Each one must be considered separately because they deal with distinct facets of the same question. As we may surmise, the Book of Ruth explores man – or, in this case, woman among others, friendship, nationhood and family in the context of redemption and return. Ruth teaches us that there is no such thing as "man is as he is," that every individual is a part of a much greater picture in the larger frame of loss, redemption and identity.

The Book of Jonah, on the other hand, is a story of an individual's flight from the Divine, of rejection of the world that appears so arbitrary and unfair. It tells of throwing off the burdens of a Divine claim to justice in a world that is so obviously unjust, so full of suffering and capriciousness.

Yet both books answer questions. This work is about the answers that we find when we engage in a careful consideration of the text and its message.

I am most grateful to Torah.org, which hosted the lectures from which it arose.

I thank the Honig, Sussman, and Borofsky families for their support, and the Levin family for their assistance in memory of Yitzhak ben Michoel Levin, OB"M.

My dear wife, who has been a source of strength and support, taught me a great deal about life and living, lessons which I now share with you. I thank all my teachers who taught me wisdom. Above all, I am profoundly grateful to the Ribbono shel Olam, whose kindness endures forever.

The French translation of this work was published by *Scrip*Torah and can be obtained at josecoh@gmail.com.

RUTH

THE BOOK OF RUTH:
THE DAWN OF REDEMPTION

Introduction

THE BOOK OF RUTH has great universal appeal. On the surface, it is the story of a young woman who leaves her family and nation to cast her lot with a people and religion that she has not previously known. Her purity of thought, noble behavior and charming character gain her the respect of the Judeans and the merit of being the progenitor of a royal dynasty. Readers identify with the risk that she took, are impressed by her dignity and refined bearing, and are drawn to her purity and strength of her faith. The book of Ruth leaves one with a sense of optimism, hope and trust, and a feeling of fulfillment and completion.

However, there is much more to the story of Ruth, for it is first and above all a story of redemption and restoration. It is precisely this element, which is explicitly identified at some times while only dimly surmised at others, that touches us, giving us a sense of identification with our own struggle against alienation and despair and our own longing for restoration and return. Ruth's story involves us so deeply because it is the story of our own lives. We also long to travel from the foreign land to the place of greater purpose and serene trust.

Like Ruth, we have traveled away from our Father, as the very name of Ruth's nation, Moab ("from the father" in Hebrew), hints. Like her, we long to reach the Promised Land. The Book of Ruth teaches us that personal redemption must occur within a family, community, and nation rather than in isolation. Our families, national identities and cultural backgrounds nurture and shape us. Yet even if these given circumstances are personal limitations, we can still rise above them, use them, and approach God together with others. Ruth became the ancestor of kings because of her kindness and devotion to others. The way does not lead from Moab but rather into Judea, not by leaving society behind but by joining it, and the means to redemption within a community is kindness. R. Zeira said, "This scroll contains neither laws of purity or impurity nor what is permitted or forbidden. Why then was it written? To teach the reward of those who deal kindly with others" (*Yalkut Shimoni Ruth*, 601).

Although the Book of Ruth is a story of redemption, it is a complex story that contains three interconnected circles. The first is the seed of Elimelech returning to his people. Elimelech and his sons had left his nation, but his widow, daughter-in-law and their eventual offspring return. The second circle is the return of Lot's daughter to her rightful position in the family of Abraham. Lot's branch of the family had descended into licentiousness and carnality (see Genesis 19), separating itself from Abraham's messianic destiny for humanity. It now returns through Ruth and, later on, through David. Like all return journeys, this one was not easy and required struggle. Traces of their Moabite heritage remained a stumbling block for Ruth's descendants, David and Solomon, whose spiritual task was to cleanse themselves of the remnants of Lot's daughters' legacy. Unrestrained lust, inherent in the family's Moabite roots, destroyed the lives of three of David's sons – Adonijah, Amnon, and Absalom – while Solomon married many wives who turned his heart away from God. David himself underwent the trials of Michal, Abigail and, of course, Bathsheba. Knowing David's ancestry enables us to better appreciate his ultimate success in overcoming these temptations.

This book teaches us another lesson – that redemption requires separation. Ruth kissed Naomi and went with her to her future, while Orpah kissed Naomi and returned to her past. The Sages tell us that Orpah became Lot's daughter again that very night, cohabiting with one hundred men. It was during those encounters that she conceived Goliath, who eventually faced Ruth's descendant, David, in combat.

We face choices every day of our lives, and these choices have consequences. Even as we reclaim and redeem, we also must reject. This is not an easy process and has many potential pitfalls. Although God helps us in this daily struggle, it remains *our* struggle. No amount of Divine assistance will allow us to escape our duty to face the truth that we know but that the heart does not reveal to the mind. Before redemption comes separation: of good from evil, of that which can be redeemed from that which must be rejected and abandoned.

The third element is the Messianic redemption, which stands at the fulcrum of history. Mystics teach us that the three syllables of Adam stand for the three stages of human history – A for Adam, D for David and M for the Messiah. The redemption of Ruth is thus a parable for the entire panorama of human history, and this element is close to the surface of the text.[1]

Our approach to the Book of Ruth must differ from our approach to the Book of Jonah, which this book also contains. While there are few traditional commentaries on Jonah, we are fortunate to possess several midrashic works on Ruth. Our task, therefore, will be less to innovate than to uncover the profound wisdom of the Sages, who spoke in parables and allusions. Our study of Ruth will be an opportunity to learn how to draw from the wellsprings of rabbinic literature. I hope that as I attempt to draw up these deep, living waters, our Sages' wisdom and righteousness will impress you as much as it continues to impress me.

Let us speak first of the second cycle, which connects and binds the other two themes of redemption.

Lot's Failure

When Lot, Abraham's nephew and his faithful companion in Canaan and Egypt, chose to abandon his uncle's family, he left a void that remained unfilled for many generations. Abraham was childless and Lot was to be his heir. What would his position have been had he remained with Abraham? Although we cannot know this with certainty, it is likely that Lot would have continued to play an important role even after Abraham was granted children. Surely God would have retained a place of greatness for Lot, Abraham's devoted associate, in His plan.

Unfortunately, that is not how things turned out. Lot rejected the Abrahamic covenant, choosing the verdant valleys of wicked Sodom. His seed became the two great temporal powers of Moab and Ammon, which lay outside and were hostile toward God's people and God's plan.

Yet God never despairs. His thoughts are beyond human reckoning. As the angels rushed Lot out of Sodom, they told him: "Arise, take your wife and the two daughters who are here, lest you be caught in the sin of the city"

---

[1] This series ran originally on Torah.org in the form of a commentary. It is only while preparing it for publication that I came across an article by Professor Yehudah Liebes entitled *"Sefer zaddik yesod olam"* in *Sod ha-emunah ha-shabta'it* (Jerusalem: 1995). In footnotes 21 and 22, he lists several obscure commentaries on Ruth that approach Ruth from a kabbalistic perspective as an esoteric account of redemption. Among them are *Megillat Setarim* by R. Moshe Chaim Luzzatto, *Benei Yitzhak* by Yitzhak Chanan, *Benei Yehuda* by Yitzhak Chabilio, *Migdal David* by R. Dovid Lida (some attribute the work to R. Chaim Kohen, one of the Ari's students), and *Zaddik yesod olam,* which is ascribed to the Ari. On the sources for this approach in the Zohar and the Ari's writings, see the discussion in that article. For a recent collection of essays that apparently draws upon these sources, see *A Pearl in the Sand: Reflections on Shavuos, Megillas Ruth and the Davidic Kingship* by Moshe M. Eisemann (1997 and 2005).

(Genesis 19:15). On this the Sages comment: "'Two daughters' – this refers to Ruth the Moabite and Na'amah the Ammonite" (who married Solomon, King of Israel [I Kings 14:21]). Similarly they say, in a statement that is also open to interpretation, "I found My servant David" (Psalms 89) "in Sodom" (*Genesis Rabbah* 50:15).

This is what *Shem mi-Shmuel* (Shavuot, 670) writes regarding this passage. "Royalty was not to be found in Israel and had to be imported from Moab… for the shell of Moab is arrogance (that hides within it true royalty of spirit and aristocracy of behavior), as is written, 'We heard the pride of Moab; he is exceedingly high'" (Isaiah 16:6). This is why the soul of David was caught in captivity within the shell of Moab so as to be able to liberate royalty from the trappings of arrogance and pride and to combine it with the holiness of "authority over others for the sake of Heaven."[2]

This suggestion follows the kabbalistic worldview that sees history as the process of drawing good out of evil, in which it is imprisoned as a fruit is enclosed within a peel. In our world, the good is often intermixed confusingly with evil, and our task as human beings is to draw out the good so that it can join the good that has already been separated from evil.

Moab could contribute yet another aspect to the trait of kingship in Israel. Lot took some of the kindness and graciousness of Abraham's house with him to Sodom, though he applied it wrongly. Although he risked his own life to protect his guests from the Sodomites, he was willing to deliver his own daughters to their abuse. His descendants, following the same pattern, displayed heartless insensitivity to their own cousins as they passed near their land in their time of need.

Therefore,

> An Ammonite or a Moabite shall not enter into the assembly of God; even to the tenth generation shall none of them enter into the assembly of God for ever; because they met you not with bread and with water in the way, when ye came forth out of Egypt; and because they hired Balaam the son of Beor from Pethor of Aram-naharaim against you, to curse you. (Deuteronomy 23:4, 5) [3]

As every administrator or manager knows, it is difficult for a ruler to apply mercy and severity in proper measure. A policy that benefits one group or population invariably hurts or deprives another.

---

[2] Probably quoting *Benei Yitzhak* 55a, see *Sefer ha-gilgulim* 1:2:9.
[3] In general, the quotes are from the JPS 1917 translation. I attempted to modernize the language and at times change it when it appeared to me to be inaccurate or mistaken.

Saul, the first king of Israel, failed on both of these scores – excessive humility, which is inappropriate for a king, and misapplied kindness. "Why was he punished? Because he forgave an insult to his honor" (Maharsha, *Yoma* 22b)." His "hiding among the vessels" almost led to Israel's destruction (1 Samuel 10). He was merciful to his enemies and merciless to his friends, sparing Agag, the king of Amalek, and persecuting his loyal servant David. His tragic inability to combine the use of power and kindness, of justice and mercy, was his downfall. "He who is merciful when he should be pitiless will end by being cruel when he should be merciful, and falls by the sword" (*Kohelet Rabbah* 7:36).

David's challenges were also twofold – to bring the aristocratic bearing of Moab into the Jewish monarchy and to use the kingly kindness that he inherited from his great-grandmother in proper balance with the ruthlessness that his office required. When he failed to keep a proper balance between the two, he was severely punished (see *Shabbos* 56a). That he ultimately succeeded is in great measure thanks to his noble ancestor, Ruth the Moabite.

Thus far, we concentrated on the ideas of redemption and restoration that operate just below the surface of the Book of Ruth. We focused in particular on how this descendant of Lot and of Eglon, King of Moab (*Sanhedrin* 105b), brought back certain qualities of kingship to the nation during the phase of its history known as "the times when the judges judged."

When the Sages say that Ruth is a daughter of Lot, they mean that she is his spiritual offspring. In terms of actual descent, she was his great-great-great granddaughter. The Sages also say that she was the grand-daughter of Eglon, the king of Moab (*Sanhedrin* 105).

The text itself corroborates Ruth's royal lineage. Elimelech and his sons are described as Ephratites, one translation of which is "princes." One would naturally then expect that even in Moab they would marry into the royal family. It follows that the women whom they married, Ruth and Orpah, would have been aristocrats. Besides, Ruth is a daughter of Lot in the wider sense, in that she inherited his destiny and mission. Ruth was Lot's spiritual descendant. Assuming that every nation has its own spiritual qualities, we may also say that she was Lot's daughter through her access to Moab's national spiritual legacy. Families as well as nations have different spiritual destinies.[4] On a deeper level, this refers to families that share a

---

[4] As Rav Yosef Dov Soloveitchik used to say: "The Torah views nations as families, as per "You only have I known of all the families of the earth; therefore I will visit upon you all your iniquities" (Amos 2:2, see also Genesis 12:3).

unique characteristic, something that non-family members do not possess. You might call it a soul, although this English word is too narrow, particular, and personal. The infusion of the Moabite quality of royalty prepared the ground, setting the stage for the eventual development and success of the monarchy in Israel.

What makes a successful ruler? Ancient philosophers thought that it was the ability to maintain a balance between opposites – compassion and steadiness, strategic expansiveness and tactical vision, national priorities and individual needs (see *Kuzari* 3). Beyond that, a Jewish king must be able to be both a follower and a leader – a leader of his people and a follower of God's law and the voice of His prophets. Saul failed in this. David excelled because he inherited the ability to lead from Judah and the inclination to follow from Lot.

We all know that we carry our parents' legacy with us through life, sometimes as a burden, sometimes as a blessing. However, we often do not appreciate the extent of our indebtedness to the generations that preceded us. The simple fact is that as families share similarities, inclinations and proclivities – so do nations. Some call these assortments of qualities "national character" while others appeal to the collective unconscious of the entire human race, but, whatever they may be, these roots are deep, extending to the distant past, to the crucible out of which the nations arose. Some nations are by nature intolerant of authority and rule by consensus, while others crave direction and seek a heavy hand and control by a ruler or rulers (see the Netziv on Genesis 9:25). "There is a land that produces warriors and a land that produces weaklings" (Rashi on Numbers 13:18). It was known for many generations that one particular family in Judah produced powerful leaders.

> She said: "What, have you broken a path for yourself?" Therefore he called his name Peretz (Genesis 38:29).
>
> Saul said of David: "If he came from Peretz, he will rule, for a king breaks (*poretz*) a path for himself and no one can stop him. If he came from Zerach, he will merely be a prince. (*Yevamot* 76b)

A leader must forge his personal path without caring what others might say or think. On the other hand, leaders who cannot also follow often bring themselves and their people to disaster. These two manners of behavior must be in balance. Witness the results when the later kings of Judah refused to follow in the ways of the Lord.

A reader of Ruth is struck by the opacity and mysteriousness of her character. She never expresses doubt or vacillation, never wavers or questions. No complaint escapes her lips. Unlike Naomi or Boaz, she speaks little and obeys. She follows Naomi to Bethlehem, walks after the reapers, carries out Naomi's instructions to meet Boaz on the threshing floor and then waits patiently for him "to arrange the matter." Even when she gives birth, the text tells us that "a child is born to Naomi." Ruth is the perfect follower. I do not mean to imply that she did not make brave and difficult choices; on the contrary, her steadiness and courage are exceptional and inspiring. However, her choices – whom to follow and where to direct her steps – were those of a follower rather than a leader. Ruth recognized her nature and wisely chose good role models, but she did not lead.

Lot was also a follower. At first he faithfully followed Abraham, going with him into the land of Egypt, where apparently the sophistication and hedonism of the Egyptians appealed to Lot. To his credit, he did not switch allegiance immediately, nor did he betray his uncle and aunt. It must have been a deed of great courage for a "follower" to withstand the temptation to assimilate into the majority culture, but he resisted for a time, and for this he was greatly rewarded. "God remembered that Lot knew that Sarah was Abraham's wife and he heard that Abraham represented her as his sister but he did not reveal it, for he cared for him. Therefore, God had mercy on Lot" (Rashi on Genesis 19:29).[5] However, Lot had already decided in his heart. It was Egypt, or something like Egypt, for him. After they returned from Egypt, Lot settled in Sodom, a place "like the garden of God, like the land of Egypt" (Genesis 13:10). Yet although he sat at the city gates, his attempts at leadership failed, for he was and remained a follower.

In order to understand this aspect of Lot, we must look at his father, Haran, Abraham's brother, who was also a follower.

> Terach (the father of both Abram and Haran) complained about Abram to Nimrod because his son had smashed the idols. Nimrod threw Abraham into a fiery furnace. Haran sat and said to himself: "If Abram wins, I will follow him. If Nimrod wins, I will follow him." When Abram was miraculously saved, they asked Haran, "To

---

[5] Abraham was a self-made man. He broke completely with his family and left his birthplace at God's command. He had nothing to transmit to his children except for his passionate love of God, and as we know by experience, this particular passion does not transmit well in isolation. He therefore remained childless. It took a miracle and a change of name to enable him to transform his burning passion and love for God into a tradition that he could transmit to his offspring. Lot was supposed to have corrected this deficiency by augmenting the Abrahamitic heritage with the capacity to follow – that is, to live and function in a community. His departure created a gap that was not filled until the advent of Ruth.

whose party do you belong?" He said, "Abram's." They threw him into the furnace and he was consumed. (*Genesis Rabbah* 38:12)

The Sages picked up here on something basic and essential that allows us to appreciate the extent of Abraham's break with his sterile past, which is represented by his name change from Abram to Abraham. "Abram cannot father children but Abraham will father children" (Rashi on Genesis 14:5). This extra-Biblical story is not a fanciful invention that aims to fill in a gap in our knowledge of Abraham's family or to resolve exegetical difficulties. Rather, it is an excellent example of how the Rabbis taught profound psychology and theology in simple garb. This insight into the difference between Abraham and his family also allows us to understand what the Sages say about Terach, who was also a follower. He first obeyed Nimrod and later followed Abraham to the land of Canaan. Abraham, the iconoclast, pressed forward in pursuit of his unique destiny, rejecting his family's beliefs and lifestyle. However, without the ability to follow, one cannot build a nation. Abraham was not a follower. It was Lot's task to preserve the character trait of "following" in Abraham's family.

The crucial ability to follow was to have been Lot's contribution to Israel's destiny. When Lot left Abraham's covenant, it threatened to be lost forever. God restored it through Lot's descendant, Ruth. Mixed with the courage and independence of Peretz, it set the stage for the emergence of David, who led his people in God's ways. May we merit, speedily and in our day, to see his descendant, who "will teach us of [God's] ways and we shall walk in His paths, for Torah will come from Zion and the word of God from Jerusalem" (Isaiah 2:3).

The Setting, or What Ruth Found in Judea

It came to pass when the judges judged....

The Book of Ruth opens with a description of a time "when the judges judged." Such an introduction aims to explain something about the time in which the events described in the book took place and therefore provides important background.

Rabbinic sources have the following to say about this first verse (Petihta to *Ruth Rabbah* 2):

[At the time after the division of the land by Joshua], the land became precious to them. One person busied himself with his field and another with his vineyard, still another with his doorpost.... They refrained from dealing kindness to Joshua [at his burial] and the Holy One, blessed be He, thought to shake up the entire world [i.e., became angry], as it is written, "The earth was shaken up and disturbed" (Psalms 18).

Woe to the generation that judges its judges! When the judge said: "Remove a splinter from between your teeth," the accused would say, "First remove the beam from between your own eyes" (*Bava Batra* 15b; see also *Ruth Rabbah* 5:10).

This is a description of anarchy. Rather than say, "In those days there was no king in Israel; everyone did what was right in his own eyes" (Judges 21:24), which describes only the political situation, the Book of Ruth recounts it in a way that emphasizes its effect on individuals. It was a time – perhaps similar to the time in which we ourselves live – when people distrusted authority, avoided communal obligations, and held their private lives to be superior to and more valuable than public life. In those days, as in ours, the leaders' faults attracted far more attention than their virtues did. The Israelites were occupied, each with his own little plot of land and his own vineyard, jealously guarding the doorpost of his own private world from intruders.

In such times, leaders are seen not as noble individuals who sacrifice selflessly for the common good, but rather as opportunists who are tainted by self-interest and personal, and therefore petty, needs. If our leaders cannot be trusted, neither can our neighbors. Cynicism is corrosive. In an atmosphere of mutual suspicion it becomes difficult to view others benevolently and to behave with kindness and charity. Since the people felt that they owed Joshua nothing, they neglected to pay him last respects.

When there is no justice, there is also no sense of security, and everyone lives in fear and suspicion of their neighbors. Only this can explain how a prominent prince of the people, Elimelech, could abandon his community, including his extended family, at such a difficult time and go to another country where his material needs would be better met.

As we pointed out in the introduction, Ruth restored kindness to this era of anarchy. She certainly had reason to be bitter, suspicious and cynical. A young, childless widow, she had joined a nation she did not know, was still called a Moabite despite having left her people (2:5) and rejected as a marriage prospect (4:6). Yet she trusts Naomi implicitly and believes that Boaz will act according to the noble ideas that he appears to embody. It is not easy to trust others when the very air reeks of pseudo-sophisticated cynicism, where everyone mocks whatever they regard as naiveté and foolishness.

Nevertheless, there is a redemptive quality in the deliberate refusal to live negatively. It inspires and often brings out the best in others. It also sets the stage for the final redemption, which is one of the lessons of the Book of Ruth.

Parallel Universes

Those who have not been exposed to rabbinic literature may have noticed by now that the Rabbis teach through parable and allusion. Why did they not use simple, straightforward exposition? One reason for this is the pedagogical imperative. It is well known that the best way to learn is through a story. The Rabbis painted a colorful world of relationships, events and connections so that we could perceive and accept some fairly complex ideas. It is quite clear that the Sages had traditions regarding the intended significance of every story and character in the Bible. To this end, they went beyond what is directly described in the Scriptures, leaving us images, stories and characterizations that palpably embody major teachings passed down by tradition.

I do not mean to imply here that midrashic stories are not historical. They are always eminently plausible and can usually be seen to reside in the verses, present within them by hint or allusion. They always contain a kernel of historical truth. Nevertheless, a question remains: "Why did the Sages choose to share this particular story with us rather than some other one?" Proper understanding of the midrashic method calls for proper appreciation of its message. One starts to study Midrash by discovering the key, the underlying idea or interpretation that is central to various and sometimes disparate rabbinic comments.

I hope that at this point my readers are convinced that that the Sages understand the Book of Ruth as teaching the workings of redemption in history. First, there is the idea is that good and evil are mixed in this world, much as twilight is a mixture of light and darkness. Redemption consists of separation of good and evil, of light and darkness, and this occurs when we make correct moral choices. On the national level, this process may take generations, each generation in its own unique circumstances replaying the drama of its forebears. Step by step the good is rewarded and set apart from the bad until only pure evil remains, which is then destroyed. To drive this point home, the Sages often trace patterns that are not literally in Scriptures, though they are reasonable, plausible and make exegetic sense.

Let us look at how this principle works regarding the characters of Ruth and Orpah. I will list a number of rabbinic comments side by side with minimal discussion.

1. Ruth and Orpah were sisters. This implies that they faced the same choice.

> Ruth and Orpah were descendants of Eglon, king of Moab (*Ruth Rabbah* 2:9) Ruth was also the descendant of Eglon, the son of Balak (*Sotah* 47a).

2. Although Balak was evil, he did some good and it was rewarded.

> As a reward for the forty-two sacrifices that he offered, he merited that Ruth would descend from him (Sotah 47a).

3. His descendant, Eglon, another king of Moab, also did some good that merited reward.

> God said to Eglon: "Because you rose from your throne to honor me, I swear that you will have a descendant [David] who will sit on my throne" (*Ruth Rabbah* 2:9)

4. Orpah followed the same pattern. Although, unlike Ruth, she did not go beyond the honor that her ancestors gave to the Almighty, she was also rewarded for it.

> In the merit of the four tears that Orpah spilled for her mother-in-law, four mighty fighters descended from her (*Sotah* 42b).

Although Balak, Eglon and Orpah do not move beyond what they as Gentiles were expected to do, they (or rather their descendants) are rewarded with another chance. However, after three tries the process stops. The warriors who descended from Orpah, Goliath among them, represent complete and unadulterated evil and are destined to fall by the hand of the anointed king, David.

Thus, early in the book of Ruth we encounter three characters who fail to fulfill their personal, familial or national process of redemption and two who succeed. As descendants of Er, son of Judah, Machlon and Kilyon could have rectified the sin of Er and Onan who "did not wish to give seed to their brother." However, they were stingy and did not share their wealth with their brothers in Bethlehem. They chose flight over sharing, and so they perished. Ruth redeemed them when she pursued levirate marriage to Boaz.

Orpah could have rectified the sin of her ancestors, the kings of Moab. When she turned back, she gave up that opportunity, and she was lost.

Ruth and Boaz rose to the challenge. Boaz was a descendant of Peretz, the son of Yehuda and Tamar. By descent and constitution, Ruth was a daughter of Lot. It would have been natural for Ruth and Boaz to repeat the patterns of the past but they did not. Instead, when they met on the threshing floor, they rose to the pinnacle of spirituality, assuring their personal portion within the sacred and the spiritual future of their descendants.

Every man and woman exists within this continuum of heredity and tradition. Each family and nation is given their allotted number of chances. This is as true of individual failings as of communal ones. "So also all these God does, two or three times with man" (Job 33:29) (see also Maimonides, Laws of Repentance 3:5).

To summarize, a careful correlation of various sayings of the Sages scattered among disparate midrashic sources leads us to several conclusions. First, the Sages possessed a tradition of interpretation, a set of exegetical keys widely shared across sources that were remote from one another in time and space. Second, they expressed and transmitted this tradition by setting up a parallel universe populated by the same characters from the books of Tanach, but with richer detail and background. (All such detail is designed to reinforce and transmit the received interpretative approach and a specific set of teachings.) Finally, echoes of many of these teachings can be found in the later books of the Kabbala, which also deals with substantive questions of meaning and purpose, albeit from a more explicit perspective.

Ambiguity and Authority in the Book of Ruth

> It came to pass, in the days when the judges judged, that there was a famine in the land. A certain man of Bethlehem in Judah went to sojourn in the plain of Moab together with his wife and two sons. The name of the man was Elimelech, the name of his wife Naomi, and the names of his two sons were Mahlon and Chilion, Ephrathites of Bethlehem in Judah. They came to the plain of Moab and sojourned there. Elimelech, Naomi's husband, died, and she was left with her two sons, who took wives from among the women of Moab. The name of one was Orpah and the name of the other was Ruth, and they dwelt there about ten years. Both Mahlon and Chilion died, and the woman was bereft of her two children and of her husband. Then she arose with her daughters-in-law that she might return from the plain of Moab, for she had heard in the plain of Moab that God had remembered His people by giving them bread.

A great deal happens in the first five verses of Ruth. Famine, exile, death, bereavement and loss – these are trials that test the souls of human beings, stretching our capacities to the breaking point. Where is God in all this?

Absent! His name does not even come up until the sixth verse, "for she heard that God had remembered His people by giving them bread."

Were all these tragedies a punishment for some sin or were they only a few more mishaps among the many that accompany our lives in this world? If we were reading this story elsewhere rather than in the Bible, would we recall that Providence directs and supervises all things? How different is the introduction to the story of Ruth from that of most other Biblical books, in which God is from the outset an active, determining and omnipresent force! Compare it to the introduction to the story of Job. There, from the outset, we know who is behind the scenes, deciding, planning and arranging matters. It is as if the narrator of the Book of Ruth wished to conceal the Director. In this matter-of-fact retelling of events with no direct attribution to God, the Book of Ruth most resembles the Book of Esther and no other Biblical book.

Closer inspection reveals that deliberate ambiguity is a feature of this story. In fact, such ambiguity is prominent throughout the Book of Ruth. In a recent article,[6] Mordechai Cohen points out a number of other such examples, among them the one in 2:20. As background, in 2:20 Boaz has just recognized Ruth as a relative and instructed his lads to help her glean in his fields. Since Hebrew does not use capitals, both of the following translations are possible and correct.

> Naomi said to her daughter-in-law, "Blessed be he of the Lord, for he did not abandon his kindness to the living and to the dead."

> Naomi said to her daughter-in-law, "Blessed be he to the Lord, Who did not abandon His kindness to the living and to the dead."

See the difference. The first reading praises Boaz for his kindness while the second one praises God. Ambiguity! Also, look at the following verse:

> It so happened that Ruth happened to come to the portion of the field that belonged to Boaz (2:3).

Readers of the story are struck with wonder. Was it really a coincidence that Ruth just happened to arrive at the field that was owned by her future husband? Surely the narrator does not mean it as it reads, for such a reading disagrees with the overall context of the canon. Nevertheless, it is surely not accidental.

---

[6] Cohen, Mordechai. "Hesed: Divine or Human? The Syntactic Ambiguity of Ruth 2:20." In *Hazon Nachum: Studies in Jewish Law, Thought and History,* edited by Y. Elman and J.S. Gurock. Ktav, Jersey City, NJ: 1977.

These verses are emblematic of the narrative's intentional ambiguity. On one hand, the hand of God is so evident that it cannot be denied, while on the other, the Author deliberately hides Himself in expressions and semantic structures that suggest randomness and chance.

In this, the Book of Ruth reflects life itself. At times, God is as distant as heaven is from earth, though at other times, He is as close as our own breath. These two perspectives are concurrent and complementary, and we oscillate between them in an attempt to understand and overcome the challenges of religious life.

AMONG THE FAMILY

Elimelech

THE BOOK OF RUTH opens with the presentation of several characters. Such early introduction to the "players" is quite unusual in Biblical writing. Much more common is the pattern in which single characters are introduced and their immediate and more distant forebears are listed and described, after which the characters' own stories are related. The focus is usually on one person rather than on the group. It follows, therefore, that these characters must be important in setting the tone and outlining the theme of the book.

Now it is true that Machlon, Kilyon, and Elimelech pass quickly from the scene and Orpah follows them soon afterwards. Yet they throw a long shadow over the entire story. As we explained in the introduction, the restoration of Elimelech's seed by Boaz through levirate marriage to Ruth constitutes the first redemptive cycle of the book. This is why Elimelech and his family are introduced at the story's very beginning.

Who was Elimelech? The text does not tell us but the Sages do, and so, we will engage in "reverse engineering," trying to grasp how they understood this complex personality and then to appreciate how they came to their interpretation. We will not focus on the details as much as on the concepts behind their exegesis. We must be aware that the Sages taught in "riddles and parables" (Proverbs 1:2) and that our task is to translate and restate their message in the conceptual language that we use today.

Although the clues are scarce, the first one is Elimelech's name itself. We assume that names of Biblical characters are not accidental but reflect the essence of their bearers' task or destiny, or that they memorialize significant events of their lives and the life of the nation. This makes perfect sense when we consider that certain Biblical individuals were called by several different names during their lifetimes and could receive new names at any time. There were no central registries or even surnames at the time, and names served a much more fluid purpose then than they do today.

For example: "He called his name Noach, meaning, 'He will give us comfort (*yinahamenu*)'" (Genesis 5:29). Here the name reflects the man's essence. Another example: "The name of one was Peleg, for in his days the entire world became divided (*niflega*)" (Genesis 10:25). This name was given in memory of the Dispersion that occurred after the Tower of Babel episode, which happened during Peleg's lifetime. "The ancestors, since they knew their genealogies, would derive names from events. We, who are not certain of our genealogies, derive names from our ancestors. Rabbi Shimon ben Gamliel said: The ancestors who used the power of Divine Inspiration drew names from [future] events; we who do not have access to Divine Inspiration draw names from our forebears" (*Genesis Rabbah* 37:7).

What does the name Elimelech mean? Ordinarily it would be translated as "My God is King." However, the Sages read it with a slight difference in pronunciation as *elai* (to me) *melech* – "For he said, 'Kingship is due to me'" (*Ruth Rabbah* 2:5). What could have led them to this interpretation? It seems that they are pointing out a certain disconnect between the bearer's name and his behavior. Would someone who truly believes that his God is King abandon his people during a famine? It must be that the name is not as noble as it may at first appear. In addition, they may have asked why a private individual would carry a name that signifies royalty. We know of Abimelech, son of the leader Gideon, and Abimelech, the King of Gerar. The name of Achimelech, the High Priest who gave aid to David at Nob, reflects his elevated stature (*Leviticus Rabbah* 1:3) and Malchizedek was the king of Salem (Malkiel in Numbers 25:24 deserves a separate discussion). When kings ruled, "My God is King," denoted not only political but also spiritual power. "Gideon said to them: I shall not rule over you and my son shall not rule over you. God shall rule over you" (Judges 8:22).

The second clue that this name is significant comes from how the verse presents it. It purposely draws our attention to it, for it first tells us that "a man went out" and then tells us that "the man's name was Elimelech." The usual pattern is the reverse; first we are told a man's name and familial antecedents and only then about his actions. Here a gap exists between the man and what he called himself.

Finally, the description of Elimelech's departure is sparse, bereft of detail. This suggests that the Narrator was not happy with this character, for when God approves of a journey, it, the participants, their families, and even their livestock are described in loving detail (See Ezra 2:66–67, after the commentary *Nachalat Yosef*).

The resolution to these irregularities is primarily exegetical. The Sages reasoned that Elimelech must have misread his destiny, thinking that he would be king. He was correct that kingship would come from his offspring; yet he was also wrong, for he himself was not fit to become king of Israel. Instead, it was God who demonstrated His sovereignty by bringing about the chain of events that led to the establishment of the Israelite monarchy.

Apparently Elimelech abandoned his people because they scorned their leaders. They rejected him as they had rejected Joshua. While he was right to respond to their rejection in kind, nevertheless his response may have contained a personal element.

"The man's name was Elimelech. How did Elimelech know that strict justice was [rampant] in the world? When he saw that his generation scorned great men, he said, 'Surely I shall depart from here so that I will not be caught among them'" (*Zohar Hadash* 77a).

Elimelech was one of the great men in Israel. When the years of famine came he said, "Now all of them will come to my doorpost, each with his begging cup in his hand. He arose and fled from them" (*Ruth Rabbah* 1:4). Apparently he was willing to help, but only if he wore the mantle of authority.

Is this the behavior of a leader who loves and cares for his people, even if they do not fully deserve his respect?

Ezekiel castigates the leaders of Israel as being "foxes in the ruins" (10:3). The Midrash explains:

> What does a fox watch out for in the ruins? When it sees people coming, it immediately runs away. You, the leaders, did not stand among the ruins as Moses did. What was Moses like? He was like a faithful shepherd whose corral fence fell as darkness approached. He stood and surrounded it with rebuilt walls from three directions. A space remained that he did not manage to rebuild. He stood in the opening and blocked it with his body. A lion approached and he fought off the lion. A wolf approached and he fought the wolf. You, leaders, did not stand at the opening like Moses. Had you done so, you would have been able to even withstand God's anger. (*Petihta Ruth Rabbah* 5)

Elimelech appears to have been a man of faith who was unable or perhaps unwilling to be completely faithful. He possessed all the qualities of leadership except for deep love and concern for his people and disregard for his own worthiness and rights. Even if he was not fully aware of this failing, God was.

Can we dismiss the sincerity of members of the clergy who do not always live up to their convictions? On the other hand, can we forgive and excuse their deficiencies and the harm that they cause?

While humans cannot see beyond these two alternatives, God has another choice. He deals out divine justice, punishing evil and rewarding the good. Although Elimelech was punished for his failings, the good within him was preserved and rewarded, allowing him to become the progenitor of Israel's royal line.

Machlon and Kilyon

The Book of Ruth also tells us almost nothing about Machlon and Kilyon. We read that they were the sons of Elimelech and Naomi and the husbands of Ruth and Orpah. Besides that, we know almost nothing about them. However, the Sages made their remarkable names the starting point of their interpretation. These Hebrew names imply so much that no serious interpreter can afford to overlook them. In Hebrew, Machlon invokes either forgiveness or dissipation and profanation, while Kilyon is clearly derived from the Hebrew word for destruction.

The first meaning of Machlon is expounded in the following passage.

> Machlon was called so because the Holy One, blessed be He, ultimately forgave him because he opposed his father's plan and strove with [or against] him for justice. Kilyon was so called because he was wiped completely from the world…. Ruth, the wife of Machlon, joined the Jewish people because God forgave him, so that his name is remembered. Orpah, the wife of Kilyon, did not join the Jewish people, for God destroyed Kilyon and his name was not remembered in Israel. (*Zohar Hadash* 71a)

The translation that is explicated here follows the first meaning of the name Machlon – that is, forgiveness. The full significance of the statement that we just read will become clearer as we proceed. For now, note how the meanings of the names serve as a key to interpreting the entire story of Ruth.

When the text gives us too little information from which to form a larger interpretative picture, recourse to wider context and other Biblical sources becomes imperative. Look at how the following Talmudic passage exemplifies this exegetical technique. I do not mean to imply, God forbid, that the Sages' interpretations are not based on ancient tradition but merely ask you to put that position aside temporarily in an attempt to learn from the rabbis how to read a Biblical text.

> Sons of Shelah, the son of Yehuda: Er… and Yoash and Saraf who became husbands in Moab and those who live in Lehem, and these matters are of great depth (I Chronicles 4:21–23).

> Rav and Shmuel disagree. One says: "Their names were Machlon and Kilyon. Why were they called Yoash (despair) and Saraf (conflagration)? Because they despaired of redemption and became

liable to destruction by fire." The other one says, "Their names were Yoash and Saraf. Why were they called Machlon and Kilyon? [One was called] Machlon because they profaned their bodies, [while the other was called] Kilyon because they deserved destruction at God's hand for having become husbands in Moab – they married Moabite wives. Those who live in Lehem – this is Ruth the Moabite, who settled in Bethlehem. The matters are of great depth – the Profound One of History enunciated them: "I *found* David, My servant [in Sodom]" and [regarding Lot] "Your two daughters *who are here*." (*Bava Batra* 91a)

Here, the Sages not only identified previously unknown individuals with known Biblical characters but also placed them squarely within the framework of descendants of Shelah, son of Yehudah. More remarkably, they draw our attention to the fact that Shelah called his son, the progenitor of Machlon and Kilyon, by the name of his deceased brother, Er. As we see time and again, in one pithy statement the Rabbis succeed in alluding to a number of profound teachings (See *Yalkut Reuveni, Va-yeshev* 157a and *Kohelet Yaakov,* entry Er). We will attempt to merely gain a surface understanding of this passage by demonstrating that it uses an essential rabbinic exegetical technique that is well suited for when information is scanty: recourse to patterns. To understand what they are driving at, we will start with the principle that history is a series of cycles in which later generations are granted the opportunity to repair the mistakes and missteps of the earlier ones.

Although this idea applies to the destinies of individuals as well as of nations, it is invoked most aptly in intergenerational sagas of families and may be familiar to some of our readers from certain classics of Western literature. The pattern to which the passage alludes is that of two brothers, both of whom are given an opportunity to lay claim to history. One "steps up to the plate," establishing a line of descent or even a nation, while the other one fails and is spiritually lost. This pattern is well known to us from the book of Genesis. Yet failure is not always final. Often there is a second chance and an opportunity to return, sometimes taken, sometimes wasted. This pattern includes Isaac and Ishmael, Esau and Jacob and, according to the Rabbis, Er and Onan.

> Yehudah took a wife for Er his first-born, and her name was Tamar. Er, Yehudah's first-born, was wicked in the sight of God, and God slew him.

> Yehudah said to Onan: "Go to your brother's wife and perform the duty of a husband's brother to her, and raise up seed to your brother." Onan knew that the seed would not be his, and it came to pass that when he went in unto his brother's wife, he spilled upon the ground rather than give seed to his brother. His deed was evil in the sight of God, and He slew him also. (Genesis 37:7–10)

We see the same situation occurring over and over in Yehudah's family. In fact, we encounter it three times. Two brothers are seemingly destined for perdition, yet one is saved and the other one perishes.

1. Both Er and Onan sin. Er is ultimately redeemed by Yehudah's levirate marriage to Tamar, but Onan is lost.
2. Similarly, both Machlon and Kilyon die, but Boaz restores Machlon via levirate marriage to Ruth.
3. Lastly, as we have just seen, the name of Er returns to Yehudah's line in Chronicles through his third son Shelah, who gives his firstborn the name of Er. Through this son, Shelah becomes an ancestor of Machlon who, together with Kilyon, loses his chance at redemption, but is later redeemed by Ruth. I would add that Yehudah and Tamar also have two children, Peretz and Zerach. Peretz becomes the ancestor of Boaz, who redeems Machlon through Ruth and ultimately begets the Davidic line. Redemption through the father, redemption through the mother!

Lot undergoes the same process. Ruth, one of his descendants, also has the opportunity for redemption. Lot's two youngest daughters committed grievous sins, as did Er and Onan. Like them, one is saved through Ruth and the other is lost with Orpah.[1]

The story of Boaz and Ruth is not only a narrative about two individuals who find each other but an account of the cosmic spiritual forces that bring them together. As we will see, their encounter at the threshing floor replays all the paradigms, only this time correct choices are made, sin is overcome and the cycle of redemption can finally be completed.

Look how much we have learned from our Sages. We mined the names for information, explored other relevant Biblical passages, and plumbed the depths of recurring patterns. As a result we emerged with a much broader appreciation of Machlon and Kilyon and of the idea of redemption as it is alluded to, carefully formulated and painstakingly developed in the book of Ruth.

---

[1] See Zohar 188a on Genesis 25:24 and the discussion by R.A.Z. Naiman in his commentary on Ruth in *Edrei tzon*, 14–16.

How did Machlon and Kilyon lose their Yiddishkeit?

> A certain man of Bethlehem in Judah went to sojourn in the plain of Moab, he, and his wife, and his two sons.... They came into the plain of Moab, and sojourned there.... They took wives of the women of Moab: the name of the one was Orpah, and the name of the other Ruth; and they dwelt there about ten years.

These verses describe an all too familiar pattern of decline and estrangement. Machlon went to sojourn, hoping to return to Judea as soon as he could, as soon as the famine ceased.

> "To sojourn in the land are we come, for there is no pasture for thy servants' flocks. The famine is sore in the land of Canaan" (Genesis 47:4). The verse teaches that they did not come to assimilate there but to reside temporarily. (Passover Haggada)

While the patriarch was alive, the old country and its religion exerted sufficient pull upon the children. Yet once he died, "they took wives of the women of Moab" in violation of Torah law, which prohibits such unions. As we will see later, rabbinic interpretation of the verse in Deuteronomy 23:4 does allow marriage to a Moabite woman convert, but would they have known that? As we will soon see, this dispensation seems either to have been forgotten or had never been applied until a later time. It must be that Machlon and Kilyon assimilated and married Moabite women without converting them.

Alas, the pattern of assimilation to the surrounding culture is a sad refrain in Jewish history. The slow slide into complete estrangement can be arrested in the first several generations as long as the descendants retain some awareness and affection for their heritage. At times, the return is actually triggered by the Gentile partners, who experience and are drawn to the values that still persist in some attenuated form among their assimilated Jewish spouses. This appears to have happened to Ruth and Orpah and to their mother-in-law – who, as the first generation, is still securely attached, living and breathing the pure Judaism of her native culture. The experience of this tug and pull has been well chronicled in literature and film (for example, *The Jazz Singer*) and is part of the personal memory of so many families.

Rabbi Uziel Milevsky of blessed memory wrote in his commentary on the Passover haggada, *Ohr Someach Haggada*, that the four sons are emblematic of this process of estrangement. The wise son is the first son, the first generation, the one who has not yet taken a step away from his heritage. The second son symbolizes the second generation, who is in a rush to throw off the shackles of his religion in order to gain acculturation and acceptance in the glittering Gentile world around him. The third son – the third generation – no longer knows much, for he was never taught. However, he vaguely remembers his grandfather and retains positive feelings and associations about Jewish matters. The fourth generation is represented by the son who does not know how to ask. This son knows practically nothing but he is still a Jew and he still sits at the Passover table. There is a fifth son, however, who is not mentioned in the haggada: this is the son who, regrettably, is no longer at the table. He is gone, lost to his family and to the Jewish people. How sad, yet how true!

You may recall the rabbinic interpretation that Machlon left Judea because he did not wish to share his wealth with the destitute during the famine. It is not surprising that he made his way to Moab instead of to Egypt. Moab was also known for its lack of generosity – "they did not greet you with bread and water when you were on the way out of Egypt" (Deuteronomy 23:5). "What led them to marry Moabite women? The fact that they behaved like Ammon and Moab in regards to generosity" (*Yalkut*). Naomi did not escape censure either, though she did eventually arrest and reverse the spiritual decline. "Naomi was fallen, but she rose by returning to the Land" (*Lekach tov*). "Then she arose with her daughters-in-law in order to return from the plain of Moab, for she had heard in the plain of Moab that God had remembered His people by giving them bread" (Ruth 1:6).

"She departed from the place where she was" (Ruth 1:6–7) – from that state of mind, that state of descent and spiritual decline.

"… to return from the plain of Moab…"

The word "return" is used fourteen times in the book of Ruth (4:15 contains the same root but has a different meaning). This indicates that it is a key word, one that encodes and conceals the key to interpretation. This tells us that the concept of return is the key to understanding this book.

Yet even as this noble family descended and assimilated, squandering its spiritual riches in pursuit of mediocre goals, it encountered two precious souls who were ascending.

Here is the paradox of a great person who falls, yet in the very act of failing inspires others. Even dying embers can start a fire if they fall upon parched ground. This phenomenon is widespread even in our own day, for many sincere converts were first attracted to Judaism through involvement with Jews who were in the process of turning their backs on their heritage.

Orpah and Ruth walked together with Naomi as she returned to her people, the people whom God had blessed by giving them bread. With this, we complete the first cycle of return and begin the second: the return of Lot's offspring to Abraham's covenant.

Orpah

Orpah is a mystery. Who is this young woman who initially throws in her lot with Naomi but then abandons her and returns to Moab? After flashing in front of our eyes, she fades into obscurity. What does she represent? What does her character mean to us and to the understanding that we seek?

It is tempting to see Orpah as Everywoman, an ordinary individual who, like so many of us, is attracted by the spiritual but never seems to fully commit to it. Orpah would love to be the heroine of the Book of Orpah, if there were one, but simply cannot muster the energy. She cannot manage to sacrifice her ease and everyday comforts on the altar of the Big Idea. Her sin is one of omission, cowardice, and lack of vision. She is a good person who means to do well but simply is not cut out for self-transcendence and mighty deeds. While we regret Orpah's lack of vision, we can understand her and feel sorry for her, and deep in our bones we feel sympathy for and a sense of recognition regarding the choices that she has made.

Cynthia Ozick, a well-known American writer and an observant Jew, wrote an insightful essay on Ruth. Here, as she writes about Orpah, she expresses this very thought:

> Her prototype abounds. She has fine impulses but she is not an iconoclast. She can push against convention to a generous degree, but it is out of generosity of her temperament, not out of some large metaphysical idea…. She is certainly not a philosopher, but neither is she, after ten years with Naomi, an ordinary Moabite. Not that she has altogether absorbed the Hebrew vision… she is somewhere in between. In this we may suppose her to be one of us: a modern, no longer a full-fledged member of the pagan world, but always with one foot warming in the seductive bath of those colorful, comfortable, often beautiful old lies (they can console, but because they are lies they can also hurt and kill); not yet given over to the Covenant and its determination to train us away from lies, however warm, colorful, beautiful and consoling lies…. So Orpah goes home; or more to the point, she goes nowhere. She is never to be blamed for it. If she is not extraordinary, she is also normal… it is not the fault of the normal that it does not or cannot aspire to the extraordinary. What Orpah gains by staying home with her own people is what she always deserved: family happiness. She is young

and fertile; soon she will marry a Moabite husband and have a Moabite child.

What Orpah loses is three thousand years of history. Israel continues; Moab has not. Still for Orpah… [it] may not be a loss at all. Orpah has her husband, her cradle, her little time. She once loved her oddly foreign mother-in-law. And why shouldn't open-hearted Orpah, in her little time, also love her Moabite mother-in-law, who is like her own mother, and who will also call her "daughter"?… Normality is not visionary. Normality's appetite stops at satisfaction.[2]

A fine interpretation, beautifully expressed – but not in the spirit of the Truth of the Sages. The idea that spiritual cowardice is normal, that self-sacrifice is not to be demanded of us common folk, that we have no right to judge others because we are all flawed, that all paths are essentially equal although some may bring better results than others, is so much in the spirit of our times, so post-modern, imbued with moral relativism and the belief in humanity's impotence against its nature, yet contains such distrust of our finest asset – the power of free choice.

The weakness of this perception of Orpah is not only moral but also exegetical. A serious deficiency of this approach is that it gives short shrift to the character of Orpah as a foil and counterpart to Ruth. If Ruth's choices were momentous, Orpah's choices must have been as well.

Far from being a sympathetic character with understandable weaknesses, the Sages' Orpah undergoes a profound spiritual upheaval that immediately leads her and her descendants deep into the side of impurity. That very night, they tell us, she fell far indeed.

"The night that Orpah parted from her mother-in-law she cohabited with a hundred men from a hundred nations. R. Tanchum said: also with one dog, as it is written, "The Philistine [Goliath] said to David, Am I a dog?" (Ruth Rabbah 2:2).[3]

One thing must be clear. The first principle in interpreting the Sages' ancient wisdom is that the more striking and the more outrageous the metaphor, the greater the profundity that lies beneath its surface. We already know that the key to interpreting this book in that it is about redemption. As we will soon see, the Sages viewed the parting of Orpah and Ruth as representing the separation of good and evil in the prelude to redemption.

---

[2] Ozick, Cynthia. "Ruth." In *Reading Ruth: Contemporary Women Reclaim a Sacred Story*. Edited by J. Kates and G. Twersky-Reimer, 211–233. Ballantine: New York, 1994.
[3] This is one of several possible translations of an ambiguous phrase.

Kabbala teaches that in our world, good and evil are inextricably intertwined. Humanity's task is to separate them and put each one to its rightful place.

On the road to Bethlehem, Naomi called both Orpah and Ruth "my daughters." This means that Orpah also could have been the mother of David. Once Orpah gave up the possibility of becoming a direct ancestor of the Messiah, she did not simply go back to her normal, everyday existence. Consciously or not, she fell into the deepest evil, causing her descendants to be found among those who, like Goliath, "reviled the camp of the living God." The lesson for us everyday folk is that a spiritual universe does indeed surround us on all sides, that there are momentous choices to be made, and that our decisions matter and are sometimes enormously important to us, our descendants and the entire world, for God fashions history out of human choices.

It used to be that humanity perceived itself as very small and God as immense, filling all space and allowing human beings no place for self-expression. Later, when human beings felt themselves to be so large and important as to fill the entire universe, they restricted God to a small and useful role within their world. With advent of modernity, everything changed. We, in our own time and place, see ourselves as taking up a tiny part of a meaningless and essentially empty universe, and as for God, we are not even entirely sure where in the void He resides. We can understand and justify anything because we value nothing. The episode on the road to Bethlehem teaches the opposite: this world of choices that God graciously created and gave into our power is our world to pollute or to redeem, and in this holy work of history, God is our partner.

According to the Sages, Ruth and Orpah were sisters, descendants of Eglon and Balak, kings of Moab. The burden of this legacy both informed and influenced their choices. We will yet discuss how Providence and human choice interact to shape the history of individuals and nations. For now it suffices to say that as soon as Orpah stepped off the stage of history, she sank low indeed.

Naomi always understood that without her guidance, Orpah might slip. Therefore, when she tried to send her daughters-in-law back, she kissed each of them. As *Ruth Rabbah* on this verse points out, her kiss was not a mere expression of emotion but rather a ritual. So Zohar Hadash comments on the first verse of the Song of Songs: "'Song of Songs' – clinging of body to body; 'kiss me from the kisses of your mouth' – clinging of spirit to spirit."[4] Naomi breathed into Orpah something of her own spirit so that it would

---

[4] See also Tanya 1:45

accompany and support her in her life among the idols of Moab. Yet when Orpah finally left Naomi, she returned the kiss because she no longer wanted Naomi or her God. She was going back to what would be, for her, a new life without the burdens of Naomi's gift.

Nevertheless, what Orpah had learned in the home of the Judeans refused to be forgotten. We might say that it pursued her, giving her no peace. We can only imagine what feelings of frustration, anger and self-loathing Orpah experienced when she returned to the environment in which she had grown up but that now felt foreign, discomfiting and revolting to her. Yet she could no longer turn back. Her choice was final and irrevocable.

To put it differently, Orpah experienced a profound failure. It is common for people in such situations to feel such an overwhelming sense of defeat and contempt for what they have done that they thrust themselves into the very depths of degradation. They do this both in order to punish themselves and to drown their pain as they vainly attempt to assert the rightness of their actions to themselves and others.

"The night that Orpah parted from her mother-in-law, she cohabited with a hundred men from a hundred nations. R. Tanchum said: Also with a dog…." (*Ruth Rabbah* 2:20)

It is crucial at such times to break one's fall. To what may this be compared? To a mountain climber who loses his footing and slides down the steep incline. If he manages to grab onto a branch or an outcropping of rock and break his fall, there is hope. He may yet reverse his course and retake the heights. If not, he is truly lost and falls to the deepest depths.

R. Chaim Shmulevitz used this thought to explain a strange episode involving the prophet Samuel and King Saul. When Samuel informed Saul that God rejected him as king of Israel, Saul reacted in a truly perplexing fashion. Instead of arguing or at the very least begging forgiveness and asking the prophet's intercession to reverse the decree, he asks that Samuel join him at a public meal "to honor me in the eyes of the elders." Of what significance is this honor when it is not destined to last? What purpose would be served by Samuel's participation in this empty charade? Yet the prophet agreed.

> Saul has just been humiliated in an unprecedented way. He had been the hope of Israel, the chosen and anointed one. He was now totally rejected, a bitter disappointment, a discarded relic in the course of history. God has become "disgusted" with him. If he remained in that state of disappointment, he could never recover and all hopes of a comeback would be gone. He pleaded with Samuel, "Give me

some dignity so that I may break my fall, so that I may continue and perhaps salvage something of my life." (*Reb Chaim's Discourses,* ArtScroll, 1998, 16)

Orpah did not do as Saul did. In telling us what happened to her that night, the Sages not only present Orpah and Ruth as a metaphysical parable of good and evil, but they also teach an important psychological and moral insight. The hundred men from a hundred nations represent the direction in which humanity has traveled ever since Sinai – toward rebellion against the Almighty and his onerous rules. The addition of the dog to the parable makes a point about romanticism. These are not Byronian rebels rising up against injustice. This is not a stand of the individual against tyranny or an act of moral heroism. Rather, this rebellion leads to the loss of the Image of God, to the generation whose "face is the face of a dog" (*Sotah* 49b). It leads us away from what is finest in humanity into the inner recesses of degradation, and not, as the Romantics imagined, to full expression of humanity's grandeur *qua* humanity.

The ultimate outcome of Orpah's failure of nerve was that she joined the forces of evil. "She returned to the plain of Moab but because she was wanton, they did not accept her. She then went to the land of the Philistines, where she bore six sons out of wedlock who all fell by the hand of David, Ruth's descendant" (*Zohar Hadash,* Ruth 81b).

In reward of the four tears that Orpah shed over Naomi, the punishment of her son Goliath was suspended for forty days (*Ruth Rabbah* 20:2). The exegetical basis for these statements seem to be identification of Orpah with Haruphah in II Samuel 21:15–22, which speaks of the mighty warriors, including Goliath, who fought against David (as per R. M. Eisemann, *A Pearl in the Sand: Reflections on Shavuos, Ruth and Davidic Kingdom,* 1997).

"The sons of the 'one who kissed' fell before the sons of the "one who clung" (*Sotah* 42b).

The power of Naomi's kiss did not help Orpah. Instead it was returned and misdirected into a course that opposed God's plan for humankind. Orpah did not simply fade into obscurity, but rather produced the worst enemies of Israel. No longer capable of attaining redemption, the only promise that the future held for her was that of utter destruction in the course of history.

> And she said: "See, your sister-in-law has gone back to her people and to her god; return after your sister-in-law."
>
> And Ruth said: 'Entreat me not to leave you, and to return from following after you; for wherever you go, I will go; and where you

lodge, I will lodge; your people are my people, and your God my God. Where you die, I will die, and there will I be buried. May God do so to me and more if anything but death should part you and me."

When she saw that she was bent on going with her, she left off speaking unto her. The two walked together…. (Ruth 1:15–18)

When Orpah kissed Naomi in return, when she "gave back" Naomi's kiss, it became apparent that Orpah intended to go back not only to her people but also to her gods. Such is the nature of a kiss; it is a momentary contact destined by its very shape and transience to be final, to signify separation. With it, Orpah established her independence and that she would no longer follow "after" Naomi. Orpah was now going to go her own way, free of the influence and perhaps even the memories of her former mother-in-law.

This posed a choice to Ruth. Naomi and Ruth both recognized that Ruth was a follower and not a leader. With Orpah striking on her own path, whom would Ruth follow? The word for "sister-in-law" that is used here is very unusual for the context. What we translate as "sister-in-law" is, in the original Hebrew, a word that signifies a levirate relationship – in other words, familial similarity, intense closeness and a shared destiny. Naomi was suggesting that Ruth should follow Orpah who, as her own sister, a Moabite and a kindred soul, perhaps would be a more appropriate mentor for Ruth than Naomi.

In our culture, followers are seen as weak while leaders represent the ideal. This is not so in other cultures, where following a deserving teacher is more ennobling (and usually more productive) than blundering in spiritual wonderlands on one's own. To be a disciple presupposes humility and wisdom and is certainly harder than exploring freely, unencumbered by the likely criticism and instruction, but also without guidance. It is regrettable that so few people in our individualistic and intensely egocentric society choose the mentoring option, where every youngster raises his or her head and says, "I shall reign." Since Ruth herself knew that she needed to follow in order to grow, she was presented with a clear choice. Whom would she follow: Naomi or Orpah?

Ruth responds that she is not after vague, diffuse, amoral spirituality, at which Orpah so excelled. She seeks to join Naomi and her people, to follow the God of Israel and be bound by His Law. "Entreat me not to leave you, and to return from following after you… your people shall be my people, and your God my God."

Picking up on this subtext, the Sages interpreted the exchange between Ruth and Naomi in terms of specific religious laws. Although it may also be possible to interpret this conversation as being about basic religious beliefs (see Malbim ad loc. and Mamonides, Laws of Forbidden Relationships 14:2), the Talmud in *Yevamot* 47a–b frames it in legal terms. Ruth wanted to be bound by religious law and Naomi obliged. Ruth could only learn from Naomi if she lived as Naomi did. I quote Rashi's formulation (ad loc.) of the Talmudic statement:

> From this our Rabbis said: "We inform a convert who seeks conversion of some consequences so that he/she has an opportunity to withdraw, for from Ruth's response we can infer what Naomi told her. She said to her: It is forbidden for us to go beyond a specified distance on the Sabbath. Ruth responded: Where you go, I will go. [Naomi said:] Among us a woman may not be secluded with a man who is not her husband. She answered: Where you lodge, I will lodge. [Naomi said:] Our nation is separated from other nations by six hundred and thirteen commandments. She said: Your people shall be my people. [Naomi said:] We are forbidden to serve idols – she said: Your God is my God. [Naomi said:] Our courts use four types of capital punishment – she answered: Where you die, I will die. [Naomi said:] There are two separate cemeteries, for those who are executed by stoning or burning metal and for those who are executed by the sword or by hanging. She said: There I will be buried.

Much has been written about the significance of these examples and how they represent all of Judaism. We need not concern ourselves with this issue right now. It is sufficient to point out that conversion to Judaism represents not an acceptance of a credo or belief system but a commitment to join the Jewish people, to live as they live and to share their way of life and their destiny. Although being clear about what one believes is also necessary, Jewish spirituality is actualized within a community and a nation, and expressed through action. Holding a belief and expressing it are easy matters, but the daily living of a faith through all demands of body, family, community and polity represents true commitment. Once Ruth made that commitment, she was transformed.

> R. Abbahu said: Come and see how precious converts are to the Holy One, blessed be He. Once [Ruth] made her commitment, the verse equated her to Naomi, for it says: "the two walked together" (Rashi).

The Two Mothers

> Orpah kissed her mother-in-law, but Ruth clung to her. (Ruth 1:14).

Orpah has gone, but Ruth clings to Naomi. This description of their relationship is significant, for the word "clinging" is usually used in Tanach to indicate an intense commitment of one individual to another or of a human being to God. So we find in the following:

> "To love God… and to cling to Him" (Deuteronomy 30:20, see also 10:20, 11:23).

> "I clung to your testimonies" (Psalms 119:31).

> "Therefore shall man leave his father and mother and cling to his wife" (Genesis 2:24).

> "And his soul clung to Dina, the daughter of Yaakov" (Genesis 34:3).

This choice of words may contain a clue to a larger question, one that bothered many commentators. What exactly is the relationship between Ruth and Naomi? The relationship of these two women, a daughter-in-law and a mother-in-law, presents many difficulties. Why did Ruth follow her mother-in-law with such devotion? Ruth's decision to go with Naomi is implausible on the surface. A young woman, she is ready to give up her homeland, her people and even, as Naomi points out, a chance for marriage, children and personal happiness. For what? For an old woman, her mother-in-law? One might expect that the older woman, weighed down with loss and bitterness, would cling to the younger one, but this is not the case. It is the opposite. When Ruth clings, she clings tightly. Yet although Ruth is strong and optimistic and never complains, in Bethlehem she is merely an extension of Naomi.

> Then said Boaz: When you acquire the field from Naomi, you also acquire Ruth the Moabite, the wife of the deceased, to perpetuate the name of the dead upon his inheritance" (Ruth 3:5).

Ruth is clearly a spirited individual with great inner strength. It is she who provided materially for herself and for Naomi by gleaning in the fields. It is she who took the initiative, ultimately bringing salvation to herself and Naomi. Yet Ruth is not the one who proposes marriage to Boaz; it is Naomi's idea. Not only is Naomi responsible for Ruth's success; it appears that her child, too, is also credited to Naomi.

> So Boaz took Ruth and she became his wife; and he went in unto her, and God granted her conception, and she bore a son.

And the women said unto Naomi: "Blessed be God, who has not left you this day without a near kinsman, and let his name be famous in Israel. And he shall be for you a restorer of life and a nourisher of your old age; for your daughter-in-law, who loves you and who is better to you than seven sons, has borne him."

Naomi took the child, laid it in her bosom, and became its nurse. Her women neighbors gave it a name, saying: "A son is born to Naomi," and they called his name Obed. He is the father of Jesse, the father of David. (Ruth 4:13–17)

It is as if the two women merge and the child of Ruth is really the son of Naomi. The symbiosis is underscored at the child's birth by the use of an idiom that we first encountered in the story of Chana. Here, Chana's husband is consoling her for her barrenness. Compare it to what the women say to Naomi.

Elkanah, her husband, said to her: "Chana, why do you weep and not eat? Why are you grieved? Am not I better to you than ten sons?" (Samuel 1:8)

"… for your daughter-in-law who loves you, who is better to you than seven sons, has borne him." (Ruth, ibid.)

As I struggled to link these observations into a coherent approach, God "enlightened my eyes" by arranging that a passage from the Zohar (*Tikkunei Zohar Hadash* 117 in some editions, quoted in *Pardes Rimonim* 22:15, see 14:1 and 13) cross my path. A full discussion of the passage is beyond our limits and my abilities. It suffices for the reader to know that it identifies the two women with the only two "mother" sefiros, Bina and Malchut, when they are exiled from and separated from "Father" and "Son," the sefiros of Chochma and Yesod. These two feminine sefiros, unlike the others, not only convey and filter Divine light but also receive, transmute and transmit the light from above. On its simplest level, this passage can be understood as a psychological insight about the relationship of Ruth and Naomi. The Zohar says:

There are two "mothers," the higher one and the lower one, the Presence (Shechina) Above and the Presence Below. Of this it is written, "You shall surely send away the mother and take the chicks for yourself" – two intermediaries, one corresponding to the other. Of them it says, "and the two walked together" (Ruth 1:17).

Ruth clung to Naomi, who was her teacher and conduit of spirituality. We might say that Ruth and Naomi were two stations through which the light of redemption traveled. Ruth understood this well. Ruth was wise, accepting the role of the lesser light and willing to receive before she could give.

On the simplest level, Naomi was Ruth's teacher of Judaism, but it goes far beyond that. Ruth found her mentor and her teacher not only of religion but of religious devotion; she found her soulmate and model for living. Naomi received and transmitted, while Ruth received and gave life. Of course, Naomi taught Ruth how to be a Jewish woman but beyond that, on some level they became one soul, linked in one purpose, drawn to the same goal. Together the two mothers accomplished something rare and precious: a union of two souls hewn from the same rock and perfectly complementing each other. We might say that Ruth understood that Naomi was not only her mentor but a model of how to receive in order to give, and in fact she also received from Naomi so that she could also give. At the end of this process she brought forth life. This worked because Naomi's was just like Ruth's, though in essence Naomi's was closer to God, as the sefira of Bina is closer than Malchus to the Eternal Source. The two women "walked together" because they belonged together. Physically it was Ruth, the mother below, who conceived and gave birth, but in the spiritual realm it was Naomi, the mother above, who received the seed and transmitted it to Ruth, the mother below. The wise women of Bethlehem understood and expressed this truth.

The Mother-in-Law

She departed from the place where she was, together with her two daughters-in-law; and they went on the road to return to the land of Judah.

> Naomi said to her two daughters-in-law: "Go, return each of you to her mother's house. May God deal kindly with you, as you have dealt with the dead and with me.

> God grant that you may find rest, each of you in the house of her husband." Then she kissed them; and they lifted up their voices and wept, telling her: 'No, we will return with you to your people."

One of the most baffling aspects of this narrative is the degree of loyalty, love and affection that Naomi inspired in her two daughters-in-law, a feat rare enough among women who were raised in the same culture and who share the same spirit, much less for a Judean mother-in-law and the Moabite women who married her sons. Did Naomi feel no bitterness or betrayal after her sons' intermarriage and distancing from her heritage and their own? Would she be able to move past the hurt and disappointment to see that she had gained two daughters, two precious souls, even if their mannerisms, comportment and speech were so unlike her own ways?

Do not be deceived: the chasm between those brought up under the wings of Divine Presence and those who grew up in the shadow of the idol Kemosh was surely wide. Those familiar with the observant Jewish lifestyle appreciate the many details and customs that circumscribe, elevate and sanctify every moment of daily life. Orpah and Ruth surely had no idea of this. They must have grated, however unwittingly, on Naomi's sensibilities every single day, and yet she overlooked it.

A glimpse of this gulf can be grasped from when Ruth already lived some time in Bethlehem. Here, already committed to the Jewish way of life, she unwittingly contravenes something as basic as the public separation of the sexes, a feature of life in Judea but apparently not in Moab. Note how Naomi gently brings this to her attention.

> Then said Boaz to Ruth: "Do you hear, my daughter? Do not go to glean in another field, and do not leave here, but stay here close by my maidens…."

Boaz directs Ruth to stay with the maidens.

> Ruth the Moabite said: "He told me: Stay close to my young men, until they have finished all my harvest."

Ruth misses the point but Naomi gently re-directs her:

> Naomi said to Ruth, her daughter-in-law, "It is good, my daughter, that you go out with his maidens, and that you do not gather in any other field" (Ruth 2:8, 21–22).

As well-meaning as they may have been, these daughters-in-law must have seemed very foreign to their mother-in-law. How easy it would have been for her to disapprove of them and distance herself from them, seeking justification and sanction for doing so in the commandment, "Do not seek their welfare or their prosperity all your days forever" (Deuteronomy 22:7). Yet since Naomi, whose name means "pleasantness" and whose soul was connected to the root of lovingkindness, rose above that, her daughters-in-law adored her.

However, Naomi realized that the step that they were about to take must be based on something more profound than a personal connection. She knew that people join religious communities for one of three basic reasons, alone or in various combinations. Some are driven by personal considerations – love, friendship, a search for acceptance, anger at the place from which they have come. Others are drawn to the esthetic, mannerisms, language, social structures, and way of life of a people or a religion. A few pursue the religious idea itself.

Personal considerations rarely survive adversity. Once it is established, social identification can endure but is of little merit. A true righteous proselyte, on the other hand, is a treasure and an inspiration.

So she probes:

> "God grant that you may find rest, each of you in her husband's home." Then she kissed them and they lifted up their voices and wept. They said to her: "No, we will return with you to your people."

Is their motivation social or religious?

What Naomi recognizes, and what her daughters-in-law do not know, is that her people might not be as welcoming as her daughters-in-law imagine. What do Ruth and Orpah know of Judeans but Naomi and Elimelech, Machlon and Kilyon? These were aristocrats, people of stature and of spirit. Will the average citizen of Bethlehem be able to see beyond the foreign Moabite exterior?

Naomi recognizes that reality often falls short of ideals and that even those who should know better so often behave in ways that are limited and petty. Those who put stock in human beings are sure to be disappointed by them.

> Thus says God: Cursed be the man who trusts in human beings and makes flesh his arm, and whose heart departs from God. For he shall be like a tamarisk in the desert, and shall not see when good comes; but shall inhabit the parched places in the wilderness, a salt land and not inhabited. Blessed is the man who trusts in God and whose trust God is. For he shall be as a tree planted by the waters, and that spreads out its roots by the river, and shall not see when heat comes, but its foliage shall be luxuriant; and shall not be anxious in the year of drought, neither shall cease from yielding fruit. The heart is deceitful above all things, and it is exceedingly weak – who can know it? (Jeremiah 17, 5–9)

Coming back with two Moabite daughters-in-law would not be particularly good for Naomi's reputation either. It would be a constant reminder of her family's sin and assimilation. Although group cohesiveness is necessary to keep a religious society firm against outside influences and to preserve its uniqueness and mission, it often has other, regrettable results: lack of vision, intolerance, distrust of the stranger.

Naomi knew that she was returning to a stratified society in which Moabite women and their mother-in-law would not easily find a place where they could belong. Could she foresee that inner righteousness would triumph over social strictures? Could she believe that the best in her people would become evident? Yes, as we know, ultimately the generosity and universality of the Jewish spirit came through to their aid – but how could she have known that it would? How could she explain to Orpah and Ruth, who expected to find Bethlehem populated by Naomis and Elimelechs, who looked forward to being loved and accepted as Naomi loved and cherished them, that it would not be so? How could she crush their spirit and destroy their faith?

> Why does she send them back? So as not to suffer shame on their account, for so we have found: There were many streets in Jerusalem but the inhabitants of one would not mix with the inhabitants of another. There was a [separate] street for the royals, a separate street for priests, for Levites, for Israelites. People were recognized in the market place by the clothes that they wore. No one single group wore the same clothing as another (*Ruth Zuta* 8).

What to do? Naomi invokes the emotional power of marriage and childbearing and discounts the social aspects of moving to Bethlehem in an attempt to dissuade them.

> Naomi said: "Turn back, my daughters; why will you go with me? Have I yet sons in my womb to be husbands for you? Turn back, my daughters; go your way, for I am too old to have a husband. If I should say: I have hope, even if I should have a husband tonight and also bear sons, would you wait for them till they were grown? Would you close yourselves off for them and have no husbands? No, my daughters; for it grieves me much for your sakes, for the hand of God has gone forth against me."

Naomi makes several important points. She subtly indicates that Orpah and Ruth might have great difficulty finding husbands in Bethlehem (that the prohibition of marrying Moabites applies only to males was not widely known, perhaps not even to Naomi herself). At the same time, she introduces the concept of levirate marriage. In that she foreshadows the future and preserves hope amid despair.

She also demonstrates that she truly and deeply cares about the personal happiness of her two daughters-in-law. People in pain often cannot find it in their hearts to care for others. That Naomi is capable of rising above her tragic personal situation shows her elevated spiritual stature and vindicates the Sages' reading of her character.

Orpah hesitates, for her attachment to her mother-in-law is personal and social. Ruth rises to the heights of spiritual heroism, accompanying Naomi not only because she loves her but because Naomi is her teacher.

> And they lifted up their voices and wept again; and Orpah kissed her mother-in-law; but Ruth cleaved to her.

> A ray of loving kindness illuminates the path of these two daughters of Moab and it is reflected indirectly upon Machlon and Kilyon, who have by now receded behind the horizon. The Book of Ruth does not disclose the nature of the inner life of this family. Yet the passionate devotion of the daughters-in-law to the mother of their departed husbands allows us to appraise the purity and warmth permeating the family life of these two aristocrats of Judah. Otherwise the strong ties binding the women to this family would be utterly incomprehensible…. The strongest influence, however, emanates from Naomi. She was "refined in word and deed." Orpah and Ruth were drawn toward her like planets gravitating around the sun. (Rabbi I.Z. Lipowitz in *Nachal Yosef*)

Both Orpah and Ruth felt love and affection for Naomi. However, Ruth was also motivated by a religious ideal that led her beyond the world of feeling and emotion, concern with her personal happiness and her private life. As we continue delving into their conversation, the greatness of this remarkable personality will become fully apparent.

The Path of Despair and the Path of Return

> It came to pass in the days when the judges judged that there was a famine in the land. And a certain man of Bethlehem in Judah went to sojourn in the plain of Moab together with his wife and his two sons. The name of the man was Elimelech, and the name of his wife Naomi, and the name of his two sons Mahlon and Kilyon, Ephrathites of Bethlehem in Judah. They came into the plain of Moab and sojourned there. Elimelech Naomi's husband died, leaving her and her two sons. They took wives of the women of Moab – the name of the one was Orpah and the name of the other Ruth – and they dwelt there about ten years. Mahlon and Kilyon both died, and the woman was bereft of her two children and of her husband. (Ruth 1: 1–5)

Much can happen in the life of this family in ten years – exile, dislocation, childlessness, bereavement, and loss. Surely, in this new land, relationships were formed, connections forged and characters tested, and yet we are told nothing of them. How did Naomi merit to gain the trust and love of her daughters-in-law, a rare situation in many families? How did they grow to appreciate the religion and ideals of Israel? What brought Elimelech to the plain of Moab instead of the traditional refuge from famine, the land of Egypt? How did the princes of Bethlehem justify marrying Moabite women and what did this mean to them in terms of their religious faith? What induced Orpah and Ruth to start traveling with Naomi to a foreign land? Why did neither of them have children after ten years of marriage, and why did Naomi also have none?

Many readers feel compelled to recreate a background so that they can begin to grasp the motivations and sensibilities of these mysterious characters. None of it is in the text. Where a human writer would have felt constrained to flesh out the background for us, the Divine Author did not. For Him, the outlines suffice, for from the Divine perspective Orpah, Ruth and Naomi only begin to exist at the point of their return to the Holy Land. Everything before then is ephemeral and unreal, and everything after it is lasting and real. The story of Ruth, like that of Naomi, only begins on the road to Bethlehem. Until now, the women had sojourned in the plain of Moab, but now they are coming home.

Rabbinic sources are divided on whether Naomi had a part in the original decision to go to Moab or whether she followed her husband only out of necessity. In any case, now that he was gone, she alone held the reins of free choice.

The Midrash says, "'The woman was bereft of her children and her husband' – she became like the remnants of the meal offering" (*Ruth Rabbah* 2:10).

What does this mysterious comment mean? The factual background to this is that a small part of the meal offering is removed and burned on the altar, while the rest is ceremonially eaten. Something like what happens to a meal offering has taken place regarding Naomi.

This saying has attracted many expositions. Let us also offer an interpretation.

Meal offerings are brought to expiate bitterness and anger (Netsiv to Leviticus 2:1), as is evident from 1 Samuel 26, "Saul knew David's voice and said: 'Is this your voice, my son David?' David said: 'It is my voice, my lord king.' And he said: 'Why does my lord pursue his servant? What have I done? What evil is in my hand? Now therefore, I pray, let my lord the king hear the words of his servant. If it be God that stirred you up against me, let Him accept a meal offering...."

The word that is used to describe Naomi's bereavement is also significant for in Hebrew there are two synonyms that mean "left over," the root of *n-t-r* and the root of *n-sh-r*. The first signifies that which is left over unintentionally, while the second is used for that which is left to remain on purpose (See the Netziv on Exodus 10:19). The second form is used regarding Naomi. Perhaps this is then the meaning.

Although Naomi alone was left, she was left on purpose so that she could choose. Since her suffering came from God, it possessed a measure of holiness, and her losses had a sacrificial character. Her family was consumed but she remained, a survivor of the tragic events that claimed all that she possessed. She had moved far away from her land and from her people, and now her God was pushing her farther away and showing her "the face of anger." At such times, the choice is stark –one may, in return, become angry with God, distancing oneself further from Him, or one may justify His actions and, in some obscure way, turn the suffering into a springboard back to Him. There is nothing in between.

The two polarities of feeling – anger versus contrition – that envelop survivors of great tragedies are expressed in the following verses:

> To me he is like a bear lying in wait, like a lion in secret places. He turned aside my ways and pulled me in pieces; He made me desolate. He bent His bow and set me as a mark for the arrow. He shot the arrows of His quiver into my kidneys. I have become an object of derision to all my people and their song all the day. He filled me with bitterness, He sated me with wormwood. He has also broken my teeth with gravel stones, He made me to wallow in ashes. And my soul is removed far off from peace, I forgot prosperity. And I said: "My strength is perished, and my expectation from God." (Lamentations 3)

On the other hand:

> This I recall to my mind; therefore have I hope. Surely God's kindnesses are not exhausted, surely His mercies fail not. They are new every morning; great is Your faithfulness. "God is my portion," says my soul; "therefore will I hope in Him." God is good to those who wait for Him, to the soul that seeks Him. It is good that a man should quietly wait for God's salvation. It is good for a man to bear the yoke in his youth. Let him sit alone and keep silence, because He laid it upon him. Let him put his mouth in the dust; if so, there may

be hope. Let him give his cheek to the one who smites him; let him be filled full of reproach. The Lord will not cast off forever. Though He may cause grief, He will still have compassion according to the multitude of His mercies. He does not willingly afflict nor grieve the children of men. To crush underfoot all the prisoners of the earth, to turn aside the right of a man before the face of the Most High, to subvert a man in his cause, the Lord approves not. Who is he that says, and it comes to pass, when the Lord has not commanded it? Do not evil and good proceed out of the mouth of the Most High? Why does a living man complain, a strong man because of his sins? Let us search and try our ways, and return to God. Let us lift up our hearts with our hands unto God in the heavens. (*ibid.*)

Events are great teachers, sent by the greatest Teacher, Who gives out trials according to our capacity to bear them. When things are at the most bleak, the choices are also the most stark. One can react with anger or denial, or one can accept responsibility for being the active agent of one's own pain and return to God. Often people are broken by suffering because there is no greater rejection than to be rejected by God, and only exceptional people can distinguish between lessons and rejection. The highest courage is to absorb the lessons as lessons; the easiest course is to dissolve into blaming and victimization. The hardest thing is to acknowledge God's judgment, to surmount anger and bitterness, to trust when there seems to be no more hope. The easy, cowardly way is to deny God's culpability or knowledge, to build philosophies that take Him out of the picture and to explain away suffering as random, accidental and therefore meaningless. The courageous choice is to repent rather than become bitter or angry. Naomi certainly knew what she felt and experienced, but she also know from where within her innermost depths it came.

> She said unto them: 'Call me not Naomi; call me Marah; for the Almighty has dealt very bitterly with me. I went out full, and God brought me back home empty. Why do you call me Naomi, seeing that God has testified against me and the Almighty has afflicted me? (Ruth 1, 20–21)'

Although Naomi knew exactly who was responsible for her suffering, she went back home anyway. In the Bible, such trust is always rewarded.

The extent of Naomi's anguish is difficult to imagine. Bereft of her husband and sons, Naomi had neither possessions nor hope. She was completely empty and longed to be filled. Both Ruth and Boaz understood this.

He said: "Bring the mantle that is upon you, and hold it." She held it and he measured out six measures of barley and laid it on her, and he went into the city. When she came to her mother-in-law, she said: "Who are you, my daughter?" She told her all that the man had done to her. She said: "He gave me these six measures of barley, for he said to me: Go not empty to your mother-in-law." (Ruth 3:15–17)

Naomi had a hard road to walk, so God sent Ruth to walk it with her.

Naomi Fails the Test

So they came to Bethlehem. All the city was astir concerning them, and the women said: "Is this Naomi?" She told them: Do not call me Naomi [pleasant], call me Marah [bitter]; for God has dealt very bitterly with me. I went out full, and God brought me back home empty. Why do you call me Naomi when God Himself has testified against me and the Lord has afflicted me?"

So Naomi returned with Ruth the Moabite, her daughter-in-law, who came from the plain of Moab, and they came to Bethlehem in the beginning of barley harvest.

It is instructive to compare this anguished cry with the face that Naomi presented earlier to her daughters-in-law.

No, my daughters! I am much grieved for your sakes, for the hand of God has gone forth against me. (1:13)

The Divine name Shaddai that Naomi now used is significant because it is rarely used in Tanach except in the Book of Job. While the etymology of this name is not entirely clear, it appears to be related to the Hebrew word *shod,* which signifies destruction and ruin (Ibn Ezra on Exodus 6:3). The Tetragrammaton, on the other hand, most often refers to God as friend and ally. Naomi showed faith and trust to her foreign daughters-in-law, the young widows who looked to her for consolation, spiritual support and encouragement. To them she spoke of a kind God whose judgment one accepts because "all the Merciful One does is for the good." Undoubtedly she spoke the truth for she accepted God's reproof with gratitude.

Yet deep inside, perhaps unawares, her bitterness slowly grew and festered. Her defenses crumbled when she saw the faces of the women who had played with her as children, her relatives and former neighbors, and what she had not acknowledged came pouring out. Could she not bare her heart to these kind women with whom she had so much in common?

Naomi had forgotten that ten years of suffering have taught her wisdom that her neighbors and relatives did not possess. They had suffered famine, true, but they had suffered it as a community and now God had blessed them with bounty. Naomi alone felt the hand of Shaddai, and that made all the difference.

> Did the women have nothing to say in reply? Did they accept her and comfort her, or did they shy away, reject her? For at Naomi's side there stood her gentile daughter-in-law – the daughter of Moab, who had sinfully married Naomi's son. Perhaps Scripture tells us nothing here, because each woman in turn slunk silently to her own home. Shunned Naomi remained alone in the city square, and with her daughter-in-law, Ruth, the Moabite. (Y. Bachrach, *Mother of Royalty*. Jerusalem: 1980, 60)

Naomi returned from Moab with an attitude that the women of Bethlehem could not assimilate or accept. Accompanying her was a Moabite girl who represented a morality that threatened their homes and hearths. It had not been so long ago that

> Israel abode in Shittim, and the people began to commit harlotry with the daughters of Moab. They called the people unto the sacrifices of their gods; and the people ate and bowed down to their gods. Israel joined itself unto Baal of Peor and God's anger was kindled against Israel. (Numbers 25:1–3)

Did Naomi begin to doubt the truth and validity of her own religious perception? Did she retreat into silence in order to allow her heart to sort out the truth that she felt but could not accept? Did she need time to process the feelings that unexpectedly broke through to her awareness at that moment? Did she need to make peace with God, who had testified against her, and with Shaddai, who had not spared her, who took away Naomi and left behind a stranger called Marah?

The Sages say that the inhabitants of Bethlehem were either gathered for the funeral of Boaz's wife or in order to harvest the first barley offering when the two stragglers walked into town. Although the city was astir about them both, the women spoke only to Naomi. No one, not even Naomi, spoke to Ruth.

"When she [Naomi] saw that she [Ruth] was steadfastly minded to go with her, she left off speaking to her (1:18)." Although we do not know how long the silence lasted, we know that it was broken by Ruth rather than by Naomi. "Ruth the Moabite said to Naomi: 'Let me now go to the field and glean among the ears of corn after him in whose sight I shall find favor.' She said to her: 'Go, my daughter'" (2:2).

It appears that men recognized the character and worthiness of Ruth. The men admired her, but the women shunned her.

> He [Boaz] said: "May God bless you, my daughter. You have shown more kindness in the end than at the beginning, inasmuch as you did not follow the young men, whether poor or rich. And now, my daughter, fear not. I will do for you all that you say, for all the men at the gate of my people know that you are a virtuous woman'" (3:11)

This insight may explain the later curious interchange between Naomi and Ruth, who preferred to stay with the male reapers, and Naomi could not understand why.

> Ruth the Moabite said: "He said to me: Keep fast by my young men until they have completed all my harvest."
>
> Naomi said to Ruth her daughter-in-law: "It is good, my daughter, that you go out with his maidens, and that you not glean in any other field."
>
> So she kept fast by the maidens of Boaz to glean until the end of the barley harvest and the wheat harvest, and she dwelt with her mother-in-law. (3:21–13)

Not until the very end of the book do we find women speaking positively of the Moabite stranger. "The women said to Naomi: Your daughter-in-law, who loves you and who is better to thee than seven sons, has given birth to him" (3:14–15). Yet even then they do not call her by name.

Life was not easy for Ruth in her new chosen land and among the people she longed to call her own. Yet she did not grow bitter. Her resilience and perseverance are important ingredients in the mix of character traits that earned her the opportunity to become the mother of Israelite royalty.

The Sages tells us that all the people of the town were gathered to ceremoniously reap the first stalks of barley in order to bring them as the Omer offering (*Ruth Rabbah* 4:2). What implication of the last verse of our chapter did they bring out with this comment?

The Omer sacrifice is always offered on the second day of Passover. It seems that on the day that the Jews left Egypt and witnessed God's judgment of the Egyptians, they were granted profound spiritual insights. However, since these insights were given as gifts rather than earned, all of them were quickly lost and by the day after, the second day of Passover, the former slaves reverted to their original state. However, they did not despair. That day marked the beginning of a long, slow climb back up the scale of self-improvement that culminated fifty days later with the giving of the Torah at Mount Sinai.

The Omer offering represents victory over despair. It teaches us that even if we fail, even if we fall very far, even if we lose all the spiritual accomplishments that we earned with such difficulty and self sacrifice, a new beginning is always possible. We can and must start again with optimism and hope we will again succeed (*Idrei tzon*).

R. Tzadok ha-Cohen writes that the Jewish nation began with Abraham and Sarah. Why was it necessary for such righteous people to suffer childlessness for so many years? He answers that the beginning of Jewish peoplehood had to start in despair so that the ability to overcome despair and hold on to hope would become a part of our national character. Our people lives and survives against all expectations, even when every calculation shows that it is doomed. It is beyond natural law, for it is guided by the hand of God Himself. In this lies the great and true expectation for Israel's deliverance, and in it individuals draw a lesson for overcoming adversity and gaining hope.

> So Naomi returned together with Ruth the Moabite, her daughter-in-law, who came from of the plain of Moab – and they came to Bethlehem in the beginning of barley harvest.

Boaz

In the beginning of the second chapter we meet Boaz who, as introduced through the eyes of Naomi, is "a relative of her husband." Later the verses skillfully introduce Boaz as they want us to know him: a pious, wise and gentle man, a humble leader who cares profoundly about every individual and exudes gentleness and kindness.

Boaz enters with a blessing and generates blessing in return.

> Behold, Boaz came from Bethlehem and said to the reapers, "God be with you," and they answered, "May God bless you."

On a literary level, the purpose of this introduction is to link Boaz with the concept of blessing. We must not forget that when Boaz blesses the reapers, he also blesses Ruth, who is among them. A minor prophecy is registered here: Boaz blesses Ruth and the workers bless him, and from that moment on blessing accompanies them both.

It seems that when an angel brought Ruth to Boaz's field, the Divine Presence rested near her. Boaz sensed the illumination of the Divine Presence [among the reapers] and therefore said as a fact, "God is with you." (Bach)

The Chida expresses a similar idea in his commentary:

What Boaz meant is that the workers were engaged in leaving over the portions of the poor [the corner of the field, gleanings, and forgotten sheaves]. R. Isaac Luria had written that charity unites the Holy One, blessed be He, with the Divine Presence. Boaz expressed this by telling the reapers, "God is with you." They answered: "You are the owner of the field and the blessings belong to you."

However, we can hear another echo in this sentence. The verse implies that Boaz did not regularly visit his field for "behold," he came today from Bethlehem to the field. However, that is not a correct inference, for we learn later that Boaz even slept at the threshing floor to watch his produce. In other words, he was personally involved in the harvest. The verse also says that he came from Bethlehem, suggesting a distance, but was this field not already in vicinity of Bethlehem and within its borders? Perhaps the verse associates Boaz with Bethlehem to communicate that this event was related to the role that Boaz played at Bethlehem and which Bethlehem played as a religious center.

But you, Bethlehem Ephrathah, who are little among the thousands of Judah, out of you shall one come forth unto Me one who will be ruler in Israel, whose goings forth are from old, from ancient days. (Michah 5:1)

The Sages mine these implications in the following well-known statement, "They enacted that people should greet one another with God's name, as it says, Behold, Boaz came from Bethlehem and said to the reapers, 'God be with you,' and they answered 'May God bless you'" (*Berachot* 54b).

… violence, stealing and absence of charity and kindness became rife among the people, nor did they listen to the judges. When Boaz became a judge he enacted that people greet each other with God's name in order to fix in their hearts that God is in Heaven and sees everything and also become aware that God is always before them, including in interpersonal relationships…. (Malbim)

Things needed to change. It was time for a revival. However, one might say that moral and societal reform must take place before religious revival becomes possible. Boaz, as judge, set about educating the people, preparing them for the rest of his program of reform as his major goal. His kindness and warmth at the field were nothing more than a reflection of his private and public priorities. He was what he taught – kindness, concern for others, softness and care in speech, sensitivity and focus on each individual.

When Boaz inquired about Ruth, his servant answered, "She is a Moabite girl who has returned with Naomi from the plain of Moab." This young man did not look beyond externals to see Ruth for who she was. He saw only a Moabite woman. Perhaps he resented the fact that she did not flirt with the young men as other gleaners did (*Ruth Rabbah* ad loc.), or perhaps he was simply incapable of deep thinking. "'… She is a Moabite girl who has returned with Naomi from the plain of Moab.' This means that her actions are pleasant and comely, but that is because her mistress trained her so" (*Ruth Rabbah* 4:6). He could not give her credit, but Boaz did not allow this characterization of Ruth to cloud his perception.

Psychologists tell us that human beings' opinions tend to be influenced by the first impression. This mechanism called "anchoring" is so pervasive that many good educators choose not to see their new students' report cards from the previous year so as not to become biased regarding their abilities. Boaz refused to be "anchored."

This alone tells us something significant about Boaz's character. His ability to disregard the conventional assessment of Ruth and his appreciation of her kindness, together with his refusal to minimize or explain away her accomplishments reveal his values. Sage that he was, Boaz was humble, flexible, and capable of seeing the good within others. Where the people of Bethlehem saw only a Moabite, a stranger, or at best a Jewish woman in training, he saw an exceptional human being whom he must respect and honor despite the differences in their background, learning and experience. In this, Boaz was a fitting ancestor of King David, whose career exemplified precisely these qualities. The uniqueness of Boaz and Ruth becomes apparent in their conversation that is shortly to come, which is as profound as it is simple and sophisticated as it is good. It solidifies our perception of these two unique human beings who were so perfectly matched for their destined purpose.

Naomi or Ruth

> And to Naomi a kinsman for her husband, a mighty man of valor, of the family of Elimelech, and his name was Boaz. (Ruth 2:1)

The second chapter starts after Naomi and Ruth had just entered Bethlehem. We are now introduced to Boaz for the first time. According to the usual pattern of such introductions, we would expect a sentence such as: "There lived in Bethlehem a man named Boaz, who was Naomi's kinsman and a mighty man of valor." Had it been so written, the focus would have been on Boaz as the narrator sees him. However, the verse chooses to emphasize Naomi and who Boaz was in relation to her. The verse also uses intentional ambiguity, for it might be read as suggesting that Boaz was to be a husband for Naomi. If so, we might expect Naomi to reach out to Boaz, but she does not. Instead, the focus shifts abruptly to Ruth.

> Ruth the Moabite said to Naomi: "Let me now go to the field and glean among the ears of corn after him in whose sight I shall find favor." She said to her: "Go, my daughter."
>
> So she went, and came and gleaned in the field after the reapers; and it so happened that she lit on the portion of the field belonging to Boaz, who was of the family of Elimelech.

It is Boaz in whose eyes Ruth will find favor. Providence led her to him with Naomi's assistance.

A careful reader quickly notices that while Boaz certainly appreciated Ruth's good qualities, his heart tended more toward Naomi, who was, after all, his kin, the wife of his relative, and a part of his world and his heritage. Although the Sages tell us that Ruth was forty years-old at that time (*Ruth Rabbah* 6:2), according to the plain sense of the verses, Naomi was still fertile and not much older than Ruth, perhaps in her mid-thirties (see 1:12–13, *Ruth Rabbah* 3:7 and *Sanhedrin* 69b). Even if Naomi was older, was she not a more fitting partner for Boaz's old age? Naomi was a natural, while Ruth was a gamble. So we find that Boaz appreciated and praised Ruth for what she did for Naomi.

> Boaz answered her, saying: "I have been told all that you have done for your mother-in-law since your husband's death, and how you left your father and mother and the land of your birth and came to a people whom you never knew before." (v. 11)

Even at the point that Boaz commits to Ruth, he is still thinking of Naomi.

> She said: "These six measures of barley he gave me; for he said to me: Go not empty to your mother-in-law." (Ruth 3:17)

Naomi could have married Boaz herself, but in an act of profound self-transcendence and selflessness, she put Ruth forward instead.

> And Naomi her mother-in-law said unto her: 'My daughter, shall I not seek rest for you, that it may be well with you? And now is there not Boaz *our* kinsman…" (Ruth 3:1–2)

Why did Naomi do this? Was it simply the sense of gratitude and obligation that the older woman felt for the younger one, her who left her people and her homeland to share Naomi's fate? Or was it the sense that Ruth was more suited to play the role that history had prepared for Boaz? I believe that the answer is the latter. Naomi realized that Ruth and Boaz shared a quality that Naomi herself no longer possessed.

Significantly, Boaz describes Ruth with the same words that the verse uses to describe him. Boaz is a man of valor and Ruth is a woman of valor (3:11). The Midrash notes this fact and comments on it (*Ruth Rabbah* ad. loc.):

> R. Abbahu said: A giant marries a giantess. Whom do they produce? Men of valor. Boaz married Ruth. Whom did they produce? – David, of whom it says, "man of valor…." (I Samuel 16)

What about Naomi? Is she not closer kin for the purpose of a levirate marriage, and is she not the owner of the field that Boaz is supposed to redeem? Would she not have been more appropriate than Ruth, a stranger and a Moabite, to become the ancestor of an Israelite king?

I believe that the answer lies in the last verses of the preceding chapter. We must ask why the Scripture recounts Naomi's "breakdown" upon her return to Bethlehem. On the surface, it contributes little to the story. Yet in truth, it is essential. Naomi would have been perfect for Boaz, but Naomi no longer existed. In her place, by her own testimony, there stood another woman, weighed down by suffering, embittered and not at peace with God, a woman called Marah. This woman was not suitable to give birth to the redeemer, for redemption is all about hope in the midst of darkness, deliverance in the midst of despair, a vision of glorious and consoling future in the throes of a bitter exile.

Although Ruth has traveled through her own Gehenna, unlike Naomi she never abandoned hope. Her suffering did not scar her. She remained optimistic and trusting of God and human beings. She threw in her lot with a nation she barely knew, with people who did not welcome her and a God Whom she knew only as one who had taken away her husband and withheld children from her womb. David and the Jewish people needed an ancestor such as this.

David, too, had a hard life but rose above it. His people were destined to drink the cup of bitterness to its last dregs. Only optimism, hope and trust could guarantee their survival. Ruth, Boaz and Naomi understood that this match was beyond human calculations and preferences. It was about destiny.

The second chapter of Ruth tells us about human beings who were inspired to rise above their needs, feelings, and limitations to see and act upon God's plan. Boaz, Naomi and Ruth understood that Ruth was suited to be the mother of royalty in a way that Naomi could no longer be – and the rest, as they say, is history.

> Naomi, her mother-in-law, said to her: "My daughter, shall I not seek a place of rest for you that would be good for you?" (3:1)

The narrative now takes us forward. Three months have passed since Boaz and Ruth last spoke, the months of gathering in the barley harvest, then the months of bringing in the wheat.

> R. Shmuel Bar Nachman said: "From the beginning of the barley harvest to the end of the wheat harvest is three months," "She returned to her mother-in-law," and "Naomi, her mother-in-law, said to her, My daughter, shall I not seek a place of rest for you?," and "Now Boaz is our relative." (*Ruth Rabbah* 5:11).

Let us explore this puzzling comment.

Many commentators suggest that these three months constitute the period of time that, according to Jewish law, a widow or divorcée must wait before remarrying so as to ensure that, if she is pregnant, the father's identity will be clear for the purposes of paternity and inheritance. The allusion to pregnancy is important. At the same time as Ruth was mentally and emotionally separating from her previous life, Naomi was nurturing an important realization.

Remember that Naomi was a contender and a potential competitor for Boaz. That she knew this is evident from the way in which she describes him: "Now Boaz is our relative" and "The man is a close relation, one of our near kinsmen." It would have been simple for Naomi to claim her right to marry him and thus resume her former high status in Bethlehem. After all, Naomi was a real relative, unlike Ruth, who was related by marriage. In any case, she was a closer relative than Ruth, and it is Naomi's field that Boaz must redeem.

If Naomi were to claim her rights, this would not deprive Ruth in any way. Ruth could also marry a young man and rebuild her life. Naomi could rationalize that Ruth would probably be happy with such an outcome. Is this not the best way, the Godly way, to pursue – to give each woman what she deserves? Yet deep inside, Naomi knows differently. Naomi knows that marrying a "nice young man" is not Ruth's destiny, even if Ruth herself may not realize that. Now, after three months of inner struggle, Naomi abdicates in Ruth's favor. In her appeal, Naomi is speaking as much to Ruth as to herself. This is Ruth, the dutiful daughter-in-law who has abandoned her people and her land to assist Naomi and share her fate. The pathos of the words "My daughter…," resounds within Naomi, penetrate her soul, and reverberate in her decision, and this is why in these several sentences Naomi and Ruth are repeatedly referred to as "mother-in-law" and "daughter-in-law."

However, there is another dimension. Ruth deserves a place of rest, a *manoach*. What is this place of rest? It is not merely the removal of the stress of being single and alone. Naomi referred to that kind of alleviation and easing before, when she urged her daughters-in-law to return to Moab and remarry: "May God grant that you find rest [*menucha*], each of you in her husband's home" (Ruth 1:9). But now Naomi knows that Ruth is destined for more than that.

The switch from the feminine to the masculine version of the word is highly significant. Before, the word used was *menucha,* a state of repose that a woman finds upon remarriage; now it is a *manoach,* the rightful place, the right person, the only fitting partner in life. Why was Boaz the only place of repose for Ruth?

In order to understand this more fully, we need to return to the surprising and constantly repeated motif in this book – that Ruth performed a great kindness not only for the living but also for the dead.

"Naomi said to her two daughters-in-law: 'Go, return each of you to her mother's house. May God deal kindly with you as you dealt with the dead and with me'" (1:8). Again, "Naomi said to her daughter-in-law: 'May he be blessed by God, Who left not off His kindness to the living and to the dead.' Naomi said unto her: 'The man is kin to us, one of our near redeemers.'" (2:20)

In contrast, Boaz, when initially speaking to Ruth, carefully avoids mentioning the dead. "Boaz answered her, saying: 'I have been told all that you did for your mother-in-law since your husband's death, and how you left your father and mother and the land of your birth and came to a people that you never knew before'" (2:11). Notice that he speaks only about Ruth, making no mention of her kindness to the departed. This tells us that Ruth's kindness to the dead is a sensitive topic, one that is inappropriate to mention at this point in their relationship. However, he refers obliquely to it later on when he proposes to her in these words, "'May God bless you, my daughter.

You showed more kindness in the end than at the beginning, inasmuch as you did not follow the young men, whether poor or rich" (3:10).

The topic of kindness to the dead is explored in the following passage. Since it draws on deeply hidden and profound Kabbalistic wisdom, it will be impossible for us to understand it completely. However, everything deep has its expression and reflection on a simpler level and can be accessed there as well. I ask that the reader mentally translate from the conceptual vocabulary and imagery of a bygone era to our current time. The ability to do so is indispensable if we are to learn from the wisdom of the ancients, who spoke and thought in different mental categories than we do. As you read this passage, substitute image, remembrance, paradigm, or energy for the word "spirit" and it will begin to yield its secrets.

> When a man dies, he leaves a spirit in his wife's belly and it does not separate from there all the days of her widowhood. If she merits a levirate marriage, this "spirit" becomes the foundation of a structure "to build the house of his brother." If she does not enter into a levirate marriage and marries another man, he also places a "spirit" within her. Sometimes the latter one vanquishes the first one and sometimes the reverse.... (*Shoresh Yishai* cited in *Edrei tzon*)

The concept that a man's widow preserves within her something of his spirit, which is then embodied and redeemed through levirate marriage, is alluded to in the following midrashic passage.

"Naomi said to her daughter-in-law, 'May God bless him [i.e., Boaz], who has not taken His kindness from the living and the dead.' The living – that Boaz fed and provided for the living. The dead – that he took care of their shrouds" (*Ruth Rabbah* 5:10).

Certainly, Naomi could have married Boaz and Ruth could have found happiness and contentment with some deserving young man. To a human eye that would have been fine, even fitting. Society would see it as a good outcome, and perhaps it would have even be cited as evidence of God's Providence in human affairs. However, conventional is not identical with the good. This would not have been redemption, for then the dead would have been lost and unredeemed, the past forgotten rather than transformed, as the second best takes the place of the truly good.

Naomi understood. Her actions, her self transcendence, her commitment to the right and good over all led Ruth to Boaz and the spirit that she carried in her womb to full expression in David, King of Israel.

THE SUN RISES

Ruth

THE STORY OF RUTH chronicles her transformation from a Moabite maiden to the mother of Israelite monarchy. When did Ruth accept the religion of Israel? It is clear that as she arrives in Bethlehem, she is fully keeping the laws and customs of Israel. She gleans in the fields, participates in levirate marriage, and expresses herself in the language of Israelite religious sensibilities and concepts.

It is clear then that Ruth became Jewish before her arrival in Bethlehem. Yet did she do so before her marriage to Machlon or only on the road to Bethlehem?

It is tempting to assume that Ruth converted before her marriage. This would explain her attachment to Naomi, her suitability for levirate marriage to Boaz, and her eagerness to leave Moab for Judea. It would rescue Machlon and Kilyon ("two great leaders of Israel," Rambam, Laws of Kings 5:9), and Naomi from the opprobrium of conducting, or at least condoning, an intermarriage. It is hard to imagine that the faithful Naomi, on whose lips the name of God dwelt, would form a relationship so genuinely close and affectionate with a "daughter of a foreign god." To say that the prophets and judges of Israel did not view intermarriage favorably is to put it rather mildly (see Malachi 2:11, Deuteronomy 7:3–4, Ezra 10). Intermarriage is a basic betrayal of a Jew's innermost religious values, for it is a commitment to share love, life and one's innermost being with someone who thinks, hopes, longs, believes and dreams with a different sensibility – hence the appellation "daughter of a foreign god" (Malachi, ibid.). Accordingly, it cannot be that Machlon – who, as we already established, was a worthy man – intermarried. "R. Pedas asked the son of R. Yosi of Soko, 'Since Ruth converted [from the beginning], why did they not give her a new [Jewish] name?' He said to him: 'I received a tradition that that she had another name. When she married Machlon… they called her Ruth, for she converted when she married Machlon and not afterwards.' He responded, "But it says '… where you lean [your head], so I will lean, where you go, I go, your people shall be my people and your God shall be my God' [implying that the conversion took place only at that point]" (Zohar Ruth 79a). According to this view, Ruth converted before her marriage.

However, almost the entire consensus of rabbinic commentary disagrees. From the Aramaic Targum on Ruth to the Talmud, which derives the laws of conversion from the conversation between Ruth and Naomi (*Yevamot* 47b), it is assumed that Ruth converted to Judaism on the way to Bethlehem. Machlon and Kilyon married Moabites – "Machlon and Kilyon incurred destruction by God because they took wives of another faith" (*Bava Batra* 91b).

Even in this case, questions remain. Even if Ruth and Orpah were Moabites and did not convert, how could Naomi propose that her daughters-in-law "return to your people and your god" (Ruth 1:15)? Could she have been sending them, even as Gentiles, back to idolatrous worship? However, that is less of a problem than suggesting that Naomi advised her Jewish daughters-in-law to worship idols.

The manner in which we resolve this difficulty has ramifications for other similar situations, for example the marriages of Samson and of Solomon. As we see, although both positions have merit, they also possess exegetical deficiencies. Fortunately, these apparently disparate interpretations and their Scriptural antecedents can be reconciled.

In his work *Moadim u-zemanim* (4:316), R. Moshe Sternbuch suggests that Ruth converted conditionally before her marriage and that the conversion later took effect retroactively when she chose to leave Moab. Although an involved halachic discussion on this subject is beyond our purview, Jewish law recognizes two types of conditional conversions. The first one is conversion of a minor by a parent; upon reaching the age of majority the child can choose to finalize the conversion or to withdraw from it. The other one is a conversion that one may have undergone for ulterior motives: wealth, security, or marriage, but it could also possibly have been sincere. Although such conversions are discouraged, nevertheless, if they performed by an unscrupulous or ignorant rabbinic court, they are held in probation until circumstances change and the possibility of ulterior gain no longer exists. If the convert continues to adhere faithfully to Judaism, the conversion is valid from the beginning; if he or she abandons it, it is invalid *prima facie*. Thus, Ruth's premarital conversion was conditional, since she may have converted solely for the purpose of marriage. Yet later, when she left her native land in order to accompany Naomi in a life of hardship and loneliness, she demonstrated the purity and sincerity of her original commitment.

Although conversion takes effect with a ritual (circumcision and immersion before a court of three rabbis for men and immersion alone for women), its actual fulfillment is in the heart. Jewish law has many such rituals. For example, while mourning is observed by tearing one's clothing or sitting on the ground, it is fulfilled through the emotion that these acts engender. The commandment to rejoice on a festival is fulfilled by eating and drinking with company at a holiday meal, but its fulfillment is the feeling of joy that the meal and the company generate. Similarly, conversion involves a ritual but takes place primarily in the heart. The convert may be sure of the purity of her intent, or she may be deluding herself. When money, marriage or status is involved, only time can tell.

One of my teachers drew this parallel on the occasion of my ordination. He sat with me and explained that the document of ordination, the passing of examinations, even the countless hours spent in study and preparation are not what makes a rabbi. "Ordination is like conversion. It requires a ritual but it is effected within." It can take many years until the original motivation becomes apparent and declares itself. "May you be fortunate that your old age justify your youth" (*Sukkah* 53a).

Ruth completed and validated her original conversion by her decision to accompany Naomi to Bethlehem. However, her journey had actually begun ten years before. When she and Naomi arrive to Bethlehem during the springtime harvest, at the season of renewal, it is then that the new chapter begins.

> She went, and came and gleaned in the field after the reapers; and she happened to light on the portion of the field belonging to Boaz, who was of the family of Elimelech. (2:3)

During the several days (or perhaps months) between her arrival in Bethlehem and the episode with Boaz on the threshing floor, Ruth's reputation became firmly established. "Everyone at the gate of my people knows that you are a woman of valor" (3:11), Boaz tells Ruth. Note that at the first meeting Boaz praises her only for her kindness to Naomi. It is at the second meeting, at the threshing floor, that he bestows on her the title of a woman of valor. It appears then that Ruth's reputation as a woman of valor was only established as she walked in the fields behind the reapers, after Boaz met her for the first time. What is it about her and her behavior that created such a positive impression among the people of Bethlehem?

Let us look at some of the possible reasons for this. Through this exercise we not only grow to appreciate Ruth, but also learn lessons that elevate and inspire.

1. Ruth volunteered to go out and glean in the fields so that Naomi would not have to. She willingly took upon herself an obligation that lay upon Naomi. Ruth did not say: "You got us into this

mess. You are the one who knows these people, recognizes these fields, and enjoys the respect and regard of their owners. None of them, your relatives or your childhood friends, are lifting a finger to help two poor widows whom they know reside in their midst. They should be helping you. I am a stranger, unfamiliar with the town and the customs and ways of its inhabitants. It is not safe for me here – it is you who should go." Had Ruth said this, she would have been in the right. Yet she spared Naomi, for it would have embarrassed her to beg (Malbim). Such sensitivity was undoubtedly noticed.

2. "She went and she came." While the deliberate use of the words "went" emphasizes Ruth's offer ("I will go") and Naomi's assent, ("Go, my daughter), "she came" seems out of place. The Sages comment: "She went and she came. Ruth retraced her steps in order to identify the paths before working in the field so that she would not get lost on her way back" (Ruth Rabbah 4:6) She tested out the owners of the fields so that she would not walk after people who were not decent (Shabbat 113b). She went to the closest field (Rashi) (so that she would not have to carry a heavy load for a long distance on her way home). By doing so, she demonstrated that she was not motivated by greed and wanted only to collect as much as she and Naomi needed.

3. She chose to glean rather than set her sights on peah, the corner of the field that was left for the poor during the harvest. In this fashion she worked as hard as the owners themselves for what she took and also avoided the arguments and dissension among the poor, who descended on the corner as soon as it was left available for them. She chose to work harder but preserved her dignity (Nachalat Yosef).

The Sages saw these clues and expanded on them in Shabbat 113b. They said:

Then said Boaz unto his servant that was set over the reapers: "Whose maiden is this?" (Ruth 2:5). Is it the way of Boaz to inquire about maidens? R. Eliezer said: He saw wisdom in her behavior. She picked up two fallen stalks together but not three [the owner of the field willingly foregoes two stalks but might begrudge her the three stalks taken together]. In a collection [of teachings] it was taught: He saw refinement in her. She picked standing stalks in an upright posture but sat down to pick up the fallen ones [rather than bend down and compromise herself].

Ruth is the most mysterious, private and opaque of the book's characters. She is retiring and willingly walks behind others. She makes no complaints and all her words are pleasant, measured and appropriate. She does for others, asking nothing for herself. In the verses leading up to the first meeting of Ruth and Boaz, we begin to glimpse her character and realize that she is genuine. She is also an aristocrat in her bearing, feelings and thoughts. It is the wide recognition of this fact that enabled her to escape opprobrium for going to lie at Boaz's feet in the middle of the night and that led to his positive response to her act, which otherwise would have been considered brazen self-promotion: "Everyone at the gate of my people knows that you are a woman *of valor*."

Two Souls

> Then said Boaz to his servant, who was supervising the reapers: "Whose young woman is this?" The servant who was supervising the reapers answered him, saying: "She is a young Moabite woman who came back with Naomi out of the plain of Moab; and she said: Please let me glean and gather after the reapers among the sheaves. So she came and continued from the morning until now, though she sat in the house for a little while." (2:5–7)

Though the servant answers Boaz's question, he then volunteers information. That Ruth is a Moabite and that she came back with Naomi are exactly what Boaz wanted to know. However, the comments about Ruth's work ethic are out of place. They only make sense once we realize that Scripture often uses the device of introducing a seminal event with an apparently unrelated conversation. These conversations play an important role as foreshadowing and subtle guidance to understanding the turning point in the narrative. Other examples of this technique is Yosef's conversation with the man in the field before meeting his brothers (Genesis 47:13), David's talk with his brothers before engaging Goliath (Samuel I 17:28), and Saul's question to the maidens whom he meets just prior to being anointed by Samuel (ibid., 9:11). If so, what does this servant's response in this case contribute to our understanding of the ensuing conversation?

It would seem that just as in our own time, when people met a new acquaintance, they wanted to know their family, nation and occupation (See Yonah 1:8; Samuel I, 25:2, Genesis 32:18). Rightly or not, these things are what allow human beings to form an impression upon which future associations may be based. The servant was attempting to provide exactly this kind of information to his master and so, he told him that Ruth was a young Moabite woman, that she lived with Naomi and that she was a hard worker. Aside from what this tells us about Ruth, his words emphasize Boaz's refusal to allow this information to influence him to ignore or even disparage Ruth as other, lesser people might have done.

Boaz was a sage, a divinely-inspired leader who was deeply tuned into the prophetic tradition and shaped by the law and teachings that had been given at Sinai only a few generations before. His words to Ruth betray none of the biases and preconceptions of the people who surrounded him. Boaz's words to Ruth are filled with kindness, fatherly affection, caring and humility. At the same time, their conversation contains a good deal more than is apparent on the surface. Before we begin to analyze it, a short introduction is in order.

It is a basic tenet of Jewish Biblical interpretation that Torah must be understood simultaneously on many levels. We speak of four levels of interpretation – *peshat, derash, remez* (allusion) and *sod* (mystical meaning). Peshat is the plain meaning, which is not necessarily identical with the apparent meaning. To arrive at the correct understanding of peshat, one must combine linguistic expertise, familiarity with local and extended context, erudition, sensitivity to religious tradition, and a clear sense of the principles that one uses to resolve and reconcile discrepancies and divergent implications of traditions and texts, as well as a strong sense of interpretative balance. Derash is the inner meaning that is encoded into the text.

Whereas derash is often subjective and lies in an uneasy balance with peshat, it is especially appropriate for deconstructing conversations and for unpacking undercurrents and hidden meanings in verbal give-and-take that are within our everyday experience. Anyone who routinely participates in group meetings in business, education and other settings is aware of this phenomenon.

Consider, for example, a husband and a wife who are hosting guests who are overstaying their welcome. The husband turns to his wife and says: "Dear, what time is it?" She answers, "It's already 12:30 a.m." Oh, my," he sighs, "how time flies! You know, I have to get up early for work tomorrow." The guests take the hint and promptly leave.

What happened here? On the level of peshat, the husband asked the time, remarked on how quickly time passes and then commented that he must wake up early for work the next day. Yet deeper communication took place on the level of derash. Which interpretation is more "correct"?

When we take this matter up again shortly we will see that the conversation of Boaz and Ruth took place on several levels. First, there was the apparent substance of the conversation, that Ruth should glean in Boaz's field and that he would welcome her. On a deeper level, it was an exchange between two individuals who, as the conversation progressed, found themselves matched in intelligence, moral stature, purity of character, and conception and religious outlook. On an even more profound level Boaz and Ruth spoke of their respective paths in life, how to serve God, and where He was leading them. It is this dialogue that developed trust between these two kindred souls, making possible the encounter on the threshing floor and leading to their Divinely-ordained marriage.

Conversation

> Then said Boaz to Ruth: "Did you not hear, my daughter? Do not go to another person's field to glean, and do not leave this one, but stay here by my maidens. Keep your eyes on the field that they reap and follow them; have I not charged the young men not to touch you? When you thirst, go to the vessels and drink of the water which the young men have drawn." Then she fell on her face and bowed down to the ground and said to him: "Why have I found favor in your eyes that you recognize me, and I am a foreigner?" (2:8–10)

On the surface, Boaz merely tells Ruth to stay in his field, since he has arranged that she be welcomed and made comfortable. He "puts her on the payroll," extending to her the courtesies and benefits that he gives his employees, and for this she is grateful.

However, a careful look at the language reveals powerful currents beneath the surface. We are somewhat handicapped in that we discuss in English a complex conversation in a language that has not been spoken for two and a half millennia (rabbinic, medieval, and modern Hebrew being in truth dialects of Biblical Hebrew that do not possess the subtlety and power of their ancestor). Spoken modern Hebrew has unfortunately gradually taken on much of the syntax and structure of its dominant Indo-European neighbors and is of limited help in understanding its Biblical antecedent. Nevertheless, it is worthwhile to attempt to understand this conversation and what it may have once meant, even if the tools in our possession are somewhat inadequate.

Boaz begins his conversation by referring to his instructions to the workers, using negative expressions for emphasis. He knows that Ruth witnessed his discussion with the overseer of the harvesters from a distance and realized that it was about her. He wants to put her at ease. This reveals Boaz as a sensitive and considerate man, even of strangers. Boaz does not tell Ruth that they are related at this point because he does not want his seniority to interfere with his message.

Boaz uses the long, more formal verb forms in addressing Ruth. Biblical Hebrew possesses certain short and long verb forms; the former are more colloquial and prosaic, while the latter denote respect and deference. Boaz speaks to the poor, young and forlorn widow as if she were his equal. This shows that he recognizes Ruth's true status, which is temporarily obscured by her poverty, plain clothing and foreign speech and deportment.

It is important to recognize that saying, "Keep your eye on the field" is an important vote of confidence and trust in a culture that believes in the evil eye. To put it simply, to believe in the existence of the evil eye is to think that envy can cause physical and financial harm (see *Berachot* 55a). Boaz indicates to Ruth that he knows that she harbors no resentment or envy of those more fortunate, no matter how lowly and deprived she currently finds herself. He recognizes her innate goodness, deep optimism and unfailing trust in God's justice and goodness.

Because Boaz trusts in Ruth's purity of heart, she is emboldened to respond, "Why have I found favor in your *eyes*, that you recognize me?" She is shaken to her core by the depth of insight and caring that this man reveals. He is the first person other than Naomi who has actually *seen* her.

Thus far, the people of Bethlehem had not noticed the Moabite stranger among them. Ruth may have already resigned herself to living out her days alone and lonely among people who, although they carried God's truth, neither accepted nor welcomed her. Ruth may have accepted social ostracism as the price of communion with God.

But now everything changes. Never before has anyone peered deeply into her soul and affirmed who she is and for what she yearns – not in Moab and certainly not in Bethlehem. She may have never met anyone like this before, and now that she has, she is full of wonder and gratitude.

She falls on her face because she feels inadequate in the face of what has just been revealed to her. She prostrates herself as a pupil does to a master, for she has just met her teacher. She may yet find a path to God and goodness among these people. For the first time, she feels hope.

> Then she fell on her face, bowed down to the ground, and said to him: "Why have I found favor in your eyes that you recognize me, and I am a foreigner?" (2:8–10)

All this would be amazing enough. However, the Sages reveal to us an even deeper level in this conversation. They describe that Boaz was coaching Ruth in how to avoid common pitfalls of a recent convert.

Newcomers to religion often feel threatened by absolute demands of their newly found way of life. Before, they were independent, valued men and women. Now they are novices, beginners, those who receive rather than give. Their sense of self-worth and sometimes even their sense of self is threatened. A convert or even a Jew who is new to observance often feels unappreciated and misunderstood by the people who are comfortable with the minutiae of ritual and observance and secure in their faith.

To affirm their selves, converts may sometimes be tempted to resort to syncretism – a merging of past and future, importing beliefs from outside Judaism and affirming that he or she brings something to the community that is valuable and unique, something that only he or she can offer. "If only it could be joined to the truths that I experience here," they think. "I only I could teach these self-satisfied and smug people true values – my values!"

When the locals are less than receptive, the convert withdraws. The result can be spiritual ruin and estrangement, since arrogance and self-exaltation not only interfere with learning but also lead to heresy.

The three stages of estrangement are described in the following midrash. "Do not go to glean in the field of another" – as it is written, "You may have no other gods but Me." "Also, do not leave this field," as it is written, "This is my God and I will build a holy space for Him." "Stay close to my maidens" – "These are the righteous, as it is written, 'Will You delight in it like a bird and join it to Your maidens?'" (*Ruth Rabbah* 4:11).

That Boaz truly saw Ruth, that he understood what she perhaps realized only vaguely, cut to her heart. She fell on her face, prostrating herself in acknowledgment of the wonder that she just experienced. "A sage is greater than a prophet" (*Bava Batra* 12a).

Ruth felt inadequate as she saw herself revealed so clearly. This man was like an angel and she was but a human being. Why did he then take interest in her?

> Why have I found favor in your eyes that you recognize me, and I am a foreigner?

I suspect that Boaz was equally moved by Ruth's sincerity and willingness to follow the truth without preconditions.

> Boaz answered her, saying, "I have been told all that you have done for your mother-in-law since your husband's death, how you left your father and mother and the land of your birth and came to a

people that you never knew before. May God reward your actions, and may your reward be complete from the Lord, the God of Israel, under whose wings you came to take refuge." (2:10–12)

Boaz responds to Ruth's sense of surprise with the only possible answer that can bring her closer. In her words one message rings – I am a stranger and unworthy, while you are the leader of a blessed nation; what can we possibly have in common and why do you say all these things to me? Boaz must explain, and he does so with wisdom and tact. At the same time that he acknowledges that she is a convert, he formulates his statements carefully.

Boaz first notes that Ruth has done a mighty deed of valor. Like Abraham, she has left all that she has known for the sake of an idea. In a way, she performed a greater feat than Abraham for he walked after God, Who after all is always faithful and Who protects and rewards his servants. On the other hand, Ruth came to join a nation that she did not know. Perhaps her neighbors are narrow-minded, petty, vindictive, hypocritical, or simply unsuitable to be her people. Yet she did it anyway because kindness is so much a part of her.

The allusion to Abraham is unmistakable. Compare the following phrases:

… how you left your father and mother and the land of your birth and came to a people that you never knew before (Ruth, ibid.).

God said to Abram, "Depart from your land, your birthplace, and your father's house, to the land that I will show you." (Genesis 12:1; for another parallel see Psalms 45:11)

Boaz understood that dwelling on Ruth as a convert might not please her, so he quickly moves beyond that fact. Now Ruth is a Jew and whatever her merits in converting may have been in the past, it is belonging that she now craves most of all. He must explain to her that he marvels at something that unites them, not something that will set them apart: lovingkindness.

"That you came to take refuge under His wings…." R. Avin said: The earth has wings – "from the wings of the earth we heard songs" (Isaiah 24). The morning has wings – "If I take the wings of the morning" (Psalms 139:9). The sun has wings – "The sun of righteousness with healing at its wings" (Malachi 3:30). The Cherubim have wings – "The sound of the wings of the Cherubim" (Ezekiel 10:5). The Chayos have wings – "The sound of the wings of the Chayos" (Ezekiel 3:13). The Seraphim have wings – "Each one had six wings" (Isaiah 6:12). Said R. Avin: Great is the power of those who act benevolently, for they shelter not in the shadow of the wings of the earth, nor in the shadow of the wings of the morning, nor in the shadow of the wings of the sun, nor in the shadow of the wings of the Cherubim, nor in the shadow of the wings of the Chayos, but in the shadow of Him at whose word the world was created, as it is written (Psalms 36:8): "How precious is Your lovingkindness, O God. The children of the world take refuge in Your wings" (*Ruth Rabbah* 5:4).

This rabbinic comment skillfully shifts our attention from Ruth the convert, who comes to seek refuge under God's wings, to the shelter that He gives to all the children of the world. God gives equal protection to all His children who emulate His love and kindness in their dealings with one another.

The realization that this elderly sage views Ruth as equal, if not superior, to him and that he marvels at her spiritual accomplishments leaves Ruth speechless. A moment of deep communion has taken place, and no one but the protagonists knows it. One thing is clear: Boaz and Ruth share values and perceptions. Perhaps they are united at the roots of their souls. The metaphor of wings and lovingkindness returns when Ruth speaks to Boaz at the threshing floor.

He said, "Who are you?" She answered, "I am Ruth, your servant. Therefore, spread your wings over your handmaid; for you are a redeemer." And he said: "May God bless you, my daughter. You have shown more kindness in the end than at the beginning." (Ruth 3:9–10)

The mixing of the sacred and the personal in the innermost place of love and life is the highest peak of spiritual life. Can men and women ever deal with one another on a level beyond physical desire? The book of Ruth says that they can, though only the wholly righteous should ever attempt it (Ritva on the end of *Kiddushin*). All others must be guided by the parameters of the religious law that governs interaction between the sexes. Any impurity, any admixture of petty desire or self-interest can spoil relationships and lead us to the depths of the abyss.

R. Akiva expounded: If a man and woman merit it, the Divine Presence rests between them. If they do not, fire consumes them (Sotah 17a).

Boaz and Ruth build their relationship and their recognition and understanding of one another upon a lifetime of spiritual growth. Their quest for purity and unselfish commitment to God unite them. The name of God is constantly upon their lips. They can risk meeting upon the threshing floor in the middle of the night with no witnesses because they share a palpable awareness of God's presence. When a man and woman build their relationship on lovingkindness, they draw upon an incomparable resource and redemption becomes possible, as Ruth tells Boaz, "… for you are a redeemer."

The Understanding

> Then she said, "I have found favor in your sight, my master, for you have comforted me, and because you spoke to the heart of your handmaid, though I am not worthy to be as one of your handmaidens." Boaz said to her at mealtime: "Come here and eat of the bread, and dip your morsel in the vinegar." So she sat beside the reapers and he handed her parched corn. She ate and was satisfied, and left over. (2:13–14)

The refinement, delicacy and deliberate opacity of the communication between Ruth and Boaz in these sentences are almost more profound than any other conversation in Tanach. These two exquisite souls share a deep and abiding commitment to spirituality and the service of God, yet they are also aware that they are a man and a woman speaking heart to heart. Therefore, they take great care, showing utmost restraint and remarkable refinement in what they say and even in what they leave unsaid. They speak in highly stylized and symbolic language since they are masters of "parable and expression, words of the wise and their riddles" (Proverbs 1:1).

Before we consider the rabbinic comments on these verses, let us look closely at some of the expressions that Ruth employs. By comparing her use of these expressions with how they are used elsewhere in Scriptures, some of the idiomatic meaning, tone, and nuance will become revealed, and then we might begin to understand.

"You spoke to the heart of your handmaid." Of the ten instances of this expression, the majority are a highly personal appeal by a man to woman. Three examples will suffice.

> Her husband arose and went after her, to speak kindly to her heart and bring her back. (Judges 19:3)

> Therefore, behold, I will entice her, and bring her into the wilderness, and speak to her heart. And I will give her vineyards from there, and the valley of Achor for a door of hope; and she shall respond there, as in the days of her youth, and as in the day when

she came up out of the land of Egypt. On that day, says God, you shall call Me "my husband," and shall call Me no more "my master." (Hoshea 2:16–18)

Shechem the son of Hamor the Hivvite, the prince of the land, saw her. He took her, lay with her, and violated her. His soul cleaved unto Dinah the daughter of Jacob, and he loved the girl, and spoke to the heart of the girl. (Gen. 34:2–3)

That Ruth compares herself to the handmaidens of Boaz is highly significant. Does Boaz have handmaidens and where are they mentioned before in the verse? Boaz has no handmaidens, nor could he have any, since the Torah allows a Jewish man to own a Jewish woman only as preparation for marriage and even that in highly specific circumstances (see Exodus 21). A Jew may possess non-Jewish female slaves but surely Ruth did not aspire to be a gentile slave girl. The word that Ruth employs – shifchah – as opposed to the word amah, has special significance. In order to understand it let us look at another exchange between a man and a woman in somewhat similar circumstances.

Here, David's band protected the shepherds and sheep of Naval the Carmelite, but when David needed a favor, Naval verbally abused his messengers and flatly refused to help. As a prelude to the passage we are about to discuss, the enraged David and his men are approaching Naval's home so as to reduce it to ruins. Abigail, the wife of Naval, goes out to meet David and persuades him to spare her husband and household. Among other things she says this to him (I Samuel 25):

Upon me, my lord, upon me be the iniquity. Please let your handmaid speak to you, and hear the words of your handmaid. It will come to pass, when God has done to my lord according to all the good that He has spoken concerning you, and has appointed you prince over Israel…. When God shall have dealt well with my lord, then remember your handmaid [amah].

This is a rather forward speech for a married woman. The Sages noted this and criticized Abigail for it.

"When God has dealt well with my lord, then remember your handmaid." – R. Nachman said: This is what people say: [sometimes] a woman chatters as she weaves [Rashi: as she spoke of her husband she mentioned herself, that he should marry her if he dies]. Some say: While a goose walks, she scans what is in front of her." (Megillah 14b)

When David heard that Naval was dead, he said: "Blessed be God, Who pleaded the cause of my reproach from the hand of Naval and kept back His servant from evil. God has turned back the evil-doing of Naval upon his own head." David sent and spoke concerning Abigail, to take her to him to wife. When David's servants came to Abigail to Carmel, they spoke to her, saying: "David has sent us to you, to take you to him to wife," she arose and bowed down with her face to the earth, saying, "Behold, your handmaid [*shifchah*] is a servant to wash the feet of my lord's servants."

We see from here that the word *shifchah,* which was used by Abigail and by Ruth, carries a special connotation of marriage.

In the Torah, too, a wife may sometimes be referred to as a handmaiden. Bilhah and Zilpah, the wives of Jacob, are alternately referred to as wives or handmaidens, depending on the context. I also suggest exploring the language that Bathsheba uses in II Samuel 1 as she pleads the case of her son Solomon to David.

The Sages decode the conversation between Boaz and Ruth for us in their usual poetic style. "He [Boaz] said to her: God forbid – you are not of the maidservants but of the matriarchs." This is a play on words, since in Hebrew the words *amah* (handmaiden) and *ima* (mother or matriarch) are similar. "Come hither – R. Yochanan interprets it in six ways. 'Hither' means 'royalty' – as it says [of David], "that You have brought me hither" (*Ruth Rabbah* 5:6).

Within several sentences, Ruth has gone from a stranger to a candidate for the matriarch of a royal family. Unlike Abigail, however, she expresses her hope by using a negative – "I am not worthy to be as one of your handmaidens." It is this circumspection, refinement and humility that earn her the opportunity to join the spiritual aristocracy of the Jewish nation.

In these few sentences, a great deal has been offered and shared. Since nothing more remains to be spoken, Boaz invites Ruth to seal the agreement that they have made unbeknown to those who surround them. "Boaz said to her at mealtime: 'Come hither and eat of the bread, and dip your morsel in the vinegar.' She sat beside the reapers and he handed her parched corn. She ate and was satisfied, and left over." He, personally, and symbolically, handed her food. With all that, their understanding remains preliminary and subject to misreading precisely because it is so private, so dependent on interpretation. Their pact is reaffirmed and finally sealed when they meet again at the threshing floor and once more he hands her a gift of barley as the agreement is sealed.

"He said, 'Bring the mantle that you are wearing and hold it out.' She held it out, and he measured six measures of barley and laid it on her, and he went into the city." (Ruth 3:15)

In these few sentences, the Book of Ruth sets the stage for the fateful meeting at the threshing floor. In the process we learn to appreciate the truly elevated stature of Boaz and Ruth. The meeting in the middle of the night upon the threshing floor no longer surprises us, for we have grown to understand and respect these two pure and refined individuals from whom the royal seed is destined to issue.

The Light of the Messiah

> And when she rose to glean, Boaz commanded his young men, saying: "Let her glean even among the sheaves, and do not put her to shame. Also, pull some out for her on purpose from the bundles and leave it, and let her glean, and do not rebuke her."
>
> So she gleaned in the field until evening; and she beat out what she had gleaned, and it was about an *ephah* of barley.
>
> She took it up and went into the city; and her mother-in-law saw what she had gleaned; and she took it out and gave to her that which she had left after she was satisfied.
>
> Her mother-in-law said to her: "Where did you glean today? Where did you work? Blessed be he who took notice of you." She told her mother-in-law with whom she worked and said: "The man's name with whom I worked to-day is Boaz."
>
> Naomi said to her daughter-in-law: "May he be blessed by God, who has not left off His kindness to the living and to the dead." Naomi said unto her: "The man is kin to us, one of our near kinsmen."
>
> Ruth the Moabite said: "Yes, he said to me: keep fast by my young men until they have completed all my harvest."
>
> Naomi said to Ruth her daughter-in-law: "It is good, my daughter, that you go out with his maidens, and that you not go to any other field."
>
> So she kept fast by the maidens of Boaz to glean until the end of the barley harvest and the wheat harvest, and she dwelt with her mother-in-law. (Ruth 2:15–23)

After Boaz and Ruth ate together, circumstances returned to the way they had been. Ruth returned to gleaning in the field and Boaz to being its owner. So it went until both the barley harvest and the wheat harvest were over – a period of almost three months. Behind the scenes, however, Boaz took care of Ruth's material needs in a way that did not leave her beholden to him or even aware of his kindness. He commanded that sheaves be left for her, as if forgotten in the haste of the harvest, so that she could bring them home and accumulate a store of grain. However, Ruth did not know from where this largesse came and refused to take it. Perhaps it came from the lads who labored in the fields who perhaps meant to curry favor with her for their own reasons. Ruth kept her dignity and remained aloof, taking only the gleanings to which she was entitled.

When Ruth returned home on that first day, she carried a large quantity of grain, together with the leftovers of a prepared supper that she had saved for Naomi – parched grain, perhaps slices of bread dipped in vinegar. The poor who glean in the fields are not fed; that is not the responsibility of the field owner. Naomi, seeing the supper, assumed that Ruth had not only gleaned but had hired herself out that day – "Where did you glean and where did you work?" she asks in surprise. Naomi is concerned, for clearly some stranger was overly kind to her daughter-in-law, perhaps out of pure motives, perhaps not. Ruth tells Naomi who the man was and then is surprised in turn. Boaz is a kinsman! Naomi blesses God, since she knows that this could have come only from Him and that in some way He has a plan for them.

Ruth must have been torn between a sense of obligation and fear. Shouldn't she tell Naomi what had taken place between Boaz and herself? Would Naomi understand? Would the act of telling her sully the ephemeral, delicate and evanescent communication that passed between Boaz and Ruth? Perhaps it was not even true, for nothing was made explicit or clear. Could it be that her poverty and sorrow played tricks with her mind, evoking fantasies of things that were not and never could be? A foreigner – a Moabite beggar to boot – and the prince of the people?

Ruth communicates to Naomi in the only way that befits a refined and intelligent woman like herself – by allusion. The servants stand proxy for Boaz. "He said to me: Keep fast by my young men, until they have completed all my harvest," but Naomi does not grasp her intent.

Months pass by without another conversation. For reasons that remain obscure to us until later, Boaz does not reach out to Ruth. On the surface, the story has stalled, but behind the scenes, God is working toward His goal.

> It happened at that time that Judah went down away from his
> brothers… R. Shmuel bar Nachmani began: "I know the

calculations (Jeremiah 29)." The brothers were busy with the sale of Joseph. Joseph was occupied with his fasting and sackcloth. Reuven was occupied with his fasting and sackcloth. Yaakov was occupied with his fasting and sackcloth. Yehudah was occupied with finding a wife. And the Holy One, blessed be He, was occupied with creating the light of the Messiah" (*Genesis Rabbah* 85:2)

No one can rush the light of the Messiah. Boaz, Ruth and Naomi continued to think, consider, hope and wonder among themselves. When the time comes, they will be ready; their thinking clarified, their emotions purified, their purpose certain. Like pregnancy, the determination was growing within them for three months; when the barley and wheat harvest was completed, so was the plan. Now all the actors are ready, and in chapter 3 the Author brings it to fruition.

THE LIGHT OF REDEMPTION

The Light Breaks Forth

> "And now is there not Boaz our kinsman, with whose maidens you were? Behold, he winnows barley tonight at the threshing-floor. Wash yourself, anoint yourself, and put on your special clothing, and go down to the threshing-floor, but make not yourself known to anyone, until he is finished eating and drinking. Then, when he lies down, that you mark the place where he lies, and go and uncover his feet and lie down; and he will tell you what to do." (3:2–3)

THE PHYSICAL DESCRIPTION of the meeting between Boaz and Ruth is confused and confusing. Boaz, who previously had many workers in his employ, is now portrayed as winnowing alone. Not only is he left to do the work of winnowing the entire barley crop by himself (apparently after the wheat has been all harvested he returned to winnow the barley), but he does so at night.

Normally, winnowing is performed by throwing the mixture of grain and chaff upward. The wind carries away the chaff, which is lighter, while the heavier grain falls to the ground. Since winds tend to subside at night, the nighttime is not the best time for winnowing. Also, it seems that Boaz winnows on the low ground, which is less windy – a place to which Ruth had to "descend" – the exact opposite of an area that an experienced winnower would choose.

When Boaz finishes his work, he eats and drinks and, instead of returning home, goes to sleep. Somehow in the darkness, Ruth manages to not only find him but also to uncover his feet and to lie down without awakening him.

A partial solution to some of these difficulties is the following scenario drawn from various commentators and based primarily on the Malbim.

Ruth went to join Boaz's maidens before they left for the day. Since she went there regularly, she did not draw particular attention – hence the reference "with whose maidens you were." Boaz stayed at the threshing floor overnight for a reason. The Omer offering is cut down and prepared at night so that it may be offered on the following day (Rokeach). Boaz remains behind alone to winnow a small measure of barley, which he prepares for the Omer offering. This is why he is alone and in an area of low wind: so as to be able to do this holy work with appropriate concentration. After everyone else has left, Ruth hides on the grounds, waiting for Boaz to finish.

Boaz does not return home because it is not becoming for a religious leader to be seen walking around at night lest he be suspected of unbecoming behavior (see the extended discussion on this point in Bach's commentary). He goes down to a lower, less exposed area of the threshing floor and lies down to rest. Ruth now changes into festival clothing and descends to where she knows Boaz will rest. She lies down at his feet and waits.

Why does the Book of Ruth not make all this clear? I would venture to say that it wishes to communicate to us that we should actually be confused and perturbed. The outer form of the narrative follows the inner content and is designed to discomfit and disturb the reader. Naomi's plan itself should disturb us. Granted, it is the widow's obligation to seek to perpetuate her departed husband's name, by subterfuge if necessary, as it is written, "His wife shall go up to the gate, to the elders" (Deuteronomy 25). Nevertheless, should not have Naomi pursued a more conventional approach? Should she not have sent matchmakers to Boaz or gone to him herself with a proposal?

What she does instead is extremely risky. We know that Ruth is an outstanding woman graced with all manner of nobility, but others do not. Naomi's plan could have gone terribly wrong. What if someone had seen? What if Boaz cried out in his fright and people rushed in? Imagine a Moabite girl slipping under the cover of darkness to tempt the leader of the generation! Both Ruth and Naomi would have been irredeemably shamed.

Yet it is not as though Naomi never thought of this. She considered everything and took responsibility for this plan. The wording in the beginning of the third chapter has great depth. In these few sentences there are no less than seventeen instances of *keri u-ketiv* – words that are spelled in one way but read in another. Most of these otherwise rare variants can be read as if it is Naomi herself who descends to the threshing floor, changes into festival clothing and lies at Boaz's feet. When Naomi says, "You shall go down to the barn," the *ketiv* is: "I shall go down." The verse should be read as if she said: "May my merit go with you" (JT *Peah* 8:7).

It may be that Naomi had realized two important things. First, she knew that God had not led Ruth to Boaz's field in vain. God has inclined Boaz's heart to notice Ruth and brought about an inner connection between the two. However, she also understood that not everything in life can be planned and that a life in which every detail has its place is bereft of Divine influence. She gave God a chance by creating a situation in which He could work a miracle. It is tempting to leave nothing to chance, to plan everything in advance in order to ensure against failure, but doing so leaves God out of the picture and is not the way of those who have true faith.

Naomi knew that Ruth must act out her destiny boldly. The verses just before this chapter emphasize that Ruth was a Moabite. True, she had converted and was now a Jewish woman, but it was specifically that Moabite quality of royalty – directness, boldness, frankness – that she was to bring to the Davidic line. As we might say, she felt it in her bones. "My kidneys have advised me: Go, do as your ancestral mother, the daughter of Lot, once did, when Lot finished eating and drinking and she came to her father in the darkness" (*Zot nechamati* and Alshich).

Conventional conduct was not the right way, and Naomi knew this. The spiritual forces that Ruth's conduct would unleash brought with them an abundance of opportunities, as well as the chance of complete failure. Fortunately, Boaz and Ruth proved equal to the challenge of containing and elevating these forces and by so doing changed the course of human history.

Light and Darkness

The meeting of Boaz and Ruth on the threshing floor is the peak of the story. It is here that gripping narrative, psychological insight, historical awareness, symbolism and allusion are woven together in a parable of redemption. Before we immerse ourselves in the narrative, let us set guideposts along the way and note some of the interwoven levels along which the story develops.

1. Psychological insight – the story of two pure souls who trust one another under the most improbable circumstances. The understanding that Boaz and Ruth established during their brief conversation was sorely tested during their encounter in the darkness. Ruth tested Boaz because she was sure that he would pass the test. She also tried herself; Naomi had asked Ruth, a recent convert, to trust her body and soul to a strange man from a foreign people. Boaz could have failed in so many different ways, some of them honorable and respectable on the surface. Although many excuses were available to him, he chose the path of integrity, one that required that he maintain his belief in Ruth against all evidence.

   After all, Ruth was a Moabite, from a nation of low moral standards – and indeed, here she was, lying at his uncovered feet in the middle of the night! Yet Boaz trusted her. Above all, he trusted himself and his perception of who she was. He did not waver or question. He knew that his vision was pure, sprung from a pure heart, and he trusted that which he instinctively understood. The story of this meeting is ultimately about trusting – oneself, God and others.

2. The moral level - undoubtedly, Boaz very much wanted to marry Ruth. However, the path of integrity required that he consider Ploni Almoni, the other relative who could have wedded Ruth, and so he offered him the chance to trust as he himself trusted. Ploni Almoni did not grasp the greatness within his reach, and so he remains Ploni Amoni, "John Doe," the person with no name. Nevertheless, he deserved that chance. Boaz's conduct teaches us that no matter how exalted the purpose or how great the spiritual benefits, they never trump simple human decency.

3. The symbolic and the hidden - the symbolism of the threshing floor should be mentioned. This is a place where wheat is separated from the chaff. The motif of harvest, seed and bounty adds to the significance that surrounds and holds these verses together. Redemption is preceded by the separation of good and evil, for in our world, good and evil are intermixed. We might say that our reality is neither night nor day but a kind of twilight, when light and darkness function together, shadows appear solid and what is real looks ephemeral. It is humanity's task to separate light from darkness, to extract the good and join it to its root so that it can be redeemed. Then evil will perish on its own and the good will be transformed into Godliness as wheat becomes bread, as Boaz and Ruth become progenitors of the Messianic line. In Kabbalah this is known as *berur,* or clarification, the first condition of redemption.

   For now these kings will not yet be clarified until the days of the Messiah, for then they will be completely clarified and impurities will cease to exist, which is the mystery of the verse "He will destroy death forever" (Isaiah 25:8).

   The good in them will be clarified and join Holiness. In our days, bit by bit, this clarification is taking place every day, but with the coming of the Messiah, it will be completed (*Otzrot Chaim,* Anach 3).

History informs our understanding of the narrative. Both Boaz and Ruth came to this divinely-arranged meeting with a great deal of historical precedent. As noted in the introductory lessons, Boaz descended from

Tamar who, with all good intentions, tempted Judah in the guise of a harlot. Ruth was descended from Lot, whose daughters deceived their father into lying with them "for there is no man to come to us in the manner of all the land." Yes, good intentions sometimes lead to poor outcomes – but not this time; this time Ruth is siucessful and Boaz repeats the pattern. Boaz, as the older authority figure, stands in for Lot and Judah, while she takes the place of the younger women of those episodes.

By choosing differently, by rising above the burden of the precedent, Boaz and Ruth perform *tikkun*, or rectification, the second condition of redemption. They liberate the good intentions of Lot's daughters and of Tamar that had been concealed in the outwardly ugly form of their actions. In this way they elevated the good, making it suitable for redemption.

Since the few verses that we are about to explore are the crux of the book, they require special tools. In order to do justice to this complex narrative, we will have to move freely from one level of meaning to another – a task more fitting for poetry than for commentary. The commentator's tools are textual analysis and intellectual reflection, which are less suited for this task than those that a poet and mystic would apply. Nevertheless, we will do our best to use them, as we have done so far throughout this work.

It Came to Pass at Midnight…

> When Boaz had eaten and drunk and his heart was glad, he went to lie down at the end of the heap of corn. She came in the darkness, uncovered his feet and lay down.
>
> It came to pass at midnight that the man trembled and turned – and behold, a woman lay at his feet.
>
> He said: "Who are you?" She answered: "I am Ruth, your handmaid. Spread therefore your wing over your handmaid; for you are a redeemer.' He said: 'May God bless you, my daughter" (3:7–10)

This little passage stands out for its drama, its depth in what is said and what is left unsaid. It is full of shadows and gaps that the reader is called to fill in. As always in Hebrew Scripture, what we take from the text depends on what we bring to it. Everything is based on the traditions, experience, values and training that the interpreter brings to the task of interpretation. We will attempt to present a reading that bases itself on the Sages' comments and is guided by the assumptions we used so far. As will shortly become apparent, rabbinic interpretation is often informed by parallel passages and verses.

"Uncovering the feet" is ambiguous. On one hand it is simply a sign of submission and acceptance of leadership. Maimonides in his *Guide of the Perplexed* (1:28) cites many examples of such usage of this metaphor. On the other hand, it carries connotations of physical closeness and desire, such as in I Samuel 24:4 and II Samuel 11:8. This second meaning is made clear in Rashi's explanation of a comment in Talmud *Sanhedrin* 19b where it is said that Boaz's body became like the heads of turnips.[1] It is even clearer in the following passage:

R. Shmuel Bar Nachman said, "Cursed be the wicked. In reference to Potiphar's wife it is written, 'She said, "Lie with me"' like an animal, but of Ruth it is written, 'Spread your wing over your handmaid'" (*Genesis Rabbah* 87:4).

This comparison between Ruth and Potiphar's wife calls to mind an important idea explicated beautifully by R. Tsadok ha-Cohen in *Likkutei Amarim* 80b. He writes that every element seeks to join itself with a similar element. If a woman on a low spiritual level seeks out an elevated man, it is either a sign that something within him still requires correction or that an element of goodness within her seeks redemption. The impure does not desire to attach itself to the pure, except for one of those two reasons.

For example, why would the wife of Pharaoh's chief executioner wish to attach herself to a pious Jewish man? She must have done so out of a desperate search for meaning and redemption. This is why Joseph was initially tempted somewhat by his master's wife, for he understood that she could not be attracted to him unless they shared something on a deeper level. In the end, it was her daughter Asnat who ultimately married Joseph.

The comparison between Potiphar's wife and Ruth emphasizes that Ruth wanted Boaz solely for his goodness and righteousness. He, in turn, sensed that her motives were pure.[2] Ruth uses a significant word that Boaz had said

---

[1] However, the plural form of "turnips" presents a difficulty for this interpretation. For a possible alternate explanation, compare with *Sanhedrin* 94a, where Jethro's flesh is said to become "sharp points," perhaps referring to what we call "goose bumps."

[2] This train of thought can be traced to the Ari ha-Kadosh. "Through this you will understand the concept of the *yefat to'ar*…. It is known that those who went out to the optional war were righteous, to the extent of not speaking between prayers. How then could it be that such great saints were affected by the desire to defile themselves with a foreign woman? This is why the Torah informed us that if he longs for her, this is nothing more than a spark of holiness intermixed in that nation that is found in the non-Jewish woman – specifically, a spark that is related to the soul of this man is within this woman. He therefore desired her. So the Torah permitted him to cohabit with her, and through the spirit that he injects into her during intimacy, as is known, perhaps the good within her will overcome and push away the bad, and the woman will enter into holiness and convert. Nevertheless, she gives birth to a rebellious son, for it is impossible for her

to her at their first meeting: "May God recompense your work, and may your reward be complete from the Lord, the God of Israel, under whose *wings* you came to take refuge" (Ruth 2:14). In return, she asks that Boaz spread his *wing* over her, meaning his four-cornered, fringed outer garment (as many still spread a tallit in order to constitute a chuppah), alluding to the commandment of tzitzit and its power to guard against temptation (see Malbim here, and Rashash on *Kiddushin* 18b).

When a man spreads his garment over a woman, he is saying symbolically that they now wear the same cloak and face the world from beneath the same cover. Ruth was prepared to cover herself in the garments of the Sage of Israel, with everything that this entailed.

The Hebrew word *va-yilafat* (Ruth 3:8) may also be translated as "grasped." Who or what grasped Boaz? Since the unusual verb form that is used here (see Judges 16:29) is passive and not reflexive, it can be interpreted that someone other than Ruth grasped him. Certain sources suggest that a servant of Boaz may have slept with him in the granary (*Targum Ruth* on v. 14). This is the fellow whom Boaz tells later: "Let it not be known that the woman came to the threshing-floor" (3:14). Perhaps than it was he who grasped Boaz at that moment of apparent danger. However, the simplest understanding its that it was Ruth who grasped him in an attempt to prevent him from involuntarily crying out in fright.

Boaz trembled. Like Isaac, he suddenly found himself in front of a fateful choice. He could accept Ruth, trust in her and in God and bless her, or he could blame her, call her a manipulator and curse her.

> R. Akiva was to go to [lobby in] Rome. He said to his servant: Bring me something valuable from the market [to bring as a gift]. He went and brought him a pair of birds. R. Akiva asked him, "Why did it take you so long?" He said, "Because birds make one tremble and take care to watch them." R. Akiva applied it to himself: "Man's trembling leads to failure, but those who trust God will be saved" (Proverbs 29). By rights, Isaac could have cursed Jacob for having caused him to tremble (Genesis 27:33). However, "Those who trust in God will be saved" – You put it into Isaac's heart to bless his son. Although it was only right that Boaz should curse Ruth for having caused him to tremble, "those who trust in God shall be uplifted."

---

to be cleansed of all impurity" (*Likkutei ha-Ari*, Ki Tetze). A similar but shorter comment is found in *Likkutei Torah* by the Ari regarding Shechem and Dinah. Shechem's desire to elevate his spark of holiness led him to Dinah and subsequently to circumcision. Once he elevated this spark by being circumcised, Yaakov's sons destroyed what remained.

> You put it into his heart to bless her, as it is written, "May God bless you, my daughter" (*Ruth Rabbah* 6:2)

"At midnight I shall rise to praise you for your righteous judgments" (Psalms 109:15). (David said, I praise You) for the judgments that You brought unto Ammonites and Moabites and for the goodness that you did for my great grandfather and grandmother. Had Boaz rushed in with a curse, from whence would I have come? However, You put a blessing into his heart, as it says, "May you be blessed" (*Ruth Rabbah* 6:1).

When in doubt, the righteous choose to bless. When Boaz had to make a quick decision, he chose to bless rather than curse, for that was his nature. Everything else that followed was a consequence of this one, single, momentous choice. Blessed be Boaz and fortunate are we for the choices that he made and the lessons he left to us. May we be worthy of internalizing and living his lessons to the full.

> He said: 'May God bless you, my daughter; your last kindness is more than the first, since as you did not walk after the young men, whether poor or rich. And now, my daughter, fear not; I will do for you all that you said, for everyone at the gate of my people knows that you are a virtuous woman" (3:7–8).

One of the wonderful aspects of Tanach that never ceases to move and amaze me is how well it uses echoes and reflections to communicate a rich and complex vision. This is no doubt an intentional technique that enables the Author to contain a great deal of meaning in a few words. Let us compare Boaz's current statements to his first conversation with Ruth.

Our verses parallel much of the previous encounter between Boaz and Ruth, drawing out the implicit and making it explicit, securing vague impressions and fixing their boundaries, and converting a loose and approximate understanding between two parties into shared knowledge and mutual awareness.

Boaz begins by recalling that Ruth is "blessed of God." Who brought about that blessing? Boaz himself did so, as it is written, "He said to the reapers, 'God be with you,' and they said, 'May God bless you'" (2:4).

Boaz again calls Ruth "my daughter" as he did in 2:8, when he asked her not "to glean in the field of another." He reminds her that he always wanted her to stay in his field, nearby. At the same time, by addressing her once more as "daughter," he sets the boundaries of their relationship. It is and must remain for the sake of Heaven. The Sages say that "He who marries a woman for the sake of Heaven is considered as if he gave birth to her" (*Sotah* 12a) – hence "my daughter." The man must support and assist the woman in reaching her potential as a mother and wife. "A woman makes a covenant only with the man who makes her into a vessel" (*Sanhedrin* 22b).

A husband can only perform this function if, like a father, he seeks to elevate his wife and the entire household together with her. This aspiration by necessity puts him into a paternal role.

Paternalism has a bad reputation in this generation. Many perceive it as controlling, intrusive, insensitive, limiting. That may sometimes be so. However, at the heart of being a father lies the desire to benefit others, sacrifice oneself for them, and give unconditionally.

Boaz minimizes and overlooks his own needs for the good of his wife and family. Even though Boaz and Ruth were bound together in a moment of spiritual closeness, Boaz does not attempt to draw on the powers of attraction that would come so naturally in that intense and deserted environment. At this moment their relationship is filial, and so it shall remain.

Boaz recognizes that he and Ruth are inextricably intertwined in both the religious and the personal spheres. He takes great care so that one does not intrude upon, compromise or sully the other. He now alludes once more to their first meeting, during which the motif of God's great compassion was prominent.

"Your last kindness is greater than the first." Clearly the later kindness is Ruth's request for marriage – but what was the earlier one? Of the commentators' various interpretations, I propose the Malbim's: "The first kindness was the one that you did for your husband when you married, since you chose to marry a man of the seed of Israel." In other words, Ruth looked upon marriage as another opportunity to deal kindness. She did not marry Machlon out of pity. Nevertheless, this Moabite aristocrat must have had many choices other than the Israelite refugee, a stranger in her land.

Ruth, who was kind, was initially drawn to the nation whose nature was to be kind. Now, having grown spiritually and advanced in her understanding and religious development, tempered by God's wrath and sustained by His kindness, she has traveled far beyond where she had been a decade before. Yet she continues to elevate herself according to her nature.

Her marriage to Boaz repeats her previous choices, but on a higher spiritual plane. Boaz always knew that Ruth came to "dwell under the wings" of God. Now she has asked him to spread his wing over her – a mingling of the personal and the religious! Boaz knows that Ruth wishes to learn and to grow with him, and for that he is immensely grateful. It is a greater kindness than the first.

At the time of her first marriage, Ruth had not seen and understood her choices as clearly as she does now. At that time, she was a young woman guided by nothing more than a vague sense of destiny. The personal and the spiritual were perhaps less clear in her mind. Although she married a Jewish man, he was living in Moab and behaving like a Moabite. He was in the prime of youth and she liked him. It made no difference to her whether he was poor or wealthy. Although she was looking through him at the God of Israel, her vision was cloudy and confused.

Now she is no longer walking after young men, rich or poor. She lies at the feet of Boaz – and older man and a sage in Israel – and she will follow him. Ruth lives among the Judeans and has a much greater knowledge of what Judaism entails. Not all women would want this. It is indeed a greater kindness than the first one. Why? Although Ruth now understood the pluses and minuses of her choice much better, she still chose to repeat it.

Boaz is careful about the manner in which he speaks to Ruth. He wishes to strengthen her self-esteem and her self confidence. "I will do for you all that you have said." This echoes Ruth's unquestioning acceptance of Naomi's advice – "All that you say, I will do." Boaz, however, introduces one additional word, "for you." Because Ruth followed Naomi and now she is "walking" after Boaz, he pays her the respect of affirming her individuality and autonomy – "I will do *for you* all that *you* have said."

In addition, Boaz must reassure Ruth. "Undoubtedly," he says to her, "there will be many who will see our marriage as unseemly, even tainted, considering your Moabite heritage. Yet everyone at the gate of my people – the judges, scholars and the elite – will support us because they know that you are a virtuous woman."

In his commentary on Ruth, R. Yosef David Azulai makes an interesting point. He takes us back to the passage from Proverbs 32 that we sing at the Friday night meal, "A woman of valor." Toward the end of that acrostic we find the following verse: "Many daughters have done worthily, but you surpass them all." Chida explains that every woman is uniquely precious and has an area in which she is more accomplished and expert than other women.

However, it is rare to find a woman who excels in everything. "Who can find a woman of valor? Her worth is greater than rubies." Ruth was extraordinary since she possessed all the virtues, and those who understand such things knew and appreciated this. "May God bless you, my daughter," and blessed is the union that a woman such as Ruth seeks and desires.

The Leap of Faith

> And now it is true that I am a near kinsman, there is yet a kinsman nearer than I. Stay overnight, and in the morning, that if Tob will redeem you, let him, but if he does not redeem you then will I redeem you; lie down until the morning. (3:12–13)

The reason why Boaz has not yet reached out to Ruth now becomes clear. There is another redeemer, and Boaz will not build his personal happiness upon another's loss. This unexpected development surely came as a shock and disappointment to Ruth. Now, after so much hope, expectation, longing and risk – "there is a nearer kinsman than I"? What could Naomi have been thinking? Did she not know that there was another, closer relative?

Although it would be natural for Ruth to react with anger, she does not complain. "All that God does is for the best." She will wait and trust in His kindness. More important, she will continue to trust Naomi.

It is often easier for us to trust God than those close to us. Ruth does not allow cynicism, bitterness or recriminations to enter her heart. Such unwavering trust is only possible as a conscious decision. What faith can accomplish, no blind denial will possibly achieve. The Book of Ruth tells us that having faith in God and in human beings is a decision and that the two cannot be separated. While we of limited sight have eyes of flesh, only God knows what is in people's hearts. Therefore we may not presume to know.

"God said to Samuel, 'Do not pay attention to his looks or his tall stature, because I have rejected him. It is not as human beings see: for human beings see with the eyes, but God sees the heart'" (I Samuel 16:7).

One of the hardest challenges in our cynical times is how to strike a proper balance between trust and naiveté. On one side is the abyss of cynicism and nihilism that destroys all faith, and on the other are simple-mindedness and naiveté that can leave us vulnerable to manipulation. The Sages provided a wise directive: "Respect him and suspect him." They said in Tractate *Kallah Rabbati* 9: "Always consider every person as a [potential] thief, but honor him as if he were Rabban Gamliel." In other words, maintain intellectual honesty and be prepared for self-defense, but act with all the benefit of the doubt. Ruth returns to Naomi with the same optimism and commitment as before, and she does not reproach or even question her, for what purpose would that serve?

The translation of Tob (the good one) as a proper name follows *Ruth Rabbah*. As Ibn Ezra points out, it is a deficient translation because this same individual is later called Ploni Almoni, "that certain anonymous one" (Ruth 4:1). If his name is given as Tob, he cannot be anonymous. For this reason, Ibn Ezra and the Targum translate Tob as "all right," as in "well, all right, let him redeem you"; however, it is an awkward interpretation of the verse and the cantillation signs work against it.

Contrary to this approach, interpreting Tob as a proper name is reasonable. Tob is found in Tanach (the land of Tob in Judges 11:3, 5). The men of Ish-Tob are mentioned in II Samuel 10 and we know the name Tobith from the Apocrypha.[3] However, we still have a problem. If, as most traditional commentaries assume, Tob is the name of this near kinsman, then why, when push comes to shove at the gates of the city, is he called "that certain one with no name"?

The answer may come from considering how Scripture uses irony. It is now well appreciated that irony is a common technique with which the inspired authors of Biblical books convey meaning. In this case, Tob, which means "good," is not really so good, since he passes up the chance to marry Ruth, the mother of royalty. He represents conventional piety, not the deep and passionate love and faith but its tepid reflection among human beings.

The interpretation that I now offer may be a bit too tough on Tob. Might it not be possible that he realized how matters stood between Boaz and Ruth and, like a gentleman, withdrew his claim?

Perhaps. Yet surely Scripture introduces this character for a reason. It is on an assumption that the introduction of Tob provides an important lesson that I proceed to explain how Tob is a name.

Can we really blame Tob? Do we know his family circumstances, the state of affairs in his home, his relationship with his wife and his in-laws? Perhaps we cannot blame him. Yet his goodness is a sham for it conceals timidity and smallness of spirit. He is quite willing to make a business transaction and purchase Naomi's land... but to marry a convert, and one from Moab to boot?

Tob is evidently a good businessman. He does well enough with property, but is cautious when it comes to women. He is secure within the boundaries that tradition and social convention prescribe and with the patterns of behavior that his ancestors taught him. He has no interest in disrupting his orderly existence. Tob knows that whatever his purpose in life may be, it is not marrying Moabite women. He refuses to compromise his standards "lest I destroy my inheritance." He expects that this Moabite convert will change his life, and Tob is content with his life. When he rejects

---

[3] The name Toviah is found in II Chronicles 17:8.

Ruth, Tob fades into obscurity because he has forgone his chance at greatness.

In a certain way, Tob is the Jewish version of Orpah. One comes to this conclusion not only by textual consideration but also through form analysis. Remember the chiastic structure? This is an arrangement in which each topic in the beginning of a story corresponds to the one at the end, with the central idea in the middle. In this case, the episode on the threshing-floor is at the center and the chiastic structure envelops it. Consider the following division of the book of Ruth into topics.

1. Elimelech and his family
2. Naomi loses her children
3. Ruth is a Moabite
4. Orpah drops out
5. Naomi proves unworthy/complains
6. Ruth proves worthy in the field
7. Boaz and Ruth meet at the threshing-floor
8. Ruth proves worthy/receives gifts of barley
9. Naomi confirms Ruth's election
10. Ploni Almoni/Tob drops out
11. Ruth is equated with Rachel and Leah
12. A child is born to Naomi
13. David and his family

Boaz swears by God's existence that he will redeem Ruth if Tob does not. The sages say that he swore to subjugate his desire. "'I am single and she is single. I seek a woman and she seeks a man.' He jumped up and swore that he would not touch her until the morning" (see Rashi).

The inspiration for this rabbinic comment may be a parallel between Boaz and another Biblical personality who underwent a similar ordeal and emerged victorious. Boaz always invokes God, as does Joseph; almost every statement by Joseph contains a mention of God's name. "His master saw that God was with him" (Genesis 40:3) – "That the name of Heaven was constant in his mouth" (*Tanchuma* Vayeshev 8). The comparison of Boaz and Joseph teaches us that the constant awareness of God's presence is the only way to overcome temptation.

The chapter is almost over. The great drama of redemption is drawing to a close. It remains for us to see how God's plan plays out in the next chapter. Yet before we do, we must discuss Joseph at greater length and understand Naomi's emerging role.

Heroism and Humility

"Stay overnight, and in the morning, if Tob redeems you – but if not, then I will redeem you. Lie down until the morning."

She lay at his feet until the morning; and she rose up before one man could recognize another. For he said: "Let it not be known that the woman came to the threshing-floor."

He said: "Bring the mantle that you are wearing and hold it out." She held it and he measured out six measures of barley and put it on her, and he came to town. (3:13–15)

The similarities between Boaz and Joseph do not end with the fact that they constantly invoked the name of God. Both descended from strong women who pursued their men: Boaz from Tamar and Joseph from Rachel (see Genesis 30 and 38). We might say that these facts were written into their spiritual DNA. Both were tempted in similar circumstances, and both overcame the temptation. Both earned a place in history and in the Bible because they conquered their desires. However, there was also a crucial difference between them. Joseph performed a heroic deed, a mighty act of self control, that had cosmic significance. The Sages in *Genesis Rabbah* (87:10) compared his escape from Potiphar's wife with the rolling back of the waters of the Red Sea before Israelites as they fled the Egyptians.

"The sea saw and fled" (Psalms 114:3)" – in the merit of "and he left his garment in her hand and fled" (Genesis 39:12).

Yosef's self-control became a symbol for all generations. "If a person says, 'I did not serve God because I was too much under the sway of my desires,' they say to him, 'Were you more subject to them than Joseph was?' (*Yoma* 39b). What the Sages tell us in *Genesis Rabbah* is that the mystery of Jewish survival in Egypt began with Joseph's refusal to be drawn into intimate relations with an Egyptian woman. This was a heroic act, for there are few other images as impressive and awe-inspiring as the rolling back of the mighty sea.

Boaz, on the other hand, was a quiet hero. His courage was wholly internal in accordance with his name, which means 'within him is strength'. His courage and heroism were of the everyday, mundane variety, drawn from a multitude of small daily deeds. He performed no theatrics and perhaps did not even realize that the way he lived was extraordinary, elevated and holy. A soft-spoken man, Boaz dwelt with his God among his people, benevolent and considerate, modest and pious, despising honor and clinging to kindness. Boaz changed the world one mitzvah at the time.

Boaz's temptation was even greater than Joseph's. "Ruth was single and with him in bed, but Joseph was tempted by a woman who was married and not with him in bed" (Rashi on *Sanhedrin* 19b). Moreover, at that time one could legitimately betroth a woman through marital relations, as the first Mishna in *Kiddushin* teaches. It would have been both easy and tempting to rationalize. There was no obstacle before Boaz, neither religious law nor fear of discovery. In fact, he could easily have found a perfectly legal argument for taking Ruth as his wife right then and there in order to fulfill the commandment of procreation. Ruth might have accepted that in good faith. But Boaz, a man of integrity, handled this trial as he did all the challenges of everyday life. He did nothing out of character that night, for that was how he lived his life – in humility and modesty. "Rabbi Yehoshua said: Joseph's heroism, Boaz's humility!" (*Sanhedrin* 19b; this line of thought comes from *Nachalat Yosef*).

As dawn broke, the ground burned under the feet of Boaz and Ruth. Although it would have been best for Ruth to leave right away, Boaz behaves in his characteristic fashion. He speaks to Ruth slowly and deliberately, sensitive to her dignity and her feelings. He measures the barley as she holds her mantle, and he does not spread it on the ground out of respect for her. He honors Ruth for herself, as he honors all people.

Nevertheless, the business of giving Ruth a gift is fraught with risk. Imagine if someone had seen them! He would think: a woman spent the night with Boaz and is now receiving her pay. It would have been better that Ruth leave right away, covered by her mantle, but Boaz pays no heed to the fears that might motivate a lesser man. Boaz does the right thing and more, since from the text it appears that he walks with Ruth, carrying the barley for her until he enters the city.

> Behold, God passed by, and a great and strong wind rent the mountains, and broke in pieces the rocks before God; but God was not in the wind; and after the wind an earthquake; but God was not in the earthquake; and after the earthquake a fire; but God was not in the fire; and after the fire a still small voice (Kings 1:19).

God is found less in heroics than in the still small voice that whispers inside people of conscience. Quiet heroism, humble deeds of valor, and inner accomplishments bring about redemption, for "blessing is found only in that which is hidden from the eye" (*Taanit* 5b).

> Boaz did not know that the Holy One, blessed be He, had decided to bring forth from him David, Solomon, all the other kings and the King Messiah. Of Lot's daughters it is written, "When she rose up";

of Ruth it is written: "She arose before one man would recognize another." On that day she was raised up and Boaz was joined to her to set the name of the dead upon their inheritance and to set up all these kings and all men of stature in Israel. In Genesis 10:31 it is written, "He [Lot] did not know when she lay down." Of Ruth is says, "She lay at his feet until morning." Corresponding to her [the daughter of Lot] rising up in Genesis, it says of Ruth, "She arose before one man recognized another." This is why there is a dot over the vav of *ve-kumah* [and her rising up] [and an extra vav in the word be-terem, "before"]. (Zohar 1:110b)

The numerical value of the letter vav is six. We will now address the six measures of barley that Boaz gave to Ruth and their significance.

Boaz and Naomi

… he measured six measures of barley and laid it on her, and he went into the city.

When she came to her mother-in-law, she said: "Who are you, my daughter?" And she told her all that the man had done to her. And she said: "He gave me these six measures of barley, for he said to me: Do not go empty to your mother-in-law."

Then said she: "Sit still, my daughter, until you know how the matter will fall; for the man will not rest until he has finished the thing this day." (3:15–18)

The six measures of barley are mystifying and it is tempting to see them as symbols. "If you say actually six grains of barley, is it the way of Boaz to give just six grains? Perhaps it is six *seah* of barley? Is it possible for a woman to carry six *seah* of barley? It must be that [it is a symbolic act], hinting that she will produce six sons who are blessed with six blessings and they are: David, the Messiah, Daniel, Chananiah, Mishael and Azariah" (*Sanhedrin* 93a).

On a simpler level of interpretation, it may refer to some smaller and unspecified measure of grain; in fact the Hebrew word for barley, *se'orim,* can also be vocalized as *she'arim* (measures), a usage known to us from Genesis 26:12, though this interpretation is marred by its inconsistency with the Masoretic vocalization. Alternatively it may refer literally to six *seah,* which Boaz carried almost all of the way until he came to the city and only then transferred them to Ruth. An early riser who saw them might assume that

Ruth had gone early to the granary to bring her gleanings home and that Boaz, who had met her by chance, was assisting her.

A novel interpretation arises from the verse that follows. We begin by noting that Naomi's question to Ruth – "Who are you, my daughter?" – is hard to understand. Did she not recognize Ruth and if she did not, how could she call her "my daughter"? *Ruth Rabbah* 7:4 suggests: "She said to her, 'Are you still single or are you now a married woman?' She said to Naomi: 'I am single.'" The *Nahalat Yosef* suggests a fascinating interpretation that is rich with psychological insight. Naomi asked Ruth, "Do you still belong to me? Are you still mine or has Boaz taken you away from me? Whose are you now, my daughter – mine or his?"

The wise and sensitive Boaz, who realized that there was a deep and complex relationship between Ruth and her mother-in-law, foresaw this reaction and acted to prevent it. He did not assume that Naomi was above feelings of resentment and abandonment. Instead, he signaled to Naomi that she would remain an important part of Ruth's married life. "'He gave me these six measures of barley, for he said to me: Do not go empty to your mother-in-law." The six measures of barley were a message to Naomi in which Boaz promised to restore what she had lost and feared that she might be losing again.

At the peak of Naomi's success her family consisted of Elimelech, herself, Machlon, Kilyon, Orpah and Ruth: six individuals, hence six measures of barley. Boaz is reassuring Naomi that when he redeems Ruth, he will not leave her behind. Thus reassured, Naomi gives her consent. "Then said she: 'Sit still, my daughter, until you know how the matter will fall; for the man will not rest until he has finished the thing this day."

There is one more thought that deserves expression.

When the Jews first saw the Manna, they said to each other, "Man hu." In Hebrew it means, "It is a prepared portion"; however, in the cognate language, Aramaic, it is a question that means, "Who is he?" This recalls Naomi's question to Ruth. The Hassidic master Yaakov Yitzhak Horowitz, the Chozeh of Lublin, explained it as follows: those who ate manna reached new and elevated levels every day, so much so that every day a man no longer recognized his fellow and asked, "Who is he?" (*Sippurei Chassidim* [Zevin], Beshalach). In a similar vein, after David slew Goliath, Saul did not recognize him even though the two had met only a short while before. Why did Saul not recognize David? Before, David had been a simple page, but now he possessed great stature.

When Ruth walked through the portals of Naomi's dwelling, she was taller, straighter, more radiant and infused with illumination of the events of that blessed night. Naomi did not recognize this stranger who so resembled and yet appeared so different from her daughter-in-law, and she asked in wonder and confusion: "Who are you, my daughter?"[4]

---

[4] In the same vein, R. Shimshon Raphael Hirsch writes in his commentary at the end of Parshas Va-yetze that when Yaakov left Beer Sheva and encountered the vision of the angels, he marveled and was moved. Twenty years later, as he returned to the Land of Israel, the verse states that the angels met him, for after twenty years of striving and growth, he had grown to such an extent that they marveled at him.

THE CIRCLE CLOSES

At the City Gate

> Now Boaz went up to the gate and sat down there. Behold, the near kinsman of whom Boaz had spoken passed by, and he said: "Hey, Ploni Almoni, turn aside, sit down here." He turned aside and sat down.
>
> He took ten of the city elders and said, "Sit down here," and they sat down. (4:1–2)

As they entered the city, Ruth went home and Boaz continued toward the gate. From many other Biblical references we know that the city gate is the place where public activity, court sessions and prophetic exhortations take place. Excavations at various archaeological sites suggest that Israelite settlements had two walls surrounding the city, with two gates facing each other. The system of double gates allowed for detailed inspection of large parties before they entered the city. The space between the gates was paved and served as the plaza in which various activities could take place without disturbing the city's inhabitants.

Boaz received Divine assistance. As soon as he entered this area, "Behold, the near kinsman passed by."

"Was he standing behind the door? R. Shmuel Bar Nachman said: Even if he had been at the end of the world, the Holy One, blessed be He, would have transported him there, so that that saint would not be sitting and worrying as he waited" (*Ruth Rabbah* 7:6).

"Boaz did his part, Ruth did her part and Naomi did her part. The Holy One, blessed be He, said: I will also do my part" (*Ruth Rabbah* 7:7).

It is clear that Boaz was respected and valued. When he spoke, people listened. When he asked for ten elders, no one protested that he was busy or did not have the time. The kinsmen and the elders obeyed him immediately and without question. Perhaps this is the source for the Sages' identification of Boaz with the judge Ivtzan.

Who was Ploni Almoni? We have previously pointed out that the Sages understood that his name was Tob. The name itself is found in the Bible in Zechariah 6:10 and Samuel II, 10:6. Here, however, he is called Ploni Almoni, an appellation that in Hebrew has come to signify "John Doe," a generic name for a person whose actual name we do not know. In Tanach this appellation is also found in II Kings 6:8 and I Samuel 21:3, as is noted in the Mesorah to our verse. There it means "unspecified."

While the term may refer to someone who is timid and retiring by nature (Targum), it also implies criticism. While modesty and refinement are certainly great virtues, a man must be in charge of his natural qualities and not be controlled by them. We have suggested previously that Tob lost the opportunity to have his name recorded in the Bible because he did not seize the opportunity to marry Ruth on the account of his retiring disposition. He was a good man, which is what Tov means in the Holy Tongue; however, his goodness was a type of timidity with which he was born, not something for which he strove and attained through a lifetime of self-discovery and inner change.

There is an appropriate time to use every quality of character in the Creator's service. There is a time to draw back and a time to be bold. Tob's lesson to us is that even as we respect the modest and the humble, we must remember that in this regard the mind must lead the heart and not the other way around.

It is interesting to realize that Boaz and Tob represent two different kinds of redemption. Tob is the redemption that almost happened but was never completed. Boaz, on the other hand, is the true and final redemption.

It is explained in the Zohar that this alludes to the future redemption, may it come speedily and in our day.

> "If Tob redeems you" – this refers to your good deeds – then let it happen that way. If not, God forbid – that is, if you do not return to Him, even so "I will redeem you." It is possible to say that this is the meaning of the verse, "True, I am a redeemer, and also there is a redeemer closer than I" (Ruth 3:12). God is called "close," as it is written: "God is close to all who call him" (Psalms 145:18). It also says [in the description of returning to God in Deuteronomy 30:14]: "This matter is close to you." This redemption is closer to you than I am; "it is in your mouth and your heart" (Chatam Sofer, Sermons 302, 74).

With this, we can also understand the significance of the two names of the would-be redeemer, Tob, meaning "good," and Ploni Almoni, meaning "obscure" and "silent." There were so many times in Jewish history when the final redemption seemed imminent. The circumstances were right, the people were ready, and at times there was even an apparently fitting redeemer, such as King Chezekiah or Bar Kochba, a noble leader worthy of the role and claiming the mantle of the Messiah. Yet in the end, the redemption did not occur. The moment passed, the redeemer failed in his mission, the Jewish people's hope dissipated and the Jews suffered distance from God once more.

The reasons for this were never clear. Sometimes it was the failure of the would-be redeemer, while at other times the failure may have stemmed from the people themselves. Yet always, the true Redeemer is just around the corner, calling the elders together, arranging his marriage with his bride, sitting down to bring matters to completion. The belief in the ultimate redemption is one of the basic principles of Judaism.

The book of Ruth demonstrates how suffering, abandonment and despair can end in deliverance and joy. It shows us that the road to redemption is strewn with many disappointments and false starts. In the end, however, we believe that we will merit to welcome the descendant of Ruth and Boaz and for that we need patience, persistence and hope.

> He said to the redeemer: "Naomi, who returned from the plain of Moab, is selling the parcel of land that was our brother Elimelech's; and I thought to disclose it to you. Buy it before them that sit here, and before the elders of my people. If you will redeem it, redeem it; but if it will not be redeemed, then tell me so that I may know; for there is no one else to redeem it beside you; and I am after you." He said: "I will redeem it."
>
> Then said Boaz: "On the day that you buy the field from the hand of Naomi – you [written as "I"] also acquire Ruth the Moabite, the wife of the dead, to raise up the name of the dead upon his inheritance." And the redeemer said: 'I cannot redeem it for myself, lest I mar my inheritance; take my right of redemption yourself, for I cannot redeem.' (4:3–6)

We have interpreted the enigmatic figure of Ploni Almoni as representing a potential redemption that did not come to fruition. Facing it is the towering figure of Boaz, who stands for the Redemption that will actually take place – soon, with God's help, and in our day. There are commentators who perceived in these two individuals an allusion to the two Messiahs, the Messiah who stems from the tribe of Joseph (the Messiah of the house of Joseph) and the Messiah who descends from David and the tribe of Judah.

The former, who represents the spiritual qualities of Joseph and the northern tribes of Israel, is meant to accomplish the work of uniting the Jewish people and vanquishing its enemies and in that way prepare the world for the final redemption by the descendant of David. The descendant of

WHAT THE BOOKS OF RUTH AND YONAH TEACH

Joseph will ultimately be killed at the gates of Jerusalem in a massive counterattack by the united armies of all the nations. The final redemption will then be accomplished by the descendant of David in the manner and spirit of the tribe of Judah. Both *Pirkei de-Rabbi Eliezer* 19 and Tractate *Sukkah* 52b refer to this tradition, which is elaborated for the first time in *The Book of Beliefs and Opinions* by R. Saadiah Gaon.

In these sources, the details of his mission and leadership are few and contradictory. What we learn about his enemies and his work is unclear and confusing – like Ploni Almoni, that redeemer with the obscure name who came close to redeeming Ruth but did not. That the Messiah from the tribe of Joseph can be represented by Tob, a descendent of Judah, is not problematic, for these figures represent the spiritual rather than familial proclivities of the two tribes, and some kabbalistic sources suggest the this Josephite Messiah actually stems from the tribe of Judah (*Margaliyot ha-yom* on *Sanhedrin* 94a).

> "I cannot redeem lest I destroy my inheritance" – from here you see
> that there are two redeemers, the near redeemer and the far-off
> redeemer. The near redeemer is from the Right side and the far-off
> redeemer is the Messiah who comes from Joseph…. (*Zohar Hadash*
> 88a)

Ploni Almoni was meant to prepare Boaz and Ruth for their mission, but he declined to do so. The conversation between Boaz and Ploni Almoni is enigmatic. Boaz offers Ploni Almoni the sale of the field, and the latter is willing to purchase it. However, Boaz then clarifies that Ruth is a part of the deal and at that point, Ploni Almoni declines. Did he not see from the beginning that Ruth also deserved redemption? Why did Boaz present his proposal in such a convoluted manner? What would have happened to Boaz's promise to Ruth, had Ploni Almoni accepted his offer and married Ruth?

It is possible to suggest that what Boaz actually offered was to divide the redemption of Ruth into two parts, just as the two Messiahs divide the work of redemption between them. Ploni Almoni would redeem the land and Boaz would marry Ruth. If Ruth had a male child, when he reached majority, the field would revert to him "to raise the name of the dead upon the inheritance."

Ploni Almoni did not accept this proposal "lest I destroy my own inheritance," for he did not wish a semi-heir to complicate his affairs. This novel interpretation also explains why the verse reads with the word "you" even though it is spelled with the word "I." (A similar explanation is offered by S.G. Rosenberg in *Esther, Jonah, Ruth Deciphered,* 2004). If so, the allusion to the two Messiahs gains a new basis in the verse.

On a simpler level, Ploni Almoni refused to marry Ruth because he was afraid.

> R. Shmuel Bar Nachman said: He was mute regarding Torah knowledge [a play on the shared root of *ilem* and *almoni*]. He said: "The first ones died because they married them. Shall I go and marry her? I will not marry her. I will not introduce a blemish into my seed." He did not know that the law that permits marriage to a Moabite woman, unlike a Moabite man, has already been (re-) innovated (*Ruth Rabbah* 7:10).

Understanding the prohibition (or the non-prohibition) of marriage with Moabites is crucial to the story of Ruth. We will now discuss it at greater length.

No Moabite Shall Enter

At first glance, the Book of Ruth appears to disregard the Torah law that does not allow Moabites to join the Jewish people. Although the Torah prohibits marriage to Moabites, Ruth is not only welcomed but is an ancestor of King David and, through him, of the Messiah. In this chapter, we will focus on this prohibition and its relevance to what we learn here.

Deuteronomy 23 states:

> A *mamzer* [child of an adulterous or incestuous union] may not enter God's marriage group. Even after the tenth generation, he may not enter God's marriage group. An Ammonite or Moabite may not enter God's marriage group. They may never enter God's marriage group, even after the tenth generation. This is because they did not greet you with bread and water when you were on the way out of Egypt, and also because they hired Balaam son of Beor from Pethor in Aram Naharayim to curse you. Do not despise the Edomite, since he is your brother. Do not despise the Egyptian, since you were an immigrant in his land. [Therefore,] children born to [members of these nations] in the third generation [after becoming proselytes] may enter God's marriage group.

The Talmud in *Ketubbot* 7a tells us that Boaz gathered the ten elders in order to publicize an ancient law that had fallen into disuse. This Sinaitic ordinance explained that while male Moabites or Ammonites were barred from joining the Jewish people, this restriction did not apply to Moabite and

Ammonite women. *Yevamot* 77b suggests that the verses themselves modify the prohibition. "… because they did not greet you with bread and water when you were on the way out of Egypt, and also because they hired Balaam son of Beor from Pethor in Aram Naharayim to curse you." The statement of a reason for the law that follows the law indicates that only the males are prohibited. After all, "It is the way of men to greet with bread and water" and "It is the way of men, and not women, to engage in hostile action or to wage war." The Oral Law explains that in this one exceptional case the stated reason for the Law can modify its application, a matter otherwise of Tannaitic dispute (*Bava Metzia* 115a).

To clarify: Although there are exceptions,[1] we usually follow the view that the stated purpose of a law does not determine the details of its application. Yet in this one unusual case, the Oral Law that stems directly from Sinai teaches us otherwise.

There are several indications from the Tanach itself that this Sinaitic law operated from the earliest times. There is the case of Rehoboam, whom Na'amah the Ammonite bore to Solomon and who ruled over the kingdom of Judea after him. There are also several verses from the Book of Ezra that, when read carefully, suggest that the returnees from the Babylonian exile also understood the prohibition against marrying Moabite converts to apply only to the males (see the work *The Rabbis' Advocate* by R. David Nieto, 1:24–28).[2]

What deeper factor makes this law an exception? Why are only male but not female Moabites prohibited? The Maharal in *Netzach Yisrael*, chapter 32, offers a profound explanation that I present in a somewhat abbreviated fashion. He begins by pointing out that all nations stem from a union of a male and female ancestor and both of them contribute equally to the physical and spiritual characteristics of the emerging people. In the language of Aristotelian philosophy, the man contributes the form while the woman provides the matter. However, this was not the case at the emergence of Ammon and Moab. In that unique case, a father and his daughters initiated the process of national emergence. Consequently, the contribution of the father, coming directly through his daughters, was overwhelming, so that the female element in Moab and Ammon remained small and undeveloped. This is why the women were exempt, since they did not possess that determinative Moabite quality. In fact, we might say that it is precisely this

---

[1] The reason behind the law can sometimes be used "*le-chumrah.*" For full discussion see *Encyclopedia Talmudit,* "Ein dorshin ta'amah de-kro."
[2] This translation of *Matteh Dan* (Kuzari Ha-Sheini) was published in November 2006 with my commentary by Yashar Press.

that allowed Judah's seed to stamp its own quality upon the Moabite feminine substrate, taking from it only what it needed, only the positive and nothing of the negative.

This explication of Ruth's origin provides an important insight into her qualities and character. We have already noted that Ruth plays an exceedingly passive role in this book, following the direction of others and never asserting herself. Even her child "is born to Naomi." In a certain sense, this teaches us that redemption can only be bestowed upon those who are willing to receive it. The forces that oppose redemption will not benefit from it, but shall be utterly destroyed. The overpowering revelation of Divinity at the core of redemption will overwhelm all of creation so that only those who are willing to open themselves to receive it will survive, while the rest, either unable to receive it or who resist it, will be shattered.

> Know that that just as the powers of holiness are sustained through the light of the King's Countenance, the powers of impurity derive their vitality from the same source. When the Presence is revealed, all draw toward it…. When the effusion of spirituality overtakes them and they are not suitable for it, they are harmed. This is why the firstborn of Egypt and their gods were destroyed as God went forth in the midst of Egypt. (Netziv, commentary on Exodus 11:3).

For Redemption and Exchange

> This was the custom in former time in Israel concerning redemption and exchange, to confirm all things: a man would draw off his shoe and give it to his neighbor, and this was the attestation in Israel. So the near kinsman said to Boaz: "Buy it for yourself." He drew off his shoe (4:7–8).

Boaz and the unnamed relative performed a ceremony that marked both the exchange of property and realignment of familial lines. The verse informs us that drawing off and transferring a shoe was the means by which all exchanges and dealings were sealed. Anyone involved in business and commerce knows that bargaining and negotiations cannot be allowed to go on forever. There needs to be a symbolic act, be it a handshake or, in our more sophisticated times, a memorandum of understanding or the like, that concludes the process and marks the completion of the deal. Removal of a shoe probably served this purpose at that time.

Why the shoe? The Shelah (siddur, Birkat ha-shachar) suggests that wearing leather symbolizes humankind's mastery over its environment. Human beings hunt animals and rule over their skin and flesh. Removing a shoe, which is made of leather, and transferring it to another individual is a symbolic renunciation of dominance. Before two people conclude a deal, each struggles to extend his power over the piece of the world that is in the other's hands. A completed business transaction is the recognition that just as one party has the right to sole ownership of a piece of this world, so does the other party. The transfer of a shoe represents renunciation of claims and recognition of the limits to one's power and authority in the face of another human being (R. Shlomo Zalman Auerbach, quoted in *Shirat Levi*).

An even more profound understanding arises from the comments of R. Elazar (Zohar III:180a).

> R. Elazar arose and said: " ... certainly it was Torah law [if so, why was it only at that time and why was it later changed?]. This was a profound mystery and because the early ones were righteous and saintly, this matter was revealed to them. Once wicked people increased in the world, this type of transaction was performed in a different manner so as to conceal that which stems from a higher level.

In itself this is the standard teaching of the Zohar, that many rites were given in several equally legitimate forms, each one suitable and reserved for different generations, depending on each one's spiritual level and accomplishment. What is now of more interest to us is the explanation that derives from this teaching which we must try to explicate.

Let us start by pointing out that removal of a shoe is the central component of the act of *chalitzah* (releasing a childless widow from the obligation to enter a levirate marriage) and it is also a prominent feature of approaching the Divine. This establishes a connection between the two concepts. How so?

"Come and see: He said, 'Do not come hither. Cast off your shoe' (Exodus 3:5). Why a shoe? He commanded Moses to separate from his wife and to attach himself to another woman, the light of the Most High, which is the Shechina" (ibid.; see also 148).

The shoe, then, represents transition and exchange – movement. This is why, when a man elects not to wed his late brother's wife, refusing to rebuild his brother's line, refusing to remove his shoe and give it to her, it is she who takes off his shoe, illustrating his lack of generosity and charity. In the business context, it signals the end of conflict and the beginning of cooperation.

These inspired words of the Zohar yield the following understanding. The act of removing a shoe is essentially an act of reaching beyond oneself.

Just as the spiritual world spans earth and heaven, so the human spiritual form extends from earth toward heaven, imitating the Divine Image. "Thus says God: Heaven is My throne and the earth is My footstool" (Isaiah 66:1). Similarly, our heads reach far into Heaven while our feet rest securely upon the earth, and our bodies span the entire distance between the two. What separates human beings from the earth[3]? Nothing but our shoes! The act of removing a shoe represents reaching beyond ourselves to engage with that which is outside us – from earth to heaven.

"Each thing that is higher affects and influences what is lower. It is called the 'seller' and the lower one is called the 'buyer.'... From this one derives that every trade and transaction enables the joining and connecting of the giver and the receiver" (*Mikdash Melech* on Tikkunei Zohar 2:27, cited in *Idrei Tzon*).

No wonder, then, that the act of removing the shoe fell into disuse as the elevated perception that engaging another human being means reaching beyond and outside one's limitations in order to give rather than in order to take, receded from human consciousness. When business dealings became all about winning, when even the love between man and woman could not bridge the distance between their separate selves, the symbols that once had meant so much lost all their meaning. Since they no longer served their vital function, other symbols replaced them.

The Return of Machlon

> Boaz said to the elders and to all the people: "You are witnesses this day that I have bought all that was Elimelech's and all that was Kilyon's and Mahlon's from the hand of Naomi. Moreover, I have taken Ruth the Moabite, the wife of Machlon, to be my wife, to set up the name of the dead upon his inheritance, that the name of the dead be not cut off from among his brethren and from the gate of his place. You are witnesses this day." (4:9–10)

Boaz names Kilyon first and then Machlon. This is the opposite of what we find in the beginning of Ruth, where Machlon is listed before Kilyon. The Midrash *Lekach Tov* derives a moral lesson from this deviation from the usual order: "Why was Kilyon mentioned before Machlon? To teach us that we must guard against the bad ones in the family, so that Orpah should not appear and say: This field belongs to my husband, or that her son should appear and say: I am representing Kilyon." This is truly good business

---

[3] See *Ruah Hayyim* by R. Chaim Volozhiner, 1:1.

advice. Boaz was covering all bases, heading off potential trouble in the future.

The change in the order can also be understood on a deeper level. We start with the following midrash (Zohar Chadash 88b).

> R. Yuda said: "The commandment of marrying a deceased brother's wife is exalted, and he who fulfills it becomes a partner with God in the act of Creation. He is greater than Ezekiel whose prophecy of the reviving of the dead bones in chapter 37 was performed with great tumult, whereas what a levirate does occurs in stillness…. 'He gave to his fellow' (Ruth 4:7–8) – this is the rite of levirate marriage." R. Chanina said: "This is like a man who was lost in a desert, a place of robbers and brigands. When they saw him wandering, they struck him, robbing him and taking everything that he had…. A friend heard what had happened. He armed himself and went out and rescued him from them, though naked and stripped of everything. What did he do? He built him a new house, provided him with new clothing, and he began to prosper once more. This is what the verse says: "He gave to his fellow."

This enigmatic parable (note the comparison to Ezekiel) contains the idea of the transmigration of souls. The teaching that God affords certain individuals additional opportunities to fulfill their purpose on earth by sending their souls back again and again is a basic kabbalistic teaching, though not an obligatory belief. Although it was opposed by some of the greatest Jewish thinkers such as Saadiah Gaon and Maimonides, it has become more accepted in subsequent Jewish theology as kabbalistic teachings became more accessible.

Abarbanel on Deuteronomy 38 and R. Menashe ben Israel in his work, *Nishmat Hayyim* (4:7), emphasize that the concept of transmigration is an expression of God's absolute justice and mercy. It is possible for human beings, with some justification, to blame God Himself for their failure in spiritual endeavors. After all, it is He who placed the soul in an unsuitable vehicle – a body whose desires, proclivities and inclination were incompatible with that individual's purpose in life. Can a soul that has been called to asceticism and self-denial succeed if it is trapped in a body given to sensuality and strong emotions? Can the soul of a leader succeed in the vessel that is by nature cowardly and retiring? Can a great thinker overcome a dull mind and a slow intellect? Accordingly, God, Who is just and merciful, allows the soul that has not succeeded in its first sojourn to return to a different body with another set of traits so that it may now succeed or, if it fails, leave it no excuses.

This Zoharic passage connects the ritual that Boaz performed with the act of marrying one's brother's childless widow. The connection is natural on both the surface level and in the deeper sense. Compare the following three verses and note their shared language.

> … to set up the name of the dead upon his inheritance, that the name of the dead be not cut off from among his brethren, and from the gate of his place. (Ruth, ibid.)

> When brothers live together and one of them dies childless, the dead man's wife shall not be allowed to marry an outsider. Her husband's brother must cohabit with her, making her his wife, and thus performing a brother-in-law's duty to her. The first-born son whom she bears will then set up name of the dead brother, so that his name will not be cut off from Israel. (Deuteronomy 25:6–7)

> Judah said to Onan, "Marry your brother's wife, and thus fulfill the duty of a brother-in-law to her. You will then set up your brother's name." Onan, however, realized that the children would not pertain to him. Therefore, whenever he came to his brother's wife, he let [the seed] go to waste on the ground, so as not to have children in his brother's name. (Genesis 38:8–9)

If all these verses employ the same language, they must all be speaking of the same thing: in this case, the return of a soul, or *gilgul*. Of course, there is also an exegetical difficulty in drawing these three verses together. Since Boaz was not Ruth's brother-in-law, the verse in Deuteronomy about levirate marriage should not pertain to him. It is a serious enough consideration to lead Rashi to reject the comparison. However, in his commentary to Genesis 38:8, the Ramban not only explained this difficulty away but made it into the basis for a masterful elucidation.

> The ancients before the time of the Torah recognized that there is great benefit in the brother marrying his brother's widow. The brother is the first properly in line and after him, the rest of the relatives. This is because any relative who can inherit provides this benefit. It is considered to be a great cruelty when a brother does not wish to afford such a benefit to his brother. The ancient Sages, knowing of this matter, enacted it to be done in Israel by all inheritors of property, those among whom the prohibition of an incestuous marriage did not exist. They called it redemption. This is

the explanation of the matter of Boaz and the meaning of the words of the neighbors to Naomi ("a child is born to Naomi").

As explicated by others (see also Recanti, ibid.), the nature of close relatives is most conducive to host the returnee. They are compatible enough, yet at the same time different enough, to accomplish the purpose. More significantly, the common phenomenon of transmigration throws light upon the unique and singular event of the resurrection of the dead (hence the comparison of Boaz and Ezekiel by R. Yuda above). Just as transmigration is a reflection of God's unceasing goodness in giving an individual another chance, so is resurrection a second chance for humanity.

> R Toviah said in the name of R. Yoshia: What does it mean, "Sheol and the withholding of the womb will not be satisfied" (Proverbs 30)? What does Sheol have in common with the womb? One puts life into the womb in silence but the child comes out of in great tumult (screaming and wailing). The dead are placed into Sheol (the grave) in silence. How much more so will they come out of it in great tumult. Here is a response to those who deny that the Torah teaches resurrection (*Sanhedrin* 92a).

The circle closed. Boaz rectified the sin of his progenitor Onan, who had refused to give his seed to his brother. Judah redeemed the soul of Onan, who was reborn of Tamar as Peretz, who was an ancestor of Boaz. Kilyon was lost but Machlon returned through Boaz and Ruth. A child was born to Naomi: Machlon, the child whom she had once carried and now (through Ruth) carried again.

Although it is significant in itself, the story of Boaz and Ruth symbolizes all humanity. The redemption of one family stands for the cosmic cycle of redemption. David, who descends from Ruth and Naomi and from Boaz and Machlon, is destined not only to realize the private redemption of one family from Judea but to become the symbol and expectation of the ultimate redemption of Israel and of all humanity.

The Matriarchs and the Mother of Royalty

> All the people at the gate and the elders, said: "We are witnesses. May God make the woman who is coming into your house like Rachel and like Leah, who together built the house of Israel, and may you do valorously in Ephrath and become well known in Bethlehem." (4:11)

The people at the gate blessed the forthcoming marriage of Boaz and Ruth, echoing what they already understood and recognized much earlier, "All the people in the gate of my people know that you are a virtuous woman" (3:11). Ruth made her strongest impression upon the common folk, the kind of citizens who, after completing their daily chores, went to the gate to be entertained and educated and to learn from the elders. Unlike Moses, who gained fame from the top down ("Moses was great in the eyes of Pharaoh's officials and in the eyes of the people" [Exodus 11:3]), Ruth was respected from the ground up, honored first by the common people and then by the elite.

Those who are familiar with the Hebrew language will notice a deviation from the usual rules of grammar. Rachel and Leah are referred to in the masculine rather than the feminine verb form. As we noted before, such usage is common in this book. It communicates the high regard in which the matriarchs and Ruth were held, spoken of her as if she were an equal to the male heads of households who constituted the power and authority in Bethlehem. Another reason: As previously mentioned, the Moabite dialect of the Hebrew language appears not to have recognized gender distinctions. In mirroring Moabite usage, in speaking as Ruth spoke, the people paid respect to Ruth.

The comparison of Ruth to Rachel and Leah can be read in various ways. On one level, the people encouraged and affirmed the foreigner who was now joining them. They pointed out that the very matriarchs of their nation were also strangers from a foreign land (Malbim). The Dubno Maggid's commentary suggests that they subtly indicated to Boaz the advantage of marrying Ruth: that since she had no family in Bethlehem, she would be attached and devoted solely to him.

Like Rachel and Leah, Ruth left her family and her people, throwing in her lot with the man whom she married and the nation that she joined. On a deeper level, the comparison with the matriarchs presages the role that Ruth will play in the development of the monarchy and in the future redemption.

Rachel and Leah did not merely give birth and then pass from the scene. They continued to live through and within their descendants. The influence of Rachel and Leah on the character and development of their progeny was long-lasting, since their traits found expression in their descendants. The Sages frequently trace the characteristics and destinies of Biblical personalities and even of entire tribes to the qualities of the matriarchs. Therefore, just as Rachel and Leah shaped the future of their descendants, so Ruth influenced the course of the Israelite monarchy.

The Sages taught that parents of worthy children live on through them. "David, who left a worthy son, is described as [not having died but as] sleeping with his forebears; Yoav, who left no worthy sons, is described as having died" (*Bava Batra* 116a). Ruth's legacy continued to shape Israel's monarchy to the time of Solomon. Whether it is meant literally or not, "Ruth the Moabite [lived to] see the reign of Solomon, the grandson of her grandson, as it is written: '… he set up a throne for the king's mother' (I Kings 2:19). R. Elazar said: 'For the mother of royalty'" (*Bava Batra* 91b). At the peak of the unified kingdom as Solomon ascended his throne, Ruth, literally or symbolically, sat next to him. It is not for nothing that Solomon married an Ammonite who became the mother of his successor, Rehoboam.

Why is Ruth, a single individual, compared to Rachel and Leah, "both of whom together built the house of Israel"? What is meant by the emphasis that Rachel and Leah were two and that they worked together? How does this relate to the current situation of Ruth and Boaz? Why does Scripture frame it in the double context of Ephrath and Bethlehem?

I think that the intent is to call attention to Naomi and to the role that she will play together with Ruth, which is similar to the way that Rachel and Leah functioned together. Throughout this book, we have seen the close relationship between Ruth and Naomi. These two women function almost as one, distinct in body but united in outlook, values and spirit. It is as if Ruth is a proxy for Naomi, since Naomi is not only a mentor but a partner in everything that Ruth does. In this sense, Naomi is Ruth and Ruth Naomi, and the two share accomplishment and fulfillment.

Ruth and Naomi also rectify the conflict and lack of harmony between the two sisters, Rachel and Leah, that ultimately expressed itself in strife between the Kingdom of Israel, led by the tribe of Ephraim (which descended from Rachel) and the kingdom of Judah (which descended from Leah). This lack of unity led directly to the long and bitter exile that has lasted to this very day.

Both the Bach and Ben Ish Chai suggest that while Ephrath is mentioned as an allusion to Ephraim, Bethlehem is associated closely with the tribe of Judah. Jewish monarchy is then a reflection and a re-enactment of the birth of the nation, a joint product of the two camps of Israel. In this fashion, Ruth's destiny is tied not only to the past but also to the future, separation is transformed into harmony and redemption shines out upon the world.

The Strands of Redemption

> … And let your house be like the house of Peretz, whom Tamar bore to Judah, of the seed which God shall give you of this young woman. (4:12)

After comparing Ruth to Rachel and Leah, the verse connects her with Tamar. There is, of course, a great deal of similarity between Ruth and Tamar.

"Two women took risks in order to join the tribe of Judah: Tamar and Ruth" (*Yalkut Ruth,* cited in *Nachalat Yosef*).

"There were two women, Tamar and Ruth, from whom the line of Judah was built, and from whom issued King David, Solomon and the Messiah. These two women were similar: after their first husbands died, they acted to win their second husbands in order to build and shape the line of Judah" (Zohar 1:188b).

On a superficial level, Ruth rectified the act of Tamar, whose purpose was praiseworthy but whose means were impure. Where Tamar employed deception in order to carry out her levirate marriage, Ruth avoided falling into sin and temptation in a situation that was just as challenging and enticing, and achieved righteous results through virtuous means. When we combine this with the knowledge that Boaz also rectified the sins of his ancestors Er and Onan, Judah's sons, we can draw an apparently sufficient, though limited, picture of the concept of redemption.

In other words, Boaz and Ruth replayed the same situations that had led their ancestors into sin, but did not succumb as they had. However, the Sages are never satisfied with the obvious. On the basis of the same word used in two different contexts, they traced the thread of redemption even farther into the past. Let us consider the following two statements by the same rabbi. Here is the first:

> R. Tanchuma in the name of Shmuel said: What is it that it writes [of the intention of the two daughters of Lot]: "Let us produce seed from our father" (Genesis 19:32)? In the book of Ruth it also says "seed," the seed that came yet from another place. Which is it? The King Messiah. (*Ruth Rabbah* 7:14)

We now understand that Ruth rectified not only the error of Judah and Tamar but also the willful ignorance of Lot and his daughters. In all these situations we read about younger women with older men. Each time the sin lessened and the good intention within it became more prominent. Judah thought that he had been with a harlot after his wife died – a minor sin in his eyes, if a sin at all – while Lot did not know that his daughters had committed incest with him although, according to the rabbis, he should have known (Rashi on Genesis 20:33, from *Sifri*). Yet since both these sins had stemmed from a good intention, they deserved a chance to be rectified.

Before Ruth and Boaz, all the players in the cosmic drama of redemption succeeded in some ways and failed in others. On one side we see the men: Judah, his sons Er, Onan and Shela and his distant descendants Elimelech, Kilyon and Machlon. On the other are the women: the daughters of Lot, Rachel and Leah, Tamar, Orpah and Naomi.

However, we still have not gone far enough, since the root of the problem reaches all the way back to Adam and his sons. The Sages teach us that Adam included all the souls of humanity. Since the roots of the souls of all men and women were united within him, every marriage is a reflection of the first couple and a unification of the roots that create the harmony of a family.

How so? Here is the second statement by Rabbi Tanchuma:

> She called his name Seth, saying: God has given me seed in place of Abel, whom Kain killed (Genesis 4:25). R. Tanchuma, in the name of R. Shmuel, said: "She saw that the seed came from another place – this is the King Messiah" (*Genesis Rabbah* 23:5).

The fact that the word "seed" is now traced to Cain and Abel should not surprise us. Adam and Eve sinned, destroying the harmony of the world. Then Cain killed Abel – and how could such an irreparable rift between brothers ever be repaired and harmony restored? This was done through the birth of another brother, Seth – who, unlike the first two sons of Adam and Eve, was "in his [Adam's] image, in his likeness" (Genesis 5:3).

The letters of Adam are deconstructed as follows: Adam, David, Messiah. "Adam took seventy years of his life and gave them to David, son of Jesse" (*Numbers Rabbah* 14:12).

Complex ideas may be taken in different ways. Some kabbalists interpret the concepts that we have read as referring simply to the transmigration of souls, who was later reincarnated as whom, and how the people involved faced the tests that they had failed in previous lives. However, another explanation arises from the comparison of the pairs of Rachel/Leah and Naomi/Ruth as antecedents of harmony and disharmony and as preludes to redemption.

The threads of redemption bind us not only to the future but also to the past. The book of Ruth places the reader in the midst of a process that has a history and a direction, a beginning and an end. Every individual is joined with innumerable ancestors and descendants, near and far in both space and time.

It is a common and, some might say, a fatal error of Western thought to believe that individuals exist and function within a space that they alone fill and is shaped solely by their own efforts. On the contrary: like all of us, Boaz and Ruth stand in the middle of a long line of development. It is not for nothing that the genealogy of David at the end of the book first moves backward and only then forward. Long before David started his royal line, many others, men and women alike, had confronted and agonized over the same choices and temptations, in each generation clarifying and improving the outcomes of their choices.

Ruth, too, is only a station within the process. She also has ancestors and allies in a recurrent cycle of trial and triumph, or rout and restoration. At times, the lines of the men and the women meet and intertwine – Judah and Tamar, Jacob with Rachel and Leah, Lot's daughters and their father and, finally, Boaz and Ruth.

The background for each encounter is the family. The meeting between Boaz and Ruth takes place against the backdrop of Elimelech, Naomi, their sons, and Orpah, and Judah's story incorporates that of his sons and his separation from his brothers. Other examples are Lot's estrangement from Abraham and the revolt of Rachel and Leah against their father Laban in order to follow Jacob and his truth. Yet even as discord and separation are always present, repair and return are present at the same time.

At every misstep there is an opportunity to rectify, achieve harmony, and create wholeness. The actors in the drama of redemption traverse the fractured landscape of failure to partial restoration, ultimate rectification and the finall full realization of completeness.

The estrangement of human beings from God, which causes their alienation from each other, stems from the very first conflict between brothers, when Cain killed Abel. At that moment, the fabric of human communal existence was torn asunder and conflict, betrayal, violence and injustice became a daily part of human experience within a group. R. Tanchuma tells us that it was also at that moment that the seed of the Messiah came into being and that the process of clarification and rectification began. Abel was reborn in steps as Seth, Judah, Boaz and even, as the kabbalists tell us, as Moses.

The axis of conflict and harmony intersects and interacts with the axis of good and evil. Lot's two daughters were united in what they did. Although they committed a terrible sin, their unity of purpose was worth saving. From the very beginning of history, when people disagree about what is right, they have had to consider whether to go their separate ways or compromise for the sake of the common goal. The dilemma between pure truth and the common good made itself felt in the relationships of Rachel and Leah, Ruth and Orpah, and Ruth and Naomi. In a world in which conflict and disagreement are part of the human condition, there are no simple answers. The irreducible contradiction of good and evil and peace and war will only be ultimately solved by the Messiah, who will bring wholeness to humanity. Cain and Abel will finally be redeemed and harmony shall reign among mankind.

> Certainly there is peace which derives from the absolute harmony in which disparate components interact and complement one another. We think of a piece of music in which each note enriches and colors the other to produce the loveliness which so deeply touches our hearts. But, to remain with our musical metaphor, discord and dissonance also have their place…. Metzudot on Divrei Hayamim (Chronicles) notes that the very word which in Hebrew denotes music, nitzuach, connotes victory, the ability to overcome, because the beauty of music derives from the many voices or instruments vying with one another in a battle for beauty.
>
> This second form, this harmony which draws upon the disharmonious to enhance its attractiveness, needs the firm hand of the composer to assign form, location and degree. Uncontrolled, it is nothing but raucous cacophony plaguing the air and offending the senses. (M.M. Eisemann, *A Pearl in the Sand,* 70)

The Conductor knows how to conduct. In His hand, discord and conflict become the means to healing and restoration. In His plan, suffering and discord become a path to wholeness and peace. Suffering leads to healing – a greater good than the mere absence of suffering. Although Rachel and Leah had their disagreements, they also negotiated and cooperated and "together built the House of Israel."

Lot's daughters used deceit, but through Tamar and Ruth their act was elevated and became the element for achieving goodness. Oppression becomes justice and rejection is transformed into acceptance. The lesson of the Messianic idea is that disharmony is only a building block from which harmony ultimately results.

The Book of Ruth starts with Elimelech's betrayal of his people and ends with his soul's symbolic return to their midst. In the beginning are death, poverty, exile, estrangement and suffering. At the end are acceptance, joy, regeneration and life.

BACK TO THE FUTURE

Happily Ever After?

> Boaz took Ruth, and she became his wife, and he went in unto her. God granted her conception, and she bore a son. (4:13)

WHAT HAPPENS when a young Moabite woman, a stranger to the complex and nuanced world of Jewish observance and sensibility, marries a man who is securely and inextricably set within it? Our verse alludes to the hard work and supreme effort that Ruth expended to become a worthy wife to Boaz. She became "a wife to him," an unusual expression that hints at a degree of incompatibility that had to be overcome.

The Torah uses this expression to describe the marriages of several Biblical personalities but pointedly withholds it when speaking of others. Among the latter is Moses, the greatest of all prophets, whose marriage to the Midianite convert Zipporah shares certain similarities with the marriage of Ruth and Boaz.

Read carefully and delve a bit into the following verses from Exodus Chapter 6.

> Aaron took himself Elisheba, the daughter of Amminadab, the sister of Nahshon, to wife, and she bore him Nadab and Abihu, Eleazar and Ithamar.... Eleazar Aaron's son took himself one of the daughters of Putiel to himself to wife, and she bore him Phinehas. These are the heads of the fathers' houses of the Levites according to their families.

These verses emphasize "himself"; the second verse in fact repeats it twice. It echoes the foundational verse of marriage: "The Lord God said: 'It is not good that the man should be alone; I will make for him a helpmate for him'" (Genesis 2:18).

> Opposition is a help. Behold, a man who is by nature angry and irascible – if his wife goads him on in expressing this, even though it is a 'help' in the short run and while he is angry he enjoys this help, after he calms down, he feels hurt that his wife added fuel to his fire – this is 'against him.' On the other hand, if she had opposed him in the beginning and calmed him and pacified him even while

appearing as opposing, she truly helps him in a way that cannot be surpassed. (*Ha'amek Davar*, ibid.)

Now let us read the description of Moses's marriage to Zipporah.

Moses agreed to dwell with the man, and he gave Moses Zipporah his daughter. (Exodus 2:21)

The Hebrew phrase translated above as "for himself" does not appear in this description.

According to the Sages, Aaron's son Eleazar, like Moses, married another daughter of Jethro (Putiel), a sister of Zipporah (*Sotah* 43a). Why does one sister merit her marriage to be described with two instances of the Hebrew phrase that we translated above as "for himself" and the other with not even one?

This shows us that even though the daughter of Putiel was of no better lineage than Zipporah, Moses's wife, she merited to give birth to Pinchas. This was because she was a true help to Eleazar in his daily life – a daily partner [for good]. Eleazar realized that she would assist him to become an elevated person and was not disturbed by her [lack of] lineage. She was a fitting wife for him and he was thereby worthy of having a son like Pinchas…. Not so Zipporah. Even though she was righteous, she did not contribute to Moses's greatness in the least. (Netziv on Exodus 6:24)

Boaz inherited greatness; we might say that it was in his blood and his genes. A true aristocrat, he was noble in thought and deed and his elevated ancestors lived on through him. On the other hand, Ruth was a self-made woman of valor. In so many ways, attitudes, opinions, habits and perceptions, they would have been different, not fully of the same mold, perhaps not even of the same spirit.

Ruth understood that she must "become a wife for him." Rather than forcing or defending the world that she brought into her marriage, she must join the world in which Boaz lives.

Yet unfortunately, their life together did not last. Boaz disappears from the Book of Ruth after this verse. The Sages say that he passed away that very night (*Yalkut Ruth* 608). This teaches us an important insight. Though we might spend a lifetime pursuing a goal or what we think is our destiny, it may be nothing more than a delusion or a dream. Only God knows for what purpose we have been placed upon this earth.

Boaz spent many years leading Israel, teaching the people, accomplishing great things. Yet, unbeknown to him, his purpose was to wait for the

Moabite stranger who would one day appear in his field. Once he married her and produced the seed of the Messiah, his purpose in the world, together with his life, came to an end. "Boaz made one hundred and twenty engagements and weddings for his children, but they all died during his lifetime" (*Bava Batra* 91a). By ordinary human reckoning, Boaz's life was a failure. Not only did he not leave a family behind, but he finally married a convert and died on his wedding night. Yet this was the way that God planned it. We, too, do not always know where we succeed or fail, but it is always according to God's plan, and in this we find consolation.

The Gift of Progeny

> God allowed Ruth to become pregnant and she gave birth to a child. (4:13)

Ruth's pregnancy is described as a divine gift with an expression that is unique in Tanach. Apparently there was something unusual about this pregnancy, for it is introduced in an unusual manner. This language drew the attention of our Sages, who make a striking comment: "Ruth had no uterus, and the Holy One, blessed be He, etched out a uterus within her" (*Ruth Rabbah* 7:14). The Sages draw a parallel between Ruth and the sisters Rachel and Leah, both of whom were barren. Of Rachel it says, "Rachel was barren" (Genesis 29:31), while regarding Leah, they commented on the same verse: "'God saw that Leah was hated and He opened her womb' – this teaches us that Leah was barren" (*Pesikta de-Rav Kahana* 20:6).

It seems curious that the Matriarchs could not bear children naturally. It is almost as if the beginning of the Jewish people had to result from a miraculous act of new creation. So, too, with the Davidic line – it was not simply descended from Boaz and Ruth but was a direct new creation of the Almighty. As such, it represented a new chapter in human history rather than a mere continuation of the past.

However, Ruth's pregnancy represented something even greater. It stood for the entire process of the exile, the night of human history when oppression, suffering and falsehood fill the earth. It also stands for the time that the seeds of redemption germinate, sprout and grow.

> The name of the angel appointed over pregnancy is Night. He takes the drop and stands it up in front of the Holy One, blessed be He (*Niddah* 16b).... The exile is compared to pregnancy and the messianic redemption to birth, as it writes, "Zion labored and also gave birth to her children." (Isaiah 66:8) (*Torah Ohr* Vayera 55a)

We have previously cited the extraordinary insight of R. Tsadok of Lublin, who observed that the Jewish nation needed to start in childlessness, barrenness and despair. Only a nation sprung from men and women who could hope, labor and trust when there appeared to be no hope can outlast the long, bitter night of exile. What we read here is that just as Ruth's optimism and faith were finally rewarded, ours will be, too. It is this exegetical thread that may have led the Rokeach to offer the following allegorical explanation of our verse in his commentary:

> "Boaz took Ruth" – This alludes to Israel: that the Holy One, blessed be He, will return to Jerusalem and will desire to bring Himself closer to the Congregation of Israel. God will bestow pregnancy upon Zion and she will give birth... for "Zion labored and gave birth to her children" (Isaiah 66:8). This is: "She [Ruth] gave birth to a son" – son alludes to Israel or the Messiah. The Hebrew word "will give birth" has the numerical value of "Messiah the son of David."

May it be soon, and in our time.

Absorbing Ruth

> The women said to Naomi: "Blessed be God, who did not leave you this day without a redeemer, and [this child] will become well known in Israel." (4:14).

How strange – Ruth has a baby and Naomi gets the credit!

We certainly appreciate that Naomi is comforted by her grandson, who will inherit her land and live on to perpetuate the name and memory of her departed husband and son. On a deeper level, as the Malbim points out in his commentary, Machlon's own soul has returned to the newly-born body of this baby, the son of his beloved wife and of Boaz, his kinsman. Still, where is Ruth in all this?

On a deeper level, Ruth, too, has returned to her roots in the family of Abraham. By doing so, she – both within and beyond literary convention – has become absorbed into Naomi. In Kabbalah, Naomi and Ruth are identified with the sefirot of Bina and Malchut. In the process of redemption, Malchut rises to become reabsorbed into the sefira of Bina from which it originally derives (see Pardes 20:19 and also Chapter 13). However, this teaching also has psychological significance.

On the practical level, these verses raise the question of how a stranger can join a community. How can what is different become similar, and how can what is separate become one? What happens when a person of quality –

a man or woman of substantial personal achievement gained in a foreign environment – seeks to join with a people whose mores, values and perceptions are different and perhaps even antagonistic to those of the candidate? It seems that there can only be two possible outcomes – a slow process of assimilation that enriches the host and eventually erases all differences or a clash that brings about injury and ruin to both.

When the nation and the convert show each other love, humility and compassion, we have the story of Ruth. If there is mistrust and mutual suspicion, we have the story of Athaliah (see 2 Kings 11). Athaliah was a foreign princess, daughter of King Ahab and the Sidonian princess Jezebel, who married into the royal family of Judah and almost wiped out the Davidic line. The Sages comment:

> R. Choniah said: [It was only] due to the blessings of the women [Ruth] that the line of David was not utterly uprooted by force [by Athaliah]. (*Ruth Rabbah* 7:16, see also *Sanhedrin* 95a)

Ruth sought to identify with Naomi. The people accepted Ruth, and her absorption into the body of the Israelite nation helped to create the royal house. Athaliah, who was a pagan transplant both culturally and spiritually, resisted joining the House of Judah and almost destroyed it by her recalcitrance and rebellion.

The contradiction between self-actualization and submission to the community's authority is never easy to resolve. For some souls, which mesh naturally with their people's inner spiritual core, there is not even a question. For others, it is a lifelong struggle. Fortunately for us, the Children of Israel, self-transcendence and the search for the Divine do not contradict our tradition, history, heritage and community. The example of Ruth and Naomi in the context of separation and redemption provides important guidance about how to search for God as an individual, yet from within a nation and a tradition.

The Seven Sons

> … for your daughter-in-law, who loves you, has borne him, and she is better to you than seven sons. (4:15)

In these verses Naomi is no longer Marah (bitter), the woman with whom God deals bitterly. God now deals kindly with her, for He has given her a grandchild to sustain her old age and to perpetuate her name. Yet strangely, in the very next breath the neighbor women tell Naomi that Ruth is "better to [her] than seven sons." They seem to be reassuring Naomi about something. What could it be? What troubles Naomi?

Is she uncertain as to how Ruth will respond to her stewardship of the child? Are they saying: "Do not fear, Naomi; Ruth will continue to love you even though you will be bringing up this child"? Or do they perhaps sense Naomi's disappointment that she herself will never again bear children? Perhaps it is the realization that while this child will remain an only child, Ruth, who is better than seven children, will always be there for Naomi.

All these are possible explanations. What remains puzzling is why the women tell her that Ruth is better than seven sons even as Naomi is blessed with a child, as if she were suffering a calamity instead of receiving a blessing. The question becomes even stronger when we realize that this expression is otherwise used in the completely opposite situation – to comfort those who are childless.

In the Book of Samuel, Elkanah comforts his wife Hannah:

> ... but to Hannah he gave a double portion, for he loved Hannah, though God had shut up her womb. Her rival angered her much to make her fret, because God had closed her womb. As he did so year by year, when she went up to the house of God, [her co-wife Peninnah] would vex her. Therefore, she wept and would not eat.

> Elkanah, her husband, said to her: "Hannah, why do you cry and not eat, and why is your heart grieved? Am I not better to you than ten sons?" (Samuel I, 1:5–8)

According to tradition in *Bava Batra* 15b, both Ruth and Samuel were written by the prophet Samuel. If so, why does he use the expression "better than ten sons" in the Book of Samuel and "better than seven sons" in the Book of Ruth? Surely the change in number is significant.

The Sages appear to have noted this problem, for they comment as follows:

> R. Yehuda and R. Nechemia [disagree]. R. Yehuda says: Better than seven heads of families [of Yishai, the father of David] described in a later book (I Chronicles 2:15), "Etzem is the sixth [son], David the seventh." R. Nechemia says: "[Better than]

> the seven described here – Peretz, Chetzron, Ram, Amminadav, Nachshon, Salmon, Boaz." (*Ruth Rabbah* 7:16)

Therefore, the "seven" mentioned in the Book of Ruth refer to something specific – the generation of the royal line – while the "ten" in Samuel is merely an expression. It is interesting to realize, however, that the word "son" or "sons" is repeated in the first chapter of Samuel exactly seven times. In the manner of an allusion, the text in Ruth points to and amplifies the passage in Samuel.

On a yet deeper level, the "seven sons" recall the concept that we have already encountered in which David represents the pinnacle of a ten-step process that parallels that of Creation. David's reign (*malchut bet David*), which corresponds to the sefira of *malchut*, is the last step in this unfolding of the Divine plan (*Sha'arei Orah,* Chapter 1). In this regard, Naomi is the third step (Binah), while Ruth is the tenth (Malchut). The two mothers are united when goodness flows thorough them.

> "… better to you than seven sons" – that is the flow of goodness… is better for you than seven sons, the six intermediate steps combined with Malchut (referred to as "seven sons" or "seven days of construction"), which aid the beginning of the process and lead the plan to fruition. (R. Isaac Luria, *Tzaddik yesod olam*)

Put simply, Naomi and Ruth together make up a unit that advanced the development of God's plan. The neighbors told Naomi that she and Ruth were inseparable vis-à-vis the Divine plan. Naomi was the third station, Boaz the sixth, Ruth and David the tenth. This is why the genealogy of David at the end of the book reads both forward and backward (the exact elaboration of the relationship is beyond our scope; see *Idrei Tzon*).

First the three generations, going forward: Obed, Yishai, David.

> The women neighbors gave him a name, saying: A son is born to Naomi, and they called his name Obed. He is the father of Jesse, the father of David.

Then we return to the beginning and count the ten generations:

> Now these are the generations of Perez: Perez fathered Hezron. Hezron fathered Ram, and Ram fathered Amminadab. Amminadab fathered Nahshon, and Nahshon fathered Salmon. Salmon fathered Boaz, and Boaz fathered Oved. Oved fathered Yishai, and Yishai fathered David.

In Samuel I, Hannah, who was still childless, had not yet even begun this ten-step process. Therefore, Elkanah comforted her by saying that he was better to her than ten children. After the birth of Ruth's son, the plan was already in motion, and the women used the idiom of "seven" when they spoke to Naomi.

Oved

> The women neighbors gave him a name, saying: "A son is born to
> Naomi," and they called him Obed. He is the father of Yishai, the
> father of David. (4:17)

We do not know much about Oved. In fact, what this verse tells us is all
that we know about him. There are many questions. Who really named this
child? We can safely assume that, as was customary, Boaz or Ruth did so,
but apparently that name was not preserved. Only the name given by the
women neighbors was recorded: "Oved, the father of Yishai, the father of
David." Such a naming, which is highly irregular, may be the only one of its
kind in Scripture.

Who were these mysterious neighbor women? Were they the same as
"the people at the gate" or "the women" mentioned earlier? When did they
give Oved his name? From what we read, it appears to have happened after
his birth and possibly much later, after he became a father and grandfather.
There is no parallel in Tanach for such a delayed naming.

The neighbor women also introduce an editorial comment. The Sages
understood that the women, whoever they were and whenever they lived,
did not merely give Oved a name, but also described him and his life's work.

Oved means "servant."

> ... [He was named] after his father and his mother. His father
> [Boaz], an elderly man, took a wife purely for the sake of Heaven.
> He was [therefore] called "a servant of God," as it is written, "Israel
> served for a woman" (Hosea 13:2). After his mother – as it is
> written, "You shall turn back and distinguish between the just and
> the wicked, between the one who served God and the one who did
> not serve Him" (Malachi 13:18). This means: between Ruth and
> Orpah. Orpah became an emblem of shame [a play of words
> between the name Orpah and the Hebrew word for shame, *herpah*]
> while Ruth clung to God in clarity. This is why his name was called
> Oved. A righteous man married a righteous woman and the son was
> a perfected saint (Midrash Lekach Tov).

These neighbor women realized that Oved's life task was to shape his
parents' spiritual legacy. While his father was a wholly righteous sage, his
mother had come from the world of confusion, where good and evil are
intermixed and not easily separated. Although Ruth had voluntarily
abandoned the world of falsehood, she had not had the opportunity to
complete the work of choosing good. It is difficult to leave the past

completely behind and even harder not to transmit it to the next generation. Thus, for all Ruth's virtue, a faint trace of her Moabite past still clung to her descendants.

Oved's mission was to purify the legacy that he had received and to become a completed saint. How did he do this? He reached into his soul to the level that had existed before the backsliding of Lot. He discovered and united the Abrahamic roots of both his father and his mother. It was he who captured Ruth's true inheritance from Abraham from the time before it was sullied by Lot and his daughters, before Abraham's lofty teachings degenerated into the tainted origin of Moab and culminated in the sophisticated rebellion of Orpah.

Ruth took the first steps upon the Judaic path but it was left to Oved to complete the work – separating the true from the false, and good from evil, in all that he encountered.

> Now we will turn to a great and exalted place which is in the world and the branch and root of truth – Oved, the father of Yishai, the father of David. We learned that he was at the end [of a chain]; how then did the root of Truth come from such a place? However, Oved rectified himself in supernal rectification and turned back upon its foundation the root of a tree that had been turned upside down. He ascended through it and rectified himself, and was therefore called "the Servant." This is something that others did not merit. Oved came and worked and cultivated the base and root of the Tree. He [then] left the Face of Bitterness and rectified the foliage of the tree. Yishai, his son, came and reinforced it and fixed it and held himself by the branches of another, higher tree, and connected one tree to the other, so that the two trees became intermingled. Once David came, he found the trees intermingled and held securely together. He inherited kingship – and Oved caused all this. (Zohar Hadash 2:103b)

I suggest that the trees to which the above text refers are Abraham and Moab.

This simple understanding of the Zohar (and there are, of course, others that are more kabbalistically complex) is supported by the passage in *Ruth Rabbah* (8:13) that compares David to a diamond that a king once dropped in the sand. To recover it, he had to call many workers to sift the sand grain by grain.

> The Holy One, blessed be He, said to Abraham: "Take yourself out of your land. It is you whom I was waiting for. Why did I need to list

your genealogies – Shem, Arpachshad, Shelach, Eber, Peleg, Nachor, Terach? Only for you – 'Abram – that is, Abraham,' [of whom it is written:] 'You found his heart faithful before You.'" This is what the Holy One said to David. "Why did I need to list your genealogies – Peretz, Hetzron, Ram, Amminadav, Nachshon, Salmon, Boaz, Obed, Yishai? Only for you – 'I found David my servant.'"

Abraham was a diamond that represents the end of long process of sifting and selecting, rejection and election. Since the same applies to David, his genealogy is therefore central to the major message of the Book of Ruth. Although Ruth brought essential and precious characteristics to Jewish royalty, she also brought in elements that needed to be cleansed and set aside. The tension between accepting some traits while rejecting others will always remain at the core of the process of redemption.

Jesse

Jesse – in Hebrew, Yishai – was the father of David. As such, he was an important personality but, as with Oved, we know very little about him. The Biblical record tells us very little about King David's grandfather. The Sages attempted to fill this gap with several traditions, and their concept of redemption played an important role in how these traditions were conveyed. They viewed him as a great man, certainly not the clueless patriarch portrayed by the superficial reading of I Samuel 16.

According to *Sukkah* 52b, Yishai is one of the "eight princes of man" mentioned in Micha 5:4. Departing at the head of a multitude of followers, he returned with a multitude and he taught Torah to a multitude (*Berachot* 58a). Yishai inspired David to fight Goliath (*Tanchuma Buber* Vayigash 8). Yishai was one of four people who died solely because of the serpent's advice to Eve, for they had never sinned (*Shabbat* 55b). "The Sages said: Yishai lived more than four hundred years" (*Genesis Rabbah* 96:4).

We will focus upon a long midrashic passage that characterizes both Yishai and David. It illuminates the Sages' approach towards the recurring patterns in Tanach, the return of generations and the nature of repentance and redemption in history.

There is an opinion that Yishai separated from his wife after he learned that some people questioned the legal propriety of Boaz's marriage to Ruth. As a descendant of Moabites, Yishai feared that he was forbidden to marry a Jewish woman. He then separated from his wife and told his maidservant, who was not fully Jewish, to prepare herself to cohabit with him so that he could fulfill the commandment to procreate. (The Midrash invokes a conditional manumission agreement that rendered the maidservant permitted to a man with a tainted lineage.)

In the meantime, Yishai's wife was terribly distressed to lose her husband, as well as any more children that she might have had with him. Seeing her mistress's anguish, the maidservant suggested that they do as Rachel and Leah had done: change places under cover of darkness so that Yishai would cohabit with his wife instead of with the maidservant. The plan worked, and Yishai's wife conceived and bore a son, David.

When Yishai and his sons saw this, they suspected her of adultery but kept silent for twenty-eight years until Samuel came to Yishai's house to anoint the new king (*Yalkut ha-Machiri*, Psalms 118:28, retold in *Sefer ha-Toda'ah*, Shavuot, 322–323).

What might at first glance seem like a fanciful tale is actually a necessary conclusion of the process of purification and repentance throughout the generations. As we recall, we have encountered the motif of a well-intentioned woman deceiving a man for the sake of a praiseworthy goal many times: Lot and his daughters, Judah and Tamar, Ruth and Boaz. In each succeeding instance, the sin became less apparent, its evil component becoming ever more diluted by the good intention. Lot's daughters' act is abhorrent. The transgression of Judah and Tamar was technically much less severe since both were single, yet it was a transgression nevertheless. Although Ruth and Boaz overcame their natural inclinations, their encounter in a secluded place in the middle of the night was still improper. Therefore, David's ancestry contained a faint component of impropriety. In order to complete the great cosmic drama of redemption, the situation must be repeated once more, this time with no sin whatsoever, even if the Bible does not tell the story explicitly.

The Sages understood that the incident must have taken place before this part of the royal family's history had been completed. A righteous man and a worthy woman had to repeat the episode, this time within the confines of marriage. Yishai broke no law when he approached his wife. He violated no technical prohibition or moral consideration. Since both husband and wife acted out of wholly positive motives, their union was blessed with David.

One cycle ended and another was ready to begin. What is human history but a spiral that continually passes over the same ground, over the same issues but each time at a higher level. David certainly continued the personal and national work of redemption throughout his life and career and in the life of his descendents. Yet, a chapter has closed and a new chapter opened.

The ground that was gained will never be forfeited and the failures and ascents will henceforth play out on a more elevated platform.

David

The book of Ruth ends with the mention of David. Who is not inspired by the story of David, his trials and triumphs, his peaks of religious achievement and his failings and disappointments? In many ways his story resembles that of Ruth in that it is a tale of rejection and perseverance, effort and, above all choices. Moral perfection is a matter of making the right choices, and the same options present themselves anew in every age. David's birth ends the era when "the Judges judged" and begins the new period of national tribulations – the monarchy.

By now we have become familiar with the view that history is built on repetition. In every generation we climb the same peaks and agonize over the same dilemmas. Every generation takes the same examination, as it were, and if it passes, its children traverse the same terrain at a higher elevation.

The central moral issue of the period of the Judges had been how to preserve the uniqueness and purity of Israelite religion in the midst of the surrounding nations. The story of Ruth demonstrates that the Israelites succeeded in being able to absorb, transform and reshape outside influences under the authority and sovereignty of the Torah. So successful were they that Ruth the Moabite became the mother of royalty. Her great-grandson David represents the state of religious and spiritual maturity, able to reject the bad and transform the good. Henceforth, the Jewish people would never again be tempted to assimilate and disappear among its neighbors. Its struggle would now be internal – how to unify the disparate aspects of the sacred, assure that the Divine Presence rests upon it and remains at its central point, and build the Holy Temple in Jerusalem so as to remain united under the Torah. The failing of the monarchy was its later separation into two kingdoms, which led to its eventual fall. Disunity destroyed both the First and Second Temples.

David and his children continued to be tempted but – significantly – within and around rather than outside of marriage. We no longer see situations like that of Judah and Tamar or Ruth and Boaz. David and Batsheva, Amnon and Tamar, Avshalom and his father's ten concubines, Adoniyahu and Avishag, Solomon and the daughter of Pharaoh – all these were errors that occurred within the confines of an existing or potential marriage relationship. Marriage became the paradigm of the greater struggle for the heart and soul of the monarchy. Tikkun is now primary, with berur secondary to it; rectification and unification are the main aspiration, even if the separation of evil from good and the purification of good from evil continue under its umbrella.

David represents a way-station on the way to redemption. In some ways he succeeds and in others, he and his descendants fail. Their work has not stopped. The redemptive process continues — may we soon witness its completion, speedily and in our day.

YONAH

THE BOOK OF YONAH:
ALIENATION, DESPAIR, AND RETURN

Introduction

ALTHOUGH THE BOOK OF YONAH is a small book found in the Twelve Prophets, between the books of Ovadia and Micha, it is widely considered to be one of the most profound books in Tanach. In the story of one man's flight "from the presence of the Lord," an attuned reader will find a highly personal reflection about the nature of obedience and limits of autonomy, as well as the relationship between emotion and intellect, mercy and justice, and redemption and repentance.

The following chapters use a different approach from the one in the series of essays on the Book of Ruth. The forthcoming chapters, like those on the Book of Ruth, will cite the entire extent of traditional and contemporary scholarship on the message contained in the Book of Yonah. They will also introduce readers to the various skills that they will need in order to examine other Biblical books.

However, because the goal of this commentary is different, these lessons differ from the lectures on Ruth. The intent is not to provide passive knowledge or to dissect the approach of the Sages, who in any case left us very few comments on this book, but to present each lecture as an example of how to uncover deeper meaning in the text and its application to our lives.

The Sages did not leave us a "Midrash Rabbah" on the Book of Yonah. However, they left us a wealth of teachings and insights on the topics with which the book deals. We must allow their principles to guide us as we delve into its message; therefore, this work follows a framework of a commentary.

Most of us have a definite impression about Sefer Yonah. Those who know it from leafing through the Yom Kippur prayer book may remember only that a whale swallowed the prophet who refused to do God's bidding. We might see, in our mind's eye, vague images of a flight to Tarshish "from before the Lord," the storm at sea, the jaws of the waiting whale and the prophet's belated and reluctant discharge of the task that had been imposed upon him. Then there is Yonah's surprising complaint at the end of the book that God is too kind and merciful for his liking.

We would be surprised indeed to learn that this book is widely thought of as one of the most profound and meaningful prophetic books of the Bible.

Many beautiful approaches to exposition of Yonah have been offered throughout the centuries, and we will review some of them together. We will proceed from the assumption that this work speaks to the major issues that every spiritually attuned human being faces in life. What is life but a dynamic of encounter between God and human beings, the Divine intrusion into our routine and His incessant demands on our souls, especially when He refuses to take our advice about how to run the world? Against our will we are born and against our will we live our lives.

Some sensitive souls struggle with this truth every day of their lives. Others only deal with it at a time of crisis. All of us are tested if we only live long enough. The test may take the form of unexpected prosperity, a difficult divorce, the death of a loved one or a serious illness, to name only a few examples. Jarring experiences take us out of our daily routine. Events affect us unexpectedly, seemingly at random, without purpose or meaning.

Nevertheless, there is meaning, even if at times we would rather not see it. As much as we may wish to keep God out of our lives, He refuses to go away. He keeps making demands of us, shattering our smug self-sufficiency, our comfortable illusions, pretenses of who we think we are, of what we think He should be. Psychological denial, spiritual preconceptions, intellectual complacency – how we insist on retaining them, how hard we fight to hold on to them. Like Yonah, we also try to flee God's presence. We alone have the choice of resisting or running away, or of engaging, growing, submitting and, in the process, being redeemed and reborn.

Like Job, Yonah could not agree with the way in which God conducted His world. While the book of Job (with which Yonah shares many structural and philosophical parallels) presents the problem with the Attribute of Justice, Yonah could not abide the Attribute of Mercy. This prophet would have preferred a world that is more organized, certain and predictable, where the wicked suffer certain retribution and the righteous receive immediate reward – a world that functions according to preset rules, without the redundancies and paradoxes that surround us. In the end, the prophet had to experience pity and discover the echo of Divine mercy within his own heart.

Yet learning this is not a one-time event. It is a process and a dynamic. Yonah emerged from the belly of the fish with gratitude and praise, thinking that he had been reborn and redeemed, yet he was still resisting. There was still unfinished business: layers of denial and shells of self-delusion that needed to be removed in future trials. The lessons were not yet finished.

Our main tool in this process of exploration will be the principle of intertextuality, which can be defined as the assumption that Biblical authors and their audiences were familiar with the entire corpus of Biblical writing. It follows, therefore, that they used references to context, thought and idiom, construction and literary patterns found in other Biblical works. Always, the words of our Sages will serve as signposts upon this quest. This methodology, which is a mainstay of midrashic analysis, will guide us beyond the apparent disjointed meaning of individual phrases to the deeper intended significance of the text. More importantly, it will uncover for us a significance that we can apply to our own lives in the here and now. No longer will we be reading a peculiar little story of a prophet and a whale in a far away time and place; now it will become an intensely personal document for application and relevance to our own lives.

Let us journey together with Yonah. Let us descend into the heart of Jewish religious experience together with the man who sought to escape from God only to find Him and be reconciled with Him in the heart of the sea – "a compassionate and gracious God, abounding in kindness and repenting of evil." "Then he fell on his face and said: Conduct Your world according to the attribute of Mercy, as it is written: To the Lord our God belong mercy and forgiveness" (Daniel 9:9) (Midrash Yonah).

Let us embark on the study of Sefer Yonah.

Yonah the Prophet

The task of a prophet was to awaken and guide the people. Like the prophets who came before him, Yonah expected to carry out this task for his own people, the nation of Israel. Until his time, the great themes of Biblical prophecy related to the special status of Israel as a party to the Covenant, its responsibilities under this covenant and the consequences of violating its provisions.

The prophets often found themselves on both sides of the covenantal divide. As their nation's representatives, they often argued with God in order to defend their people and to lessen or postpone the consequences of its disobedience. On the other hand, they were God's messengers, devoted to Him and zealous on His behalf. While prophets sent messages to foreign kings on occasion (see Isaiah 13–23, Jeremiah 46–51, Ezekiel 25–33, Amos 1–2), they were always in the context of the events taking place in the Jewish kingdoms.

Yonah, who expected to be a prophet for his own people, found himself called to deliver a message to Nineveh, the only prophet ever charged with delivering a prophecy solely to Gentiles. Asked to step outside of the traditional prophetic paradigm, Yonah was unwilling to do so. He did not want to give up the privilege of advocating for the nation of Israel.

The Sages commented on the tension of this double role as follows:

> [Of] three prophets, one defended the honor of the father and of the son, one defended the honor of the father but not of the son, and one defended the honor of the son but not of the father. Yirmiah defended the honor of the father and of the son, as it is written, "We sinned and transgressed. You showed no compassion" (Eicha 3:42).… [T]herefore his prophecy was doubled…. Eliyahu defended the honor of the father but not of the son, as it is written: "I was exceedingly jealous for God, the Lord of Hosts." What does it say (regarding this)? "Go back… anoint Elisha son of Shafat in your stead as prophet over Israel" (I Kings 16). Yonah defended the honor of the son but not of the father. What is written there? "The word of God came to Yonah a second time." [He spoke to him] a second time and no more. (*Mechilta* 12:4)

The Sages point out that since Eliyahu defended the Father, he lost the right to represent the son, Israel. Yonah took the side of the children of Israel and sought to escape God, the other party to the covenant. This, too, was an error and God never called on him again. Yirmiah defended the people by offering a confession on their behalf, but he also defended God's right not to accept it right away. His was the way of which God most approved.

The Sages described the motivation for Yonah's flight as stemming from his concern that if the Ninevites were to repent, this would reflect poorly upon the Jewish people. Yonah said: "I will take myself outside of the Land of Israel, so as not to render Israel guilty, since the Gentiles are quick to repent [whereas Jews have been repeatedly called to repent and refused to obey] (*Mechilta,* ibid.). This explanation for Yonah's flight is adopted by Rashi, Radak, R. Yosef Karo and Ibn Ezra. Abarbanel questions it: "This is in truth a very weak interpretation, since the repentance of the people of Nineveh might shame Israel for their sins so that they [also] return to God, Who will have mercy on them."

It seems that Yonah's motives were honorable. Yet if that was the case, where did he go wrong? Did his wrongdoing consist in his refusal to obey God's call? That alone should not have been so bad. After all, other prophets such as Moshe, Yirmiah, Yeshayah and Amos resisted the initial call to prophecy. Yonah could hardly be faulted for following in the footsteps of his predecessors in this matter, nor can we view his noble self-sacrifice on behalf of Israel with anything less than admiration. But "the heart is deceitful above all things, and it is exceedingly deep – who can know it?" (Yirmiah 17:9). The verses show that there was more to Yonah's decision to escape the Divine Presence than a zealous defense of the Jewish people. Undoubtedly this is what "Yonah said" to himself as he ran away; yet the true motivation did not become apparent to him until much later. At the end, he knew.

"Yonah was exceedingly troubled and said: Behold, Lord God, is this not the thing that I said while still in my own country? Therefore I hurried to flee to Tarshish, for I knew that You are a merciful and forgiving God, slow to anger and very benevolent, and you repent of causing evil" (Yonah 4:2). This is what, unbeknownst to him, troubled the prophet. Underlying the noble self-perception lay the real reason – Yonah could not abide God's way in the world. Yonah did not want to carry out the Divine command because he did not approve of all this "excess" kindness. You might say in contemporary language that Yonah had a problem with God's style of management.

The experiences that followed humbled Yonah. The privations and suffering that he endured broke his stubborn certainty. In the depths of his despair, pain and frustration, imprisoned in the belly of the fish, at the depths of the sea, he grew ready to receive and to be guided. He learned that mercy is good because it allows for repentance, and he learned that repentance delivered him from the very depths of failure. Only humility allows real learning, and real humility is gained by going through life's trials. Yonah praised God for teaching him this truth for he saw that all this time, as he suffered, he was also being guided.

"Good and upright is God. Therefore he guides the sinners upon the way. He leads the humble with justice and will teach the humble His way." (Tehillim 25:8–9)

Prophecy

> It happened that the word of God came to Yonah, son of Amitai, as follows (1:1)….

As we discussed in the introduction, the Sages drew a comparison between Yirmiah and Yonah and between Eliyahu and Yonah. While Yirmiah was able to combine advocacy for the Jewish people with zealous defense of God's honor, Yonah fled from God's word in order to protect the Jewish people. The link between Yonah and Eliyahu is no less important and in some ways more dramatic but we will discuss it at a later time. For now, we will explore the comparison between Yirmiah and Yonah and what it can teach us.

It is significant that the very first words of the book of Yonah draw a parallel between these three prophets. Although the phrase "the word of God came to" is not common in Tanach as a description of prophecy, it is found frequently in Yirmiah (see, for example, 13:8). The same words also begin the account of Eliyahu in the book of I Kings 17:3.

The comparison to Yirmiah goes far deeper than similarity of expression, for even a superficial reader of Yirmiah will notice an affinity between the two prophets. Both are initially uncomfortable with their mission, are sent to a wicked city (Yirmiah's destination was, unfortunately, Jerusalem) in order to summon it to repentance, and both ultimately grow into their role. In addition, the thirty-sixth chapter of Yirmiah, in which he delivers the prophecy of destruction first to the people of Jerusalem and then to King Yehoiachin, mirrors a similar episode in the third chapter of the Book of Yonah. Of course, the crucial difference is that the people of Nineveh heeded God's word, while those of Jerusalem did not.

The doctrine of national repentance that both books teach ties them together.

> At one moment I may decree that a nation or a kingdom be rooted out and brought down and destroyed. But should that nation against which I had decreed turn back from its wickedness, I change My mind regarding the punishment that I had planned to bring against it. (Yirmiah 18:7–8)

This verse teaches us that political entities, like individuals, have responsibilities, can behave immorally, are subject to Divine correction, and can repent. Some thinkers claim that ordinary morality does not apply to countries or governments but only to individuals, and that everything is permitted in the pursuit of national interest. Yirmiah taught the falseness of this doctrine, but to his grief, his message was not heeded. Jerusalem and its kings refused to repent and instead became the object of divine wrath.

Yonah was called to demonstrate the other side of God's sovereignty over nations – His kindness and his Providence. When the Ninevites repented, they presented an image of what Jerusalem could have achieved. The Book of Yonah therefore serves as a foil to that of Yirmiah.

The Sages' comparisons between individuals, places or situations are supported by many connections besides the ones explicitly stated. Our discovery of these connections allows us to appreciate their words and the care with which they speak.

Running Away

> The word of the Lord came to Yonah…. "Arise and go to Nineveh, the great city, and cry out to it…." Yonah arose to flee to Tarshish from before God…. (Yonah 1:2)

Before we can consider the significance of Yonah's flight, we need to resolve a basic quandary. Technically speaking, Yonah committed a capital offense, yet God not only did not punish him but pursued him in order to bring him back. "A prophet who withholds his prophecy, one who disobeys a prophet and a prophet who transgresses his own words – all die by the hand of Heaven" (*Sanhedrin* 89a). I Kings 20 tells of a prophet who, like Yonah, did not follow God's command and was subsequently killed by a lion. Why, then, did God not only spare Yonah but also send him on an educational odyssey that has no parallel anywhere else in Scripture?

The answer lies in that Yonah appears to have received only the beginning of an order that was later fleshed out as "call to it the call that I tell to you" (3:1). Although he was told to call out to the city, he was given no specific message to deliver. Therefore, at least technically, he did not fall into the category of a prophet who transgresses his own words because his prophecy was not complete.

However, this claim raises other questions. Why was Yonah given an incomplete prophecy? Is there any parallel to this event elsewhere in the Tanach?

One may suggest that we encounter the phenomenon of an incomplete prophecy when the messenger is unprepared and not ready to assimilate the full message. There are other examples, such as in Yechezkel 3 and Numbers 22:20 (see *Genesis Rabbah* 39:9). The reason for this is that prophecy is not automatically sent and received. It requires that the prophet possess a prepared, attuned mind and that he understand, interpret and internalize the message (for more on this, see *Guide for the Perplexed* II:36).

It follows that even great individuals may not be prepared to absorb messages that contradict their own deeply-held beliefs. They may hear only a part of the communication, while the remainder may be garbled or unclear. The result is an incomplete prophecy. If this is what happened to Yonah, he may have recognized that he did not receive and interpret God's message in its entirety. Instead of trying to find the barrier within himself that caused the faulty reception, he chose to run away, for he was not ready for the kind of ruthless self-examination that understanding the Divine message would require.

How the above relates to us little people seems quite clear. "Leave the Jews alone. If they are not prophets, then they are offspring of prophets" (*Pesachim* 66b). "Every single day an echo issues forth from Horeb [Mount Sinai]" (*Pirke Avot* 6:2), "only we do not hear it; we close our ears to it" (see *Resisei Layla* 16 and *Mevo Shaarim* I:2–3). Like Yonah, the soul in this world attempts to flee God's Presence. It evades its obligations and sinks into transgressions. The Zohar states: "While in this world, human beings sin and think that they have fled from their Master" (cited in the Vilna Gaon's commentary to Yonah, *ad loc.*). God speaks daily to every Jew through His Torah and in current events, but we are not prepared. We are not willing to change ourselves in order to receive the message. We do not wish to hear what may be uncomfortable truths. Instead, we escape in an attempt to silence that still, small voice. Sometimes we drown it in the pursuit of material pleasures, even committing transgressions so as to become less fitting receptacles for God's voice, while at other times we seek to be entertained rather than educated.

Yonah ultimately reversed himself, changing his course and doing God's bidding. In this lies one vitally important lesson of this Biblical book.

The Great City

> Arise and go to Nineveh, the great city and call out against it for their wickedness has come up before me (1:2).

Yonah was commanded to go to Nineveh for it had sinned grievously against God. Truly Nineveh was a great city from its founding (Genesis 10:11–12). A capital of the rising imperial power of Assyria, it is mentioned in the Tanach for its might, fierceness and cruel policy of exiling the populations of enemy countries and disobedient vassal states, including the Kingdom of Israel, the Jewish tribes of the trans-Jordan and most of Judea. Only Jerusalem was miraculously saved. It is surprising, then, that the Book of Yonah ignores the essential facts that Nineveh was a feared and hated enemy of Israel and the capital of Assyria.

In order to understand what Nineveh really was, let us read the words of another prophet:

> Woe to the city of blood! It is all full of lies and rape; the prey departs not....
>
> Because of the many misdeeds of the beautiful harlot, the sorceress who sells nations through her harlotries, and families through her enchantments....

Behold, I am come against you, says the Lord of Hosts…. (Nachum 3:1–5)

Why is this information not mentioned the Book of Yonah? Furthermore, why did Nineveh deserve that God should send a prophet to call it to repentance and spread the message of Divine forgiveness among its inhabitants? After all, human history has no lack of wicked cities that received no second chance. Witness the different treatment accorded Babylon by the prophet Yeshaya (chapters 13 and 14). This question is very important since it guides our understanding of the entire book.

Some suggest that Ninevites had been righteous since the city was established and had turned to evil only recently. Therefore, they deserved a chance that other cities, which were wholly wicked, did not (Ibn Ezra). Others saw it as God's cleansing of the "staff of [Divine] wrath" (Yeshaya 10:5) in order to render it worthy to deliver His judgment against Israel (Radak, Abarbanel).

We will approach this question by noting the significance of Nineveh's description as a "great city." It was a city of large dimensions, containing within it "more than twelve myriad [one hundred twenty thousand] people" (Yonah 4:11). "Nineveh was a great city unto the Lord, a walk of three days" (*ibid.* 3:3). The ruins of ancient Nineveh near Mosul, Iraq, are visible to this day. Its walls are twelve kilometers long and its maximal width is five kilometers, and the extent of the settlement outside the walls is likely to have been even greater.

Yet evidently it was not only its size that made Nineveh great, since the same description appears at the time of its construction, when it was likely much smaller (Genesis 10:11–12). The suggestion that there is inherent significance in selecting Nineveh the Great City as the setting for Yonah's message of repentance may explain the repeated use of the word *gadol* (great), which occurs fourteen times in this brief book (except for 3:5, where it means "mature").

The concept of the key word has become widely accepted as a guide to Biblical interpretation since it was first used by Martin Buber some eighty years ago. In brief, it proposes that in Scripture, key words are frequently repeated within a unit of meaning, often seven or fourteen times, in order to encode the interpretive key for careful readers and to have a subliminal effect upon more superficial ones.

The phrase "great city" is echoed by the phrases "great wind," "great cry," "great fear" and, of course, the "great fish" that swallowed Yonah. The latter is particularly interesting because the Semitic word "Nineveh" sounds somewhat like "abode of the fish" ("naveh nun," *Daat mikra* n. 7 *ad loc.*), and the cuneiform symbol for Nineveh is a fish inside a house. The overall effect of such foreshadowing and characterization is to draw our attention to the important matters with which this book deals: prophecy, repentance, rebellion and redemption. The key word signals the cosmic significance of the events that this book recounts and helps shape our response to its message.

Rebels and Those Who Love Them

> The word of the Lord came to Yonah…. "Arise and go to Nineveh, the great city, and cry out to it…." Yonah arose to flee to Tarshish from before the Lord (Yonah 1:2–3)

At this moment, Yonah faced a decision. He could accede to God's demand as Eliyahu, his teacher, had done before him. Of Eliyahu it states: *"Arise and go to Tzarfat… and he arose and went to Tzarfat" (I Kings 17:9–10)*. He also could have ignored God's message, convince himself that he had not heard a thing, and remain the same as he had been before. He did neither. He chose to flee from God, which ultimately saved him, since although he had disobeyed God's call, he had not ignored it. Despite his flight, he remained alert to the message that he carried, and in the end, he could no longer ignore it. "I thought: I will not mention Him, no more will I speak in His name – but His word was like a raging fire in my heart, imprisoned in my bones. I could not hold it; I was helpless" (Yirmiah 20:9).

Why did Yonah run away, and where did he plan to go? One must be surprised, for how could a wise man, who recognizes God and how He acts, think to flee from Him? Humankind is in His hand and all is full of His Glory" (Ibn Ezra ibid). "Yonah said: Where shall I escape? If [I flee] to heaven, His glory is mentioned there: 'His Glory is over the heavens (Psalms 113). If [I remain] on the earth, His glory is mentioned there: "His Glory fills the earth" (Yeshaia 6:3)'. I will flee to a place [the ocean] where His glory is not mentioned" (*Pirkei de-Rabbi Eliezer* 10). "Yonah said: I will go outside of the Land of Israel, where the Divine Presence does not reveal itself" (*Mechilta,* beginning of Bo).

In order to understand this, we must invoke a classic Jewish teaching. Although God created the entire world in all its vastness and grandeur, He did so for a purpose. The fulfillment of this purpose depends on humankind uniting heaven and earth though divine service. In turn, God reaches out to human beings with His presence so that they may sense Him and be inspired in their task. Consequently, God makes Himself accessible, especially where human beings dwell and serve Him.

Yonah thought that unpopulated places such as the sea, where God's name is not known, do not contain the Divine Presence. Perhaps there he would be able to still the storm raging within his mind and soul; perhaps there he could find respite from the overwhelming Presence. Yet Yonah was mistaken, for, as it is written, "Where shall I depart from Your Spirit? Where shall I flee from your presence? If I ascend to heaven, there You are; if I lie down in Sheol, there You are. If I take the wings of morning and dwell in the farthest sea, even there shall your hand lead me and your right hand grasp me" (Psalms 139, 7–10).

It is related that at first, Rabbi Moshe Teitelbaum opposed the teachings of the nascent Chassidic movement. When someone brought him a new book published by one of the Chassidic masters, R. Moshe became so angry that he threw it to the floor. This was a shocking response, since Jews usually honor their books even when they disagree with them. When R. Chaim of Sanz was told of the incident, he said: "From his action I can tell that he will still join us and even become one of the great. Had he tepidly repudiated that work and commanded for it to be respectfully put away, there would have been no hope. There is no hope for the one who does not care but all the hope in the world for him who remains connected, albeit in denial and rebellion."

> It is not deliberate desecration but only indifference that the Sanctuary of Judaism need fear from its children. This seems to be the thought expressed by the dictum (regarding consecrated objects): "If the misuse (of a consecrated object or a sacrifice) was unintentional, the object is profaned, whereas if the misuse was intentional, the object does not become profane." When the act of desecration was deliberate, the sacred object retains its inviolate sanctity, for the very fact that it was singled out for deliberate violation only proves that it was indeed holy. On the other hand, indifference, a thoughtless act of desecration committed because one has forgotten the sacred character of the object and what our conduct toward it should be – this would dig the grave for the holiness of the Sanctuary, because its throne, from which it is meant to direct and penetrate our lives, is founded solely upon the awareness of those who profess allegiance to it." (Samson Raphael Hirsch, *Commentary,* Leviticus 5)

Yonah did not go astray. He merely lost his way for a time. Even in rebellion he remained engaged, and in this lay his salvation.

The Descent

> But Yonah rose up to flee to Tarshish from God's Presence, and he went down to Jaffa…. (Chapter 1:2–3)

How curious that Yonah chose Jaffa. Since Jaffa is at sea level, it is at a lower altitude than others parts of the Land of Israel. This fact should hardly need to be mentioned. Yet this descent is significant because it is not Yonah's last descent.

> … he went down to Jaffa and found a ship going to Tarshish; so he paid his passage and went down into it (1:3)
>
> … lay down and was fast asleep (*yiradam* – a word that sounds like the Hebrew word *yered* [descend]) (1:5)
>
> … You cast me into the depths… (2:4) I went down to the bottom. (2:7)

When Yonah fled from God, he began his descent. Step by step, he went lower and lower. The momentum of this downward movement reminds us that disobedience is not a one-time event but rather the start of a process. Every choice to sin begins a process of descent whose end we cannot know.

Though we may prefer not to remember it, our actions carry consequences that last long after the acts have been completed and perhaps even forgotten. At the same time, when we choose to return to doing good, we immediately begin a process of ascent, since God aids the path to repentance. "He who comes to sin is allowed; he who comes to be cleansed is assisted" (*Yoma* 39).

As soon as Yonah returned to God, God lifted him up.

> I went down to the bottom of the mountains. The earth with its bars closed upon me forever, yet You brought up my life from the pit, O Lord my God. (2:7)

So it states in *Pirke Avot* (chapter 4):

> Ben Azzai says: "One should run to do [even] a light mitzvah and flee from sin. Performing a mitzvah leads to performing another mitzvah, while committing a sin leads to committing another sin. The reward for a mitzvah is [another] mitzvah, while the wage for the sin is [another] sin."

The moment of decision is the key to decision. Often it seems that there can be no free choice, that the odds are stacked against us. How, many people ask with anguish, can we be expected to choose what is good, pure and beautiful when we have been imprisoned in the depths for so many years? For example, can a child who has been brought up among the dregs of society, abused and mistreated day after day, be expected to treat others with kindness and justice? Is free choice nothing but a fiction, a utopian but impractical ideal?

The Torah teaches us that no matter where we stand, there is always a moment of decision.[1] It exists at the instant of wavering before our conscious awareness floods our mind with doubts. In that split second, everything is possible. Before the mind overpowers the soul, the choices are perfectly balanced. In Biblical Hebrew this moment is termed "arise," "awaken" or "Go."

> God's word came to Yonah the son of Amittai, saying: "Arise, travel to Nineveh, that great city, and proclaim against it; for their wickedness is come up before Me."

The moment when the choices are exactly balanced is symbolized by the two goats offered as sacrifices on the Day of Atonement. As described in Leviticus 16:10, the two goats are identical. Either one can be elected to ascend "to the Lord" or to descend to Azazel in the desert.

R. Samson Raphael Hirsch writes in his commentary to Leviticus:

> ... clearly we have here the representation of two creatures, originally completely identical, who, at the threshold of the Sanctuary, part and proceed on two entirely contrasting paths.... Each of us has the power to resist, to be obstinate, the ability to oppose with firmness the demand made on our willpower. It is on the way we use this power that the worthiness or worthlessness of our moral existence depends.

---

[1] The claim that every person can utterly and completely change in one moment no matter what their situation and station in life may be follows Novardoker teaching. See M. Levin, *Novarodok: A Movement That Lived In Struggle and Its Unique Approach to the Question of Man.* Northvale, London: 1996, 81. This proposition is not universally shared. A better known view is that of *Michtav me-Eliyahu*, who proposed the concept of the "point of choice": that in fact each person has only a narrow plane in which he or she can make truly free decisions. Everything below this point is not a challenge, while everything above it is unattainable with the individual's current resources. The goal of servants of God is constantly to advance this point toward more elevated planes of choice thorough their decisions for good (*Michtav me-Eliyahu,* vol. 1, *Kuntres ha-bechira*).

Jaffa

When Yonah descended to Jaffa to find a ship to Tarshish, he provided a great deal of material for later commentators. This is because Jaffa was a secondary port that was much farther from where Yonah lived (and presumably received his prophecy) than other ports. The Jerusalem Talmud in *Sukkah* 5:1 reports that Yonah was the son of the woman from Tzarfat who had sheltered Eliyahu during the famine in Ahab's reign. If so, he stemmed from the tribe of Asher or, according to another opinion, his father was from Zebulun while his mother came from a town near Sidon – still from the territory of Asher. The natural port for that area would be Acre or perhaps Tyre. The choice of Jaffa is especially surprising in light of the close associations of seafaring with Tarshish and the port of Tyre.

> The burden of Tyre: Howl, ships of Tarshish, for it is laid waste! (Isaiah 23:1; see also 10 and 14)

> The king had at sea a navy of Tarshish with the navy of Hiram [king of Tyre]. (I Kings 22)

> Take up lamentation for Tyre…. Tarshish was… (Ezekiel 27)

The Talmud offers the following solution: "Rabbi Yonah said: Yonah son of Amitai was on pilgrimage in Jerusalem. He participated in the rejoicing of the water-drawing (*simchat bet ha-shoeva*) and the Holy Spirit rested upon him." According to this, Yonah went to Jaffa because it is the closest port to Jerusalem, where he was when God called him. This explanation sheds light on Yonah's repeated reference to "Your holy Temple" in his prayer from the belly of the fish.

> I said: I have been driven from Your sight. Nevertheless I shall gaze again upon Your Holy Temple… and my prayer came before You, into Your holy dwelling….

However, even if Yonah had come from the north, the choice of Jaffa as his port of departure is significant, since it shows the desperation and finality of his flight. This is because traveling to Tyre would take him northwest and, in some measure, toward Nineveh, which lies to the northeast. Yonah fled in the opposite direction, to the southwest, the most opposite direction possible. One who runs away from God does not merely step aside. Part of the psychology of escape is to go all the way, as far and in as opposite a direction as possible. True rebels do not stop at discarding several observances or moving to another, perhaps less observant subgroup. They throw away everything and often, like Yonah, must "hit bottom" (2:7) before coming back again.

Finally, it is significant that the three cities – Jaffa, Nineveh and Tarshish – define the dramatic space in which the story of Yonah unfolds. It is not for nothing that the acrostic of the first letters of their names spells "Yonah" – Y for Jaffa (Yaffo in Hebrew), N for Nineveh, and H for Tarshish (allowing for H to T interchange as per Ibn Ezra on Exodus 1:16). It is only one of many allusions in this profound book. Similarly, Yonah's name, which means "dove," alludes to Noah's dove, which was sent out "upon the surface of the waters." Like the dove, Yonah goes out twice and only succeeds on the second try.

Tarshish (Chapter 1:3)

The identity of Yonah's destination is relevant to the significance of his flight. Unfortunately, it has remained a subject of intense speculation even though there is a great deal of evidence in the Tanach and in contemporaneous sources that ought to throw light upon this question – only it does not, at least not conclusively. Let us consider some traditional identifications of Tarshish and thus seek to approach the real interest of our inquiry – why Yonah chose to flee there. Here are the leading contenders:

1. Josephus (*Antiquities* 1:6, §1), apparently reading "Tarshush," identifies it with Tarsus in Cilicia, Asia Minor.
2. Others argue for the region and city of Tartessus, a Phoenician settlement in Southern Spain.
3. In the genealogical table of the Noachides, Tarshish is given as the second son of Javan and is followed by Kittim and Dodanim (Genesis 10:4). Accordingly, Tarshish may refer to a settlement or colony of these Javanite tribes.
4. With Pul, Tubal, and Javan, it is mentioned as one of the remote places that have not heard of God (Isaiah 66:19; compare 40:9; Psalms 42:10; Ezekiel 38).
5. Tarshish appears to have had a considerable trade in silver, iron, tin, and lead (Ezekiel 27:12). It also gave its name to a precious stone that has been variously identified. It would then be located in a mining area remote from the Land of Israel.

The Targum of Jonathan often renders the word Tarshish in the prophetical books as "sea," which rendering is followed by Saadia. Moreover, the term "ships of Tarshish" is rendered as "sea-ships" (Isaiah 2:16). Jerome, too, renders Tarshish as "sea" in many instances; and in his commentary on Isaiah he declares that he had been told by his Jewish teachers that *tarshish* was the Hebrew word for "sea." Isaiah 23:1 in the Septuagint and Ezekiel 27:12 in both the Septuagint and the Vulgate render Tarshish as Carthage, apparently suggested by Jewish tradition. Indeed, the Targum of Jonathan renders Tarshish in I Kings 22:48 and Jeremiah 10:9 as "Afriki," meaning Carthage.

To my mind the deciding clue can be found in I Kings 10:22 and II Chronicles 9:21: "The king had at sea a navy of Tarshish with the navy of Hiram; once every three years came the navy of Tarshish, bringing gold, and silver, ivory, and apes, and peacocks." This verse suggests that Tarshish was located somewhere off the coast of Africa, where ivory, peacocks and apes could be procured. That this city was so distant should not be surprising, since Herodotus reported that the Phoenicians had circumnavigated the African continent in three years.

The location in Africa is consistent with the three years that the trip to Tarshish is said to take, for "once every three years came the ships of Tarshish, bringing gold, and silver, ivory, and apes, and peacocks."

Modern scholars, basing themselves on the fact that shipwrecks have been found almost exclusively in shallow waters, tended to doubt the ancients' ability to sail upon the open sea. The mariners of old were believed to have stayed close to the coast, keeping in sight of land, and their tales of heroic exploits in the midst of oceans were thought to be idle boasts. However, recent evidence is disproving these claims and supporting the supposition that the ancients made long voyages over the open sea without the benefit of astronomical tables or compasses (see http://www.archaeology.org/0103/etc/wreck.html).

That Tarshish was at the end of the known world would not be lost on the contemporary readers of Yonah, nor would they be likely to overlook the length of this trip and the low likelihood of catching the direct ship to Tarshish in the secondary port of Jaffa. As we have seen in the previous lesson, Tarshish vessels generally set sail from Tyre rather than from Jaffa. Thus, attempting to go to Tarshish would be seen as fortuitous – getting away as far as possible, to the very edge of the inhabited world.

The Rabbis commented on the implausibility of Yonah's success and the miracle therein as follows: "The ship in which Yonah went out to sea was two days' travel away from Jaffa, in order to test Yonah. What did the Holy One, blessed be He, do? He sent a storm and returned it to Jaffa. Yonah saw this and he was filled with joy. He said: I see that my way is proper before Him. Yet he did not know that God brought it about to make known that His Glory is [also] found at sea" (*Pirke de-Rabbi Eliezer* 10). While these comments may appear gratuitous at first glance, consideration of the ancient realia – that is, the actual circumstances of daily life – demonstrates how deeply they are rooted in the text. They also contain a subtle irony in that Yonah was running, but not away – rather, he was running into God's very hand. Not only that – in some deep part of his soul, he also knew it.

In addition to explaining difficult passages, this rabbinic saying contains important lessons. First, it points out to us that God is always in charge and that He uses human beings' best intentions and plans for His own purposes. "He turns wise men backwards and makes their plans foolish" (Isaiah 44:25). In addition, it illustrates an important psychological detail.

What the Sages tell us here is that a truly religious man remains inextricably connected to God, pining for and relying on Him even as he rebels against Him. So also Yonah, as he was running away from God, could not free himself from dependence on Him. He was filled with joy when he felt God's hand in the ship's miraculous return to Jaffa. He did not really want to leave his Master, only he did not admit to it. "A thief, in the midst of breaking in, calls upon God" (Ein Yaakov on *Berachot* 63a). This is true metaphysically (see Tanya I:14) as well as psychologically.

It is foolish for us to think that we can flee from God, for even in the very depths of denial, we remain connected to and dependent upon Him. Even as Yonah fled from God, he kept glancing backwards. This shows us that when we distance ourselves from the spiritual, we are only deceiving ourselves, since in reality we can never escape. At any moment, we are free to cast off the bonds of self-delusion and discover our Creator, who has been patiently waiting for us – "today, if you hearken to his voice" (Psalms 95:7).

Who Becomes a Prophet?

"He found a ship and paid the fare…." (1:3)

As we begin to explore Yonah's flight, we discover that the prophet's interaction with the sailors, the captain and, later on, the people of Nineveh cannot be separated from his personality. Careful reading shows us that those who spoke with him saw a man of great inner nobility and truth, a charismatic leader with impressive strength and resilience. Unless we understand the impression that Yonah made, much of what the book describes will remain difficult to fathom.

However, first let us reflect briefly about prophecy in general.

How does one become a prophet? How are Divine messengers chosen? A cursory examination of Tanach reveals no clear pattern. On the one hand, some of the greatest of prophets suffered from physical deficiencies or came from modest means and circumstances. Moshe, the greatest of the prophets, had a speech impediment, while Amos says of himself: "I am neither a prophet nor the son of a prophet. I am a herdsman and an inspector of wood" (Amos 7:14). Fairly often in Tanach we get the impression that God plucks people out of obscurity and endows them with supernatural gifts to use on His mission.

On the other hand, some prophets, such as Eliyahu and Isaiah, appear before us fully formed, almost as though they were angels rather than human beings.

R. Saadia Gaon (*Book of Beliefs and Opinions,* III:4) maintained that as a rule God did not select outstanding individuals for prophecy, for had He done so, the message could be ascribed to the messenger's genius or extraordinary gifts. One might confuse the messenger with the message. The genius of the prophet could obscure the genuineness of the prophecy.

On the other hand, Maimonides (*Guide* II:32) adopts the view that prophecy is a natural attainment of a pure human being who has reached the pinnacle of moral, spiritual and intellectual perfection. Any person who is sufficiently accomplished in these spheres will receive prophecy unless God denies it for some reason of His own. This is certainly a more philosophically satisfying formulation that also appeals to a certain contemporary sense of egalitarianism. Nevertheless, we should realize that it detracts in some measure from Divine omnipotence, for according to this view, God cannot grant prophecy to someone who is unworthy.

However, there is also a middle way. As the Malbim points out in the beginning of the Book of Amos, both explanations can be reconciled. Prophecy can be personal – restricted to an individual prophet or a close circle of prophets – or it can be communal, intended for the nation as a whole or perhaps even for all humanity. The former kind of prophecy would only come to a recipient worthy of it, while the latter kind may even be sent to an average person. The very fact that the individual is average and not expected to perform miracles validates the prophecy's Divine origin.

The Sages clearly saw Yonah as a remarkable individual. They comment: "The Holy One, blessed be He, does not rest His presence except on one who is strong, wealthy and wise…. How do you know that all prophets were wealthy? From… Yonah, for it says: "he paid the fare…." R. Yochanan said, "The value of the entire ship. R. Romanos says: The value of the ship was four thousand gold coins" (*Nedarim* 38a).

Imagine for a moment that you are a New York City taxi driver. As you drive your cab, looking your next fare, a well-dressed, sophisticated and influential-looking man flags you down, gets in, pushes four thousand dollars into your hand and breathlessly asks you to drive him to Mexico immediately. What would you do?

False Refuge

> He paid its value and went down into it to come *with them* to Tarshish from before the Lord. (1:3)

"Since it is self-evident that Jonah is traveling with the ship's crew, the superfluous 'with them' must be meant to express the existential isolation of one who carries the word of the Lord and to indicate that he wished to find acceptance as just one more member of society." (JPS Bible Commentary, Jonah)

By repeating that Yonah was running away with "them," the verse shows us that the sailors on the way to Tarshish are an important backdrop that illuminates the meaning of his escape. The dynamics of the situation must have been complex. While Yonah found his escape from God among the sailors, it also appears that they aided him willingly, if not in full awareness. He came to them with an open heart and they reciprocated.

Yonah entered the ship with a positive attitude toward his new society, among whom he would be spending the next several years of his life. His determination to become one of them, the love and affection with which he approached them, explain the extraordinary loyalty that they showed him even when their own lives were in danger. "As the reflection of face to face in water, so is the heart of one human being to another" (Proverbs 27:19).

The commitment of a man of Yonah's sincerity and stature must have been not only readily apparent but powerfully affective. As we will see, it started the sailors on a process of inner growth that is perceptible as the story unfolds. To gain a sense of what being "with them" means, let us consider a well-known rabbinic comment on the same expression in the story of Joseph and the wife of Potiphar.

"It happened that as she spoke to him day after day, he would not listen to her, to lie next to her or to be with her" (Genesis 39:10). "'To be with her' – in the World to Come" (*Sotah* 3a). "To be with her" means to share her fate for eternity. To be with a woman means to "cling to her" (Genesis 3:24) to the exclusion of anyone else. It signifies an eternal covenant and commitment. In his heart, Yonah made this kind of commitment to his shipmates, and when the ship was in danger, the sailors reciprocated.

In a wider sense, this illustrates that no one escapes God into nothingness. Wherever we may run, our first stop on the escape route is almost always a relationship of one kind or another. In our own society, romantic love has almost totally replaced the quest for God. So much effort and energy are expended in this often fruitless search – all to relieve the aching in our hearts for the one true Object of our love, whom we have ignored. If we do not seek the love of a romantic partner, then we seek a political affiliation, a professional society, or perhaps even a charitable association. We dedicate ourselves to causes in which we do not fully believe and profess loyalties that we do not fully share in order to be with other human beings who suffer as we do. Loneliness demands a cure, and fellow sufferers are a ready substitute. The prophets Isaiah and Jeremiah refer to this exchange of the eternal and all-powerful for short-lived alliances built on the shifting sands of mutual need in the following verses: "Cease ye from man whose breath is in his nostrils for in what way is he of value?" (Isaiah 2:22). "Be astonished, O heavens, at this, and be horribly afraid, be very desolate, says the Lord. For two evils has my people committed: they have forsaken Me, the fountain of living water to hew for themselves cisterns, broken cisterns, that will not hold water" (Jeremiah 2:12–13).

God did not permit Yonah to find refuge among other human beings. He sent a storm that tore him from that false refuge to face that existential loneliness on his own. The sailors, having been exposed to a spiritual reality they never imagined existed, will continue, on their way, profoundly changed, while Yonah will undergo rebirth in the belly of the fish and emerge, having connected once more with his Maker in the heart of the sea.

The Impact of Greatness (Yonah 1:4)

Before we begin this lesson, I wish to offer a clarification of the lesson above. My intent was not, God forbid, to render meaningless all relationships with other people or to imply that they are extraneous or harmful to proper worship. On the contrary, Judaism demands that we express our spirituality in everyday activities in community. We saw this when we read Ruth together. Rather, we are cautioned against using other people as a refuge in order to escape the demands of engagement with God. We must not flee from God to relationships; instead, we must undertake a sincere and abiding pursuit of God and His teachings and establish our families and society on a proper religious foundation. This is what Ruth did, and the manner in which she did so is the subject of the essays on Ruth in this volume.

To return to our subject: what would it be like for an average person to meet a prophet? Would the prophet's elevated spiritual stature be immediately recognizable? Would we see the Divine Presence that rests upon him or her? How would we respond to the sanctity that characterizes a person of God?

I think that the answer to this question can only be offered by those who have met spiritually advanced people, an experience no longer common in our day. The charisma, purity and transcendence that emanate from a sincere servant of God can only be communicated through experience. It is something that is sensed rather than told.

The Tanach describes many meetings between prophets and other individuals that support this fact. The story in II Kings 9 depicts the effect that an anonymous prophet had upon a group of military leaders and generals, leading to the coronation of Yehu. The Sages in *Sifri Zuta* 14:34, quoted by Rashi, tell us that this prophet was none other than Yonah.

The passage follows.

> Elisha the prophet called one of the sons of the prophets and said to him: "Gird up your loins and take this vial of oil in your hand, and go to Ramoth-gilead. When you get there, look for Jehu son of Jehoshaphat son of Nimshi. Go in, have him stand up from among his comrades, and take him to an inner chamber...."
>
> So the young man – the young prophet – went to Ramoth-gilead. When he arrived, he saw the captains of the host sitting, and he said: "I have an errand to you, Captain." Jehu said: "To which of us all?" He said: "To you, Captain."
>
> He arose and went into the house. He poured the oil on his head and told him: "Thus says the Lord, the God of Israel: I have anointed you king over the people of God, over Israel. Strike the house of Ahab your master that I may avenge the blood of My servants the prophets, and the blood of all the servants of God, at the hand of Jezebel...." He opened the door and fled. Then Jehu came forth to the servants of his lord, and one said to him: "Is all well? Why did that madman come to you?" He said to them: "You know the man and what his talk was." And they said: "It is false. Tell us now." He said: "He said thus and thus to me, saying: So says God: I have anointed you king over Israel." Then they hastened, and every man took his garment and put it under him on the top of the stairs, and blew the horn, saying: "Jehu is king."

Yehu was sitting in a company of his equals, all accomplished military leaders, all captains of large companies, men who had seen their share of heroism, treachery, suffering and defeat and were not easily impressed. Yet as soon as they saw Yonah they felt a premonition, for they saw that he was not a common person. Since they could recognize greatness, they knew that he had not come to them for trivial reasons.

Note how they attempt to drown this realization in mockery and scorn by calling the messenger a madman and denying the importance of his message. Yet as soon as Yehu shares it with them, they know that he was a prophet of God. Immediately and unanimously they embark on a dangerous and uncertain rebellion, abandoning their allegiance to the king in order to crown one who was previously their equal. Such was the impression that the "madman" made upon this group.

Now, imagine the effect that Yonah must have had upon the captain and sailors of that ship. What a scene must it have been! A sudden storm blows them off course to a small provincial port where a man awaits them. He is a man of wealth and privilege whose face glows with spiritual splendor. He hires the entire boat and they set sail immediately.

The sailors must wonder: why is this obviously prominent man in such a hurry, and from whom is he trying to flee? Could he be the king of Israel or perhaps the king of Assyria or, perhaps, someone greater than a mere mortal? As they set sail, they sense that they are no longer a part of ordinary reality but of an important drama. Moreover, under their unknown passenger's influence they find themselves experiencing longings that they had never known before. As time goes by, they become more elevated in spirit. It is no wonder that they single their unknown passenger out from all the others when the storm breaks, threatening their vessel.

Yonah's effect upon the sailors explains their behavior toward him. We will look at this more closely in the next chapter.

Dashed Expectations (Yonah 1:5)

> But God placed a great wind into the sea, and there was a mighty tempest in the sea, so that the ship was like to be broken. (1:4)

The beginning of our verse tells of a calm and stable situation. Yonah's flight apparently successful, his ship on the high seas, his new community accepting and responsive, Yonah finally finds the peace that he had craved. Yet, as so often in life, God intervenes, denying the prophet the respite that he had sought. He strikes at the very pillars that support Yonah's escape, removing precisely that upon which he had relied.

Yonah set up for himself a cozy little refuge:
1. "[Yonah said:] I escape to the sea, place where His Glory is not found" (*Pirke de-Rabbi Eliezer*)." Yonah thought that he would be

safe at sea, correspondingly, "God placed a great wind unto the sea…." The Sages tell us (see Radak) that this storm surrounded the ship from all sides even as other ships passed unmolested all around it. The miraculous nature of this storm is supported by the unusual phrasing ("placed" rather than "sent"), and the sailors' casting of lots – not the usual way of dealing with a storm. Clearly, these experienced sailors, veterans of many a sea trouble, saw something different about this one.

2. "… There was a mighty tempest." In the past, we discussed the fact that unexpressed prophecy burns like fire within prophets, giving them no rest, overwhelming their senses, their sense of propriety and, at times, even their compliance with conventional habits and customs (see Yirmiah 20:9). This feature of prophecy probably accounts for the frequent perception by the uninitiated of prophets as "madmen." Once the vision passes, consciousness returns to normal, at least for those who have unburdened themselves of their prophecies. We do not know whether the agitation ever subsides in someone who consciously refuses to accept the prophetic call. Tanach provides no examples of this.

   What is clear is that the storm outside mirrored and reinforced the storm within Yonah himself. Its behavior represents the inner psychological state of the prophet, who was caught once more in God's grasp.

3. The solace and succor that Yonah had found among the seafarers was now in danger as "… the boat thought itself at the point of breaking." As Radak and Ibn Ezra point out, the device of using inanimate objects here (the boat) to refer to sentient beings is fairly common in Tanach. In our case it means that all the people in the boat knew that it was about to be destroyed. The description of sailors as "the boat" also shows the high level of unity that they achieved under Yonah's influence. No longer a ragged band of mariners from all over the world, the men were now the ship and the ship became the men. What do we expect Yonah to do now? Will he cry out to God in prayer? Will he admit that he was wrong? Will he promise to obey from now on? Yonah did none of these.

The psychologists teach us that denial is one of the most powerful qualities of the mind. Those in the helping professions recall surprising experiences with the power and range of denial in the face of incontrovertible evidence. The human mind's ability to ignore never ceases to amaze and perplex. Neither the greatest storm nor the most pressing and obvious danger can make some individuals change their minds. Yonah's plan is now completely in ruin. His refuge is about to be destroyed. How does he respond?

> "… Yonah descended to the depths of the vessel and went to sleep" (1:5).

This enigmatic passage has occasioned much surprise and many explanations over the ages. Imagine – a rocking, pitching ship, chains clanging and men shouting, the waves roaring and wood cracking – and Yonah lies down to sleep? How is this possible?

In this situation, sleep represents withdrawal. This prophet who did not argue with God, who ran away rather than dispute His order, retreated. Where there is no physical escape, there is always an option to escape into dreams. When reality cannot be denied, fantasy can take its place. It is for nothing that the boat is now called *sefinah,* the only occurrence of this word in the Tanach. This word is related to the Hebrew root *s-f-n* – hidden, covered, obscured. It is the most appropriate word to use for one who descends into the *sefina* to escape.

We have barely begun to explore the meaning of Yonah's sleep. Much more will be said about it in the following chapters. For now, we should note the relationship between denial and repentance. As Yonah's story unfolds, we see the intertwining of withdrawal and engagement, the denial of fault and admission of sin, sleep/death and rebirth/redemption. Over the tapestry of the raging ocean we begin to perceive the awesome presence of the prophet Eliyahu. The Sages say that Yonah was the son of the Zarephite woman, born through Eliyahu's blessing and revived from the dead by his breath (see the discussion in Abarbanel on 3:4 and I Kings 17). In a certain sense, Eliyahu was Yonah's predecessor and teacher. We will see and analyze how Eliyahu responded to a similar situation, the apparent defeat of his mission, when everything he had worked for seemed to be lost and we will understand Yonah. (Those who cannot wait may glance at I Kings 18:4–5).

Although the prophets were greater than we, they struggled with the same challenges that we have. Therefore, their lives can still teach us lessons for today.

From Sailors to Men (Yonah 1:5–26)

> The sailors were afraid, and each one called upon his god. They threw the vessels that were in the ship into the sea, to lighten it for

them. But Jonah went down into the innermost parts of the ship and lay there, fast asleep.

The shipmaster came to him and said: "Why do you sleep? Get up! Call upon your God! Perhaps God will take thought for us and we will not die."

They said to each other: "Let us cast lots that we may know who has brought this evil is upon us." So they cast lots, and the lot fell upon Jonah.

Then said they to him: "Tell us, we pray you, the reason this evil is upon us. What is your occupation? Where did you come from? What is your country? Which is your nation?" He said to them: "I am a Hebrew and I fear the Lord, the God of heaven, who made the sea and the dry land." Then the men grew terrified and said to him: "What have you done?" The men knew that he fled from the presence of God, because he had told them. Then said they to him: "What shall we do to you, that the sea may be calm for us?" for the sea grew more and more tempestuous. He said to them: "Pick me up and throw me into the sea. Then the sea will be calm for you, for I know that this great tempest has come upon you because of me."

Nevertheless, the men rowed hard for land, but they could not reach it, for the sea grew more and more tempestuous against them. So they cried unto God and said: "Please, O Lord, we beseech You, let us not perish for this man's life, and do not hold us guilty of shedding innocent blood; for You, O Lord, have done as it pleased You." So they picked Jonah up and cast him into the sea, and the sea ceased its raging. Then the men feared God exceedingly; and they offered a sacrifice to God and made vows (1:5–16).

Many years ago I learned how to read Biblical texts from Nehama Leibowitz of blessed memory, one of the most influential Jewish exponents of Tanach in our generation. Among the many important things she taught me was always to be aware of titles and descriptions, and how the latter change and evolve as the narrative progresses. Nehama emphasized that close attention to this particular feature of Biblical storytelling always produces great benefits in understanding the intended message.[2] Let us employ her method as we study the following passages.

---

[2] Nehama Leibowitz described this feature of her method in a small Hebrew-language work, *Lilmod u-lelamed Tanach*. A short summary of her English-language work is entitled *To Teach*

The portrayal of the sailors in verses 5–16 demonstrates their rapid evolution from sailors to spiritual human beings to a united collective of people of stature. Let us see how they are characterized.

5. The sailors were afraid....

7. They said to each other: "Let us cast lots that we may know who is responsible for bringing this evil upon us."

13. Nevertheless the men rowed hard....

16. Then the men feared God exceedingly; and they offered a sacrifice unto God, and made vows.

Sailors are almost universally stereotyped as loutish, coarse and immoral.[3] While this may not be true in every case, it usually happens that when men cut themselves off from their families, communities and countries, their ethics and behavior tend to deteriorate. Thus, at first the text refers to this group of mariners as sailors. As stated above, when Yonah came on board "to journey with them to Tarshish away from God," he eagerly joined this small maritime community which, under his indirect influence, underwent a spiritual revolution. We must keep in mind that at this point no one knew Yonah's identity, country of origin or which god he worshipped. Without becoming aware of their inner change, the sailors rose to a spiritual level so high that the first thing that they did when the tempest struck was not to curse but instead to pray. Only later did they jettison objects overboard in order to lighten the ship.

As the storm worsened, they willingly shared the responsibility of casting lots among themselves and apparently accepted the consequences of this act. Someone was going to be thrown overboard to drown – perhaps one of their friends, perhaps themselves. We should not dismiss the acceptance of the shared purpose that this represents. Although the sailors could not know for certain who was responsible for their predicament, they could guess, and their suspicions fell upon Yonah.

> The shipmaster approached him and said, "Why do you sleep? Get up! Call upon your God! Perhaps God will take thought for us so that we will not perish." They said to each other: "Let us cast lots so that we may know who has brought this evil upon us." They cast lots, and the lot fell upon Yonah.

---

and to Learn: The Methodology of Nehama Leibowitz, by Shmuel Peerless. Urim Publications, Jerusalem 2004.
[3] This may not have been the case in antiquity. "Rabbi Judah says... most sailors are pious" (*Kiddushin* 4:14).

Yet the men loved Yonah because they recognized, even if dimly, how his presence had changed them. They wanted to protect him, and at that point, they feared God more than they feared death. They preferred to risk death themselves rather than throw him overboard.

> He said to them: "Pick me up and throw me into the sea. Then the sea will be calm for you, for I know that this great tempest has come upon you because of me."

> Nevertheless, the men rowed hard to reach the land, but they could not, for the sea grew more and more tempestuous against them. So they cried unto God and said: "Please, O Lord, we beseech You, let us not perish for this man's life, and do not hold us guilty of shedding innocent blood; for You, O Lord, have done as it pleased You."

Although the men knew that Yonah was responsible for their danger, they loved him too much to abandon him willingly. He was their teacher and mentor, the purest person they had ever known, and they did not want to lose him. The sailors could not even bring themselves to save themselves and him by bringing him in chains to Nineveh. They feared that as soon as Yonah was gone, they would revert to an existence that they would now find unbearable: a life without spiritual striving or any link to the God of Israel.

"Nevertheless the men rowed hard for land, but they could not reach it, for the sea grew more and more tempestuous against them." The Sages in *Pirke de-Rabbi Eliezer* 10 explain that when the men lowered Yonah into the sea, it grew calm, but when they pulled him up, it would rage again. They lowered Yonah into the sea three times: first to his knees, then to his chest, and finally to his neck. Finally, left with no choice, they reluctantly released him.

"'Then the men feared God exceedingly. They offered a sacrifice to God and made vows' – The sailors turned their ship around, went to Jerusalem and converted" (Pirke de-Rabbi Eliezer, ibid.).

Here is the paradox of a great man who inspires others even as he falls. The irony is that as Yonah is being cast out, the mariners are coming in. Where a lesser man might have capitulated, Yonah remains stubborn, refusing even to pray. He does not respond to God's call or turn to Him even to save himself. The Hebrew root *k-r-a* (to call), which repeats seven times in this passage, is a key word here.

Yonah felt that he was right to reject God's message (we will shortly discuss why) and was willing to die for his beliefs. Now he is about to descend to the bottom of the sea while his former companions ascend the mountain of the Lord. When the silence of the sea envelops him, he will find his voice. He will emerge shouting from the belly of the fish.

> He said: I called out to God in my affliction and He answered me. Out of the belly of the netherworld I cried out, and You heard my voice (2:2). But I will sacrifice unto You with the voice of thanksgiving. That which I have vowed I will pay. Salvation comes from God. (2:10)

Eliyahu and Yonah (Yonah 1:5)

Before we explore the main topic of this chapter, I would like to share an exchange with a student, who asked: "Why does Yonah tell the men to throw him overboard, in effect turning these good men into murderers? Why does he not leap overboard himself?"

This is an excellent question. Some commentators (see Malbim) say that Yonah went down to the bottom of the ship so that he would be killed first when the water poured in, and then the others would be saved.

I would suggest that the issue goes deeper. We should ask why the sailors were being threatened with death in the first place just because Yonah happened to be on their ship. Surely they had done nothing to deserve that!

I believe that we may find the answer along the lines that we have developed thus far. Once Yonah had joined the group of mariners, becoming its spirit and inspiration, all its members were now responsible for one another. They all were held culpable for Yonah's sins. Therefore, in order to escape certain death in the storm, they had to disengage from Yonah and eject him from their group. Yonah's jumping overboard would not have been enough. The sailors needed to dissociate themselves from him by their actions.

Let us begin the lesson.

> "Yonah descended into the bottom of the ship and went into deep slumber" (1:5).

What is the meaning of Yonah's bizarre response to the events taking place on deck? The storm rages, the ship rocks and groans, the wood splinters and the sails flap and come apart. Below, Yonah lies down to sleep and falls into deep slumber. How could anyone fall asleep under such circumstances? Was this a result of emotional exhaustion or was it the last escape of a man who had nowhere else to run?

Certain commentators (for example, Mahari Kara) suggest that what is described here as sleep is a profound depression, a gloom that settled over Yonah's mind and heart. He had been defeated. All his rationalizations and theories were crushed, all his rebellious romanticism melted away before the might of the storm and Him who sent it. Now all illusions fell away. Yonah was only a human being, helpless before the Creator's grandeur. Death was the only remaining escape, the only resistance left. As the storm howled outside, Yonah found refuge in sleep, death's closest cousin.[4]

Yonah's reaction was not all that unusual. Consider how Eliyahu and Moshe responded in a similar set of circumstances. As we explained above, according to Jewish tradition Yonah was not only a student of Eliyahu but also the child whom the latter revived from death. Eliyahu literally breathed his spirit into the child Yonah (I Kings 19). Is it then surprising that Yonah followed in his master's footsteps?

To my knowledge, the first to draw attention to this similarity was R. David Luria in his commentary on *Pirkei de-Rabbi Eliezer*. In Chapter 10:32, he writes as follows: "In the anguish of his soul he fell asleep, similar to what it says regarding Eliyahu: 'He sought death for his spirit'… and he lay down and fell asleep under a bush."

The motif of death and resurrection as it relates to sin and repentance is important to understanding the message of the entire book, since that is precisely what Yonah is about to undergo – death at sea and rebirth in the belly of the fish (the Sages tell us that the fish was pregnant [see Radak], implying precisely this idea).

Let us recall that Eliyahu fled to the desert from the wicked Queen Jezebel after his great triumph over the priests of Baal. Yet at the peak of his success, he suddenly lost everything. No one protected him. He had to run for his life alone into the desert. All his work was apparently for naught, and all his efforts to bring Israel back to God seemed futile.

> When he saw that, he got up and fled for his life to Beer-sheba, which belongs to Judah, and left his servant there. But he himself went a day's journey into the wilderness and sat down under a broom-tree, and said that he wanted to die. He said: "It is enough. Now, O God, take away my life, for I am no better than my forebears." He lay down and slept under a broom tree. Then an angel touched him and said to him: "Arise and eat."

Sleep as a Metaphor for Death

It is significant that Moshe also asked for death when he experienced what must have seemed like the complete failure of his prophetic mission

---

[4] I am indebted to S. Peters in her work *Learning to Read Midrash* (Jerusalem: Urim Publications, 2004), 66, and Y. Bachrach – see below – for this insight.

(Bamidbar 11:14–17). Though on the surface one might be tempted to understand this merely as a response to extreme stress, underlying it are essential questions about repentance. Although we are used to the idea of repentance as one of the basic concepts of Judaism, it is actually completely illogical and goes against nature and common sense. In the words of *Mesilat Yesharim* (Chapter 4):

> According to the Attribute of Justice, it would be fitting that the sinner be immediately punished and with full measure of wrath… for in truth, how can a man fix that which he has damaged, since the sin has already been committed? Behold, he killed a man, he committed adultery – how can this be repaired? Can that which had been done be made to disappear from reality?

Yet the Torah teaches us that this is exactly so. Without repentance there is only death, but with it, one can choose life. As Rabbi Y. Bachrach points out in his work *Yonah and Eliyahu,*[5] the relationship between Divine Mercy and Justice preoccupied all the prophets "because it is at the pinnacle of how humankind recognizes God [in this world] and they were willing to give their lives for it."

This question is basic to understanding the concept of repentance: indeed, how can one possibly correct that which was already done long ago? There is a great mystery in humanity's ability to repent and rebuild. It is akin to the mysteries of death and rebirth and of Divine Justice and Mercy.

Though he had no hope left, Yonah did not give in because, as we explained previously, he could not make peace with a world that was run only according to the Attribute of Kindness.

> They asked Prophecy: How shall sinners be punished? It replied, "The one who sinned shall die" (Ezekiel 18:4). They asked the Holy One, blessed be He: "How shall sinners be punished?" He answered: "Let them repent and I will accept it, as it is written: 'Good and upright is God; therefore He will teach sinners the way.'" (Yerushalmi *Makkot* 2:6, Geniza version)

As a prophet, Yonah upheld the opinion of prophecy. However, God thought differently, for His thoughts are not our thoughts. The book of Yonah is first and foremost about these central poles of religious life: Justice and Mercy.

---

5 Mercaz Shapiro, sixth edition, 1984, 50.

Biblical Linguistics (Yonah 1:6)

> The captain approached him and said to him, "Why are you sleeping? Get up! Call upon your God! Perhaps He will take thought of us and we will not perish" (1:6).

The verse that we are about to discuss represents an opportunity to answer an important question in how to interpret the book of Yonah. It is a truism that one must be intimately acquainted with the idioms, turns of phrase and expressions of a language in order to understand a text written in that language. Without that background, the reader will miss or misinterpret a great deal.

The book of Yonah contains many unusual words and expressions. Many of them are more typical of later Mishnaic Hebrew rather than pure Biblical Hebrew, while others appear to be imported from Aramaic, the lingua franca of the region. A list of fifteen of these exceptions can be found in the introduction to the Jewish Publication Society's translation of the Book of Yonah, and three of them are found in the verse above.

1. "How can you sleep?" In classical Hebrew this would be phrased as *Mah lecha ki nirdamta?* The form *Ma lecha nirdam* without the preposition and the present participle, which is found only in Ezekiel 18:22, is typical of Mishnaic Hebrew.

2. "Take thought for us" – an Aramaic form of the word as found in the Aramaic portion of Daniel 6:4. It is not the Hebrew form of Psalms 40:18.

3. "Captain" – *rav ha-hovel.* This usage is extremely peculiar. If the chief of rope pullers is intended, as most commentators suggest, the term should be *gedol ha-hovelim.* Rashi in Ezekiel 27:8 suggests that this is the term used for the sailor in charge of the wheel at the stern of the ship. Still, while the word *rav* is widely used in the Mishna to mean "great," it is never used that way in Tanach, where it always means "numerous."[6]

Therefore, we face a two-fold problem as readers. First, we must account for the book's tendency to use unusual words and expressions. Second, we must determine whether to regard these linguistic peculiarities as a general tendency or as specific and intentional clues to the author's intention.

Three approaches to these questions are consistent with Torah and tradition.

---

[6] See the Vilna Gaon's commentary on Proverbs 3:3. The JPS commentary seems to have missed this example of non-standard usage.

1. Although the language of the Bible is remarkably preserved in a range of Biblical compositions spanning almost a thousand years, it is possible that a process of language development was taking place. Ultimately, it evolved into the language that is familiar to us from the Mishna. As a late work from the end of the First Temple period, the Book of Yonah reveals the beginning of this process of change. Other late works, such as Ezekiel, Esther, Ezra/Nehemiah, Daniel and Chronicles, show similar patterns.

   Therefore, we should not ascribe too much significance to deviations from "pure" Biblical patterns. If we do so, we may over-interpret, ending up with meanings that the author never intended.

2. The Book of Yonah is written in what is known as the northern dialect.[7] It has long been proposed, primarily to explain stylistic and linguistic peculiarities of the Song of Devorah, a prophet who was also from the northern region (Judges 5), that the dialect of the northern tribes differed somewhat from that of Judea. The linguistic maps of the ancient Middle East show multiple overlapping language belts stretching from Sumerian in the far northeast to Amharic in Ethiopia. The middle of the map is dominated by Aramaic as it slowly transforms into Hebrew. There are indications in the Tanach itself (see Judges 12:5–6) of the existence of this putative northern dialect. In this view, we also should also not ascribe too much significance to linguistic deviations in the Book of Yonah.

3. As in English, there may have been a distinction between literary and colloquial language, often termed diglossia. It is reasonable to suppose that both coexisted during the Biblical period. Professor Stephen Lieberman suggested that the elite spoke and wrote Biblical language while the common folk spoke a variety of Mishnaic Hebrew.[8] (Response, Jewish Languages, 1978, 21–28). The discovery of the pure Biblical Hebrew inscription in the Siloam aqueduct constructed during the reign of Hezekiah appears to argue against this theory. However, if it is true, the use of colloquial expressions within the literary matrix in Yonah

---

[7] See G.A. Rendsburg, "Morphological Evidence for Regional Dialects in Ancient Hebrew." In *Linguistics and Biblical Hebrew*. Edited by W.R. Bodine, Winona Lake, IN: Eisenbrauns, 1992.

[8] "Response." In *Jewish Languages, Theme and Variations: Proceedings of Regional Conferences of the Association for Jewish Studies*. Edited by Herbert H. Paper. Cambridge, MA: Ktav, 1975.

would be intentional and must be noted and interpreted. We will adopt this approach here.

What could the use of colloquialisms and Aramaic expressions signify in this verse? Of course, it could serve to characterize the Gentile captain as speaking a foreign language (which tells us that even a non-Jew could see that God had sent the storm, while Yonah continued to resist the idea) or to call attention to Yonah's northern origins.

However, the deliberate use of Aramaic expressions may also remind us that Yonah had a choice. He could accept his destiny, change his course for Nineveh and spend the rest of his journey polishing his Aramaic, the language of that city (see Isaiah 36:11–12). There are a number of Biblical passages which suggest that the prophets delivered their message to the non-Jews in Aramaic, for example Yirmiah 10:11. It is because Yonah chose not to do so that we have the rest of the book.

Jews and Gentiles (Yonah 1:6–16)

The book of Yonah is unique for, alone of the Biblical books, it revolves around a Jewish prophet's interactions with the non-Jewish world. What's more, the prophet is obstinate and recalcitrant while the gentiles are uniformly good-hearted and obedient. This salient fact has not passed unnoticed by certain non-Jewish commentators, who, as much as they disliked the Book of Esther, loved the Book of Jonah. Many modern scholars are fond of the idea that along with the Book of Ruth, this book somehow represents a response to the narrow particularistic outlook that must have prevailed among the returning exiles as typified by Ezra's rejection of the Samaritans and his abhorrence of intermarriage. In their view Biblical works represent disparate and sometimes opposing schools of thought and it is up to the reader to adopt or reject them as basis for personal philosophy.

This approach can be traced to the Church Fathers, who detested the Book of Esther for its "Judaizing" tendencies but extolled the Book of Yonah for its supposed criticism of the Jews and praise of Gentiles. Ephrem Syrus (306–373), had this to say about the book of Yonah: "Praise be to God, who mortified the Jews by the means of Gentiles."

Of course, such approaches are unacceptable to believing Jews – and, in truth, to believers of all religions. As Jews we see the Bible as the particular heritage of the House of Israel. While it has much to say to the world, it speaks first and foremost to the Jewish people. It is precisely for this reason that it can afford to be so brutally honest, perhaps exaggeratedly so, about the failings of the Jewish nation, for she is capable of accepting criticism and learning from it.

We must also try to perceive the unifying strands among the many different and disparate works that make up the Bible. As pointed out in the introduction to this series, for reasons of belief and as basic method, we adopt the view that since all Biblical works were divinely inspired, they all speak of the same Truth. The principle of intertextuality requires the assumption that all Biblical writers drew from the same source and were aware of their predecessors' work. This principle is amply supported by linguistic and theological allusions to other books scattered throughout prophetic literature.

When we try to understand the setting of Yonah's story, we notice a striking feature. The Gentile characters are not the main actors but rather the supporting cast. This is evident from their one-dimensional depiction in the narrative. An astute observer realizes that the structure and phrasing of chapter 1 parallel those of chapter 3. In each of them, Yonah receives God's call, is reluctant to discharge his mission and escapes, first to the boat and later into the booth. In both, the Gentiles fear God and repent as soon as His message reaches them, expressing their acceptance in almost identical language. The captain and mariners and the King of Nineveh and his people are two dramatic pillars that support and frame the action that centers on the main character, the prophet Yonah. The focus is on Yonah and his story rather than on the Gentile bystanders.

Why, then, is the book set outside of the Land of Israel and in Gentile surroundings? I asked this question for many years. Although I could not accept facile explanations of modern scholars, I did not how to explain the matter in a way that was both theologically true and exegetically sufficient. Quite by accident I recently came across a midrash that illuminated the entire issue in a new and profound way.

Above, we discussed the significance of the prophet's name Yonah – "dove" in Hebrew – to the deeper meaning of his mission. R. Mordecai Kornfeld in his work *Torah from the Internet*[9] (Ha'azinu), cites the following Midrash from *Song of Songs Rabbah* 1:15:

> The Children of Israel are compared to a dove (*yonah*) in several ways:
>
> 1. Just as a dove's walk is pleasant to behold, so too, Israel's walk is pleasant to behold when they come out for the yearly pilgrimages.

---

[9] Judaica Press, 1998.

2. Just as a dove is modest, so is the Jewish nation.

3. Just as a dove stretches out its neck to be slaughtered, so do the Jews, as it is written: "For You we are slaughtered every day."

4. Just as a dove atones for sin [when it is offered in sacrifice], so do the Jews atone for the nations.

5. Just as you find that a dove will never leave its nest even if you take away its young, so do the Jews continue to search for the Temple Mount even after it had been destroyed.

6. Finally, Rebbi said: "There is one type of dove that, when fed, gives off a scent that attracts other pigeons to its nest. So also, when the Elders of Israel expound on the Torah, they attract many Gentiles who hear them and become proselytes."

Rabbi Kornfeld demonstrates that all of these six points were manifested in the story of Yonah.

Seen in this way, the prophet Yonah's destiny was inherent in his name. We might say it as follows in the idiom of the Midrash:

Just as Yonah brought the message of repentance to the people of Nineveh, so will the Jewish nation soon carry its ideas to the entire Gentile world. While the central drama of religious life is between the reluctant prophet and the One who sent him, the backdrop for it is the world of the Gentile. Western Civilization did not inherit the ideas of morality, compassion for the weak and the state's responsibility to its less fortunate citizens from ancient Greece and Rome. Rather, the Jewish people spread them throughout the world. Morality and science stem from the Jews. The Biblical concept of creation is that the universe is governed by sensible and understandable laws of nature that were given by the one Creator. Both the moral world and the natural law are of God.

The world is not a battleground of diverse and unrelated powers. It proceeds from an ultimate Unity and it can therefore be understood through scientific inquiry. This insight ultimately gave us science and the idea of human progress.

Although the classical world contained a great deal of beauty, it had no conscience. The Jews were the ones who gave it the ideas that make life worth living and impart meaning to an otherwise purposeless and empty existence. Far from being an accident of composition, Yonah's travails in the world of the Gentile are central to its meaning and message.

May we soon merit to see that message carried to its conclusion, as it is written: "Then I will turn a pure language to all the nations, that they may all call upon the Name of God and serve Him as one" (Zephaniah 3:9).

The Education of Yonah (Yonah 1:6–16)

> They said to him, "Tell us the reason that evil has come upon us. What is your occupation? Where have you come from? What is your country? From what nation are you?" He told them, "I am a Hebrew and I revere the Lord God of heaven, who made the sky and the dry land." (1:8–10).

After the sailors ejected Yonah, a "great fish" swallowed him. After three days in the fish's belly, Yonah finally opened his mouth and praised God. That psalm of thanksgiving is one of only three places where we find Yonah saying something of a personal nature. The first is in the verse above and the last occurs when he complains to God at the conclusion of the book.

We might have expected that once he is trapped inside the fish, the reluctant prophet finally realizes where he had gone wrong, acknowledges his sins and repents. Had the book been written by a conventional writer, at this point Yonah would confess and God would save him because of his repentance. But this is not how the Bible works. Life – and Scripture – are more complex than that. To our surprise, Yonah admits nothing and asks for nothing (you may read quickly through Chapter 2 to confirm this fact). He praises God elaborately but does not speak to Him. This "poor fit" between what we would expect to take place here and what actually happens provoked a great deal of critical inquiry in modern times.

To understand the function and nature of this psalm (which we will discuss at greater length later on in this book), let us focus on what Yonah says now and what that teaches us about his current situation. It appears that he learned certain facts from his experience and we find them expressed in his response to the sailors' questions.

In truth, the sailors asked Yonah the kinds of questions that the world asks all of us. The view out there is that people are products of their environment, education and conditioning. When the mariners met Yonah, they saw a kind of man that they had never encountered before. To them, he might as well have come from some unknown race of spiritual giants. Perhaps he was a clergyman of some kind, or had grown up in some far-off land of mysticism and spirituality. Where have you come from? What is your country? From what nation are you?

The fact that even at this time of extreme danger the sailors are more interested in who Yonah is than in how to save their own skins testifies to his strong effect upon them. "Who are you, O man of splendor and mystery, and what are your powers that have changed us so?"

The answer would not obligate them in any way. After all, they did not come from Yonah's country, wherever it was, and did not do his kind of work. He was what he was because of how he had grown up, and they were what they were because of their own antecedents. This is what they expected to hear.

Although Yonah understood all this, he did not answer as they expected. He did not even tell them that he was a Jew, for that would have played right into their assumptions. Instead, he described himself in terms of the general region – a Hebrew – or, as one would say these days, a Middle Easterner. He told them that he became who he was became he worshipped the One Creator of the world. They could also do so and become as great as he. Immediately, "The men became terrified" (v. 10), and later, "the men feared God greatly" (v. 16).

The point of Yonah's answer was not to explain that he was running away from God. He told them that shortly afterwards, "for the men realized that he was fleeing from God, for he told them" (v. 10). That verse demonstrates that his words to the sailors at this juncture were not about "why has this evil come upon us" but an answer to another implied but unstated question. Even as he answered the men's questions, Yonah was still trying to make them better people. At the same time, his answer showed what he himself had recently learned.

What had Yonah learned?

Yonah had thought that he could escape God by traveling by sea, and that he could leave God behind. He now realized that God made both "the sea and the dry land" and he would always revere God, for that is Yonah's very nature. Yonah had thought that he could melt into the international community of sailors. Now he learned, as he himself said, "I am a Hebrew."

Yonah realized that he could neither change his religious nature nor cut himself off from his spiritual roots. After his experience at sea, he gave up the illusion that he could abandon his unique identity. Yet although he now grasped that his life's mission was to serve God, he still did not understand Him or agree with the way He ran the world.

How can one serve a Master with whom he disagrees? Imagine a man who loves a woman who provokes and angers him. He reminds himself of all the sweet times in the past, the love that they once shared and all the good things that his wife still does for him. This is the central metaphor of prophetic literature in books such as those of Hoshea and Yirmiah, where we find God alternating between anger over Israel's wickedness and appreciation of their past faithfulness.

Although Yonah had been reborn in the fish's belly, he still did not understand why. He still felt that he was being forced to do something against his will. By praising God's kindness, he began the process of reconciliation. God responded to Yonah's efforts by commanding the fish to spit him onto the dry land, but he also did not speak to Yonah. He wisely waited for the right moment to speak to His prophet.

At this point, Yonah's education has only begun. It is only at the end of his mission, when he confronts God directly, that he receives an answer. However, Yonah is now preparing himself for that conversation, for he is beginning to learn that for him there is no other way.

Question, Answer, and Review (Conclusion of Chapter 1)

Although we have spent quite some time studying the Book of Yonah, there are still some background questions that we must consider before we continue.

Commentators tell us that Yonah ran away from Israel because he knew that he would not receive prophecy outside of the land of Israel. Nevertheless, he did received i in Nineveh in the third chapter, and other prophets, such as Yirmiyahu and Yechezkel, also received prophecy outside of Israel. How can we explain this apparent discrepancy?

Answer: The book of Yonah is like a labyrinth with many hidden passageways. Commentators must find their way through it to uncover the message within. They cannot succeed in this task without setting down the working assumptions and clarifying the methodology of their commentary. This is why our central question is: What is the main message of the Book of Yonah? Let us address this question and then return to the original query.

Various sages have proposed answers to our question throughout the centuries. An excellent discussion of the advantages and disadvantages of these approaches can be found in a book-length essay by A. Rivlin entitled *Yonah: nevua ve-tochacha*.[10] They are:

1. A document of national repentance.

Many Midrashic passages express the view that the Book of Yonah is a call to repentance. The Sages explain that Yonah ran away in order to spare his people Divine anger. "Yonah said: I know that the nations are quick to

---

[10] Yeshivat Kerem be-Yavne, 1999, 64–85.

repent. Now they will repent and the Holy One, blessed be He, will send his anger forth against Israel.... I shall run away instead" (*Pirke de-Rabbi Eliezer,* Ch. 10). "Yonah said: I will go outside of the Land of Israel to a place where the Divine Presence is not revealed so as not to render Israel guilty" (*Mechilta of R. Ishmael,* Pischa, 1). The commentators, such as Metsudat, understand the above to mean "a place where prophecy does not rest upon the prophets," referring to outside of the Land of Israel, setting the stage for our question.

Nevertheless, we must realize that there is another version of the midrashic phrase "to the sea, a place where the Divine Presence is not found." In this rendering (as explained in chapter 5), Yonah thought that God is present only in places where human beings live so that they may sense his Presence and be drawn toward Him. He thought that at sea he might escape the awareness of God and of the divine call that disturbed him. According to this version, the question does not even arise.

However, Rashi conflates the two versions, suggesting that both are true. If so, it seems that an answer would build on chapter 3, "Running Away." Briefly, we explained there that a prophet cannot hear something that he cannot accept. Therefore, all that Yonah heard was a command to go to Nineveh and prophesy there, but he did not hear the nature of the prophecy he was to give. In actuality, Yonah ran away from himself so that he would not have to acknowledge the command that he already carried within him. This idea is supported by *Yevamot* 78b, which explains that God's second command to Yonah in 3:1 was the same one as in 1:1. If so, the only difference between the two prophetic experiences was that Yonah had matured in the interim and became able to hear the original message. Therefore, it is not that he received prophecy outside the Land of Israel. Rather, it is there that he was first able to understand it.

(In discussions of Ezekiel and other prophets, who prophesied outside of the Land of Israel classical sources bring up both Yonah and Moshe, both of whom began their prophetic careers outside of the Land of Israel. Due to space limitations I will simply cite references for further study: *Moed Katan* 25a; *Moreh Nevuchim* II:36 and *Shemoneh Perakim* 7; Abarbanel, *Introduction to Amos;* Radvaz *Responsa* 2:842 and 6:2206 and *Kuzari* 2:14. Those interested are invited to investigate further.)

2. The Book of Yonah is about universalism versus particularism.

We do not adopt this approach for the reasons explained in chapter 17, Jews and Gentiles.

3. The Book of Yonah teaches about repentance.

While repentance is an important theme of the book (see *Megillah* 31a and *Taanit* 16a), I do not believe that it can account for many details in the first and second chapters, which do not deal directly with that concept. In addition, it would be peculiar for a book about repentance to offer us only examples of the incomplete repentance of the Ninevites (which I will explain in the next chapter). One would expect a treatise on repentance to be more focused and explicit. Instead, we learn about Yonah and the people of Nineveh, neither of whom repented fully, as we will see.

4. The book is about justice versus mercy.

This approach was first offered by R. Yehoshua Ibn Shoeb, a fourteenth-century rabbinic scholar, whose sermons have only recently been published. He writes:

> The prophecy of Yonah came to teach that the Almighty has mercy upon all his creatures, even the nations of the world (who rebel against Him), certainly the people of Israel…. We learn from this work that God is merciful. Even though the nations stole and conducted themselves with great violence, God accepted their repentance. Therefore, that would certainly apply to us, His beloved nation and the sheep of His pasture….[11]

This extraordinary suggestion, which appears to be based on Midrash Yonah, is the approach that we have adopted in this series.

While the classical commentators stress the vital national message, this approach that sees Yonah as struggling with the concept of divine mercy as the foundation of life and faith speaks more directly to modern people. In our day, we often feel alienated from history, community and even ourselves. We must make an effort to connect with the tradition that our ancestors received from infancy. Modern humanity is in flight from itself and its inheritance because they do not perceive the mercy behind the Creation.

Where can we find refuge? Surely in God's Book, which contains messages for our own time. It is miraculous how Scripture has something to say to every type of person in every historical circumstance and situation – undoubtedly the result of the divine inspiration under which it was written.

At the conclusion of Chapter 1, Yonah has learned that he cannot run away from God. As a member of the Jewish nation and a prophet, he cannot escape his destiny (see chapter 18, "The Education of Yonah," and chapter

---

11 Cited in S. Y. Agnon, *The High Holidays; Daat Mikra,* Introduction to Yonah #7; Y. Bachrach, *Yonah ve-Eliyahu,* 75.

10, "False Refuge"). However, he still does not agree that the Attribute of Mercy should run the world. Like many of us, he could not figure out how to translate abstract knowledge into inner change.

However, God, who knows what we need, sent Yonah a refuge and a womb within which to be reborn.

> God sent a great fish to swallow Yonah and Yonah was in the womb of the fish three days and three nights (2:1).

Praise and thanks to God, Who allowed and assisted us to finish our study of the first chapter of the Book of Yonah.

PART II

The Flight (Yonah 2:1)

> God prepared a big fish to swallow Yonah. Yonah was in the belly of the fish for three days and three nights (2:1).

As WE BEGIN chapter 2, we encounter some of the most profound teachings in Yonah. Yet before we do so, we must discuss the fish that swallowed Yonah and whether and how this is possible. As it happens, we cannot study the Book of Yonah without mentioning the fish. Ask most people about the Book of Yonah and it is likely that they will answer, "Oh, Yonah and the whale." How sad that such a minor detail has become the book's best-known feature.

For this reason, the fish merits a mention. Though it is a distraction from the primary goal of revealing the book's message, it remains a stumbling block to serious students, who find themselves unable to advance because of this apparently unbelievable incident. Therefore, it would be a disservice to skip over this topic completely.

Can a human being survive inside a fish for three days? If not, was Yonah's survival a miracle? If so, why does the narrator let it pass without comment?

Several attempts have been made to reconcile Yonah's three-day stay inside the fish with cetacean anatomy and physiology. One plausible explanation invokes the large and flexible pharynx of sperm whales, which have been known to swallow large octopi whole. The stomachs of sperm whales, which are large and filled with air, may also provide enough air to enable a human being to survive for some time.

Others point to the large air sacs of certain species that can accommodate a person in relative comfort. In 1891, a report circulated about a sailor who had swallowed by a sperm whale and cut out alive from its belly by his shipmates the next day. As everyone knows, no story remains unquestioned and no proof survives unopposed. Since the story was subsequently denied in 1905 by the wife of the ship's captain, the truth of that incident will never be known.

Many classical commentators maintain that it was a miracle or a series of miracles (see Ibn Ezra, Radak and Malbim). Others lessen the disruption of natural law by pointing out that this was a special fish, "a great fish" as the verse says, prepared specifically for this purpose at Creation (see *Pirkei de-Rabbi Eliezer,* chapter 10). Alternatively, the miracle may have been a minor one, consisting merely in widening the fish's belly in order to enable it to contain a person comfortably (*Yalkut* 550).

Could Yonah's stay inside the fish have been a prophetic vision that did not occur in the physical world? Although there are isolated references to those who maintained this view, we must reject it on the grounds of the widespread consensus among early and older sources that it was real event. These include Mishna *Taanit* 2:4 ("He who answered Yonah from the belly of the fish, He shall answer us"), the apocryphal books of Tobias (14:4) and Maccabees (6:8), Josephus (*Antiquities* 9:10:2) and many earlier and later commentators.

In his commentary on Yonah 2:11, Joseph Ibn Kaspi cites one such opinion with disapproval, as does Maimonides when he quotes "some of the Andalusians" in the *Guide* (1:42). However, we should remember that this view does not derive from disbelief in the possibility of miracles, as might well be the case in our time, but from an Aristotelian-based insistence that the perfect Creator created perfect rules of nature whose violation He would never allow for the sake of mere convenience. Yes, as philosophy passed from the heart of religion to its periphery, opposition to miracles began to stem from a fair measure of disbelief, but not yet at that time. There is also an attempt by the Ephodi, a rather controversial philosopher and commentator (known as Profiat Duran after his forcible conversion to Christianity, which he ultimately renounced) in his commentary on the *Guide* 3:32 to read this view into Maimonides himself. However, Abarbanel, in his commentary upon the same passage, disproves this conjecture convincingly. (Those who wish to explore this topic more fully may consult the introduction to the JPS edition of the Book of Yonah with the commentary of Uriel Simon; R. Shlomo Aviner, *Perush on Sefer Yonah,* 64; and A. Rivlin, Yonah: *Nevua ve-tochacha,* Yeshiva Kerem b'Yavne: 1999, 43–57.)

The Vilna Gaon and the Zohar read the Book of Yonah as an allegory that describes the soul's descent into the physical world and its sojourn there. However, there is no indication that they disputed the literal sense of the story. Unlike the story of Job, which one Talmudic opinion in *Bava Batra* 15a considers a parable rather than a record of actual events, no such precedent exists for the Book of Yonah. In my opinion, those who propose an allegorical interpretation of Yonah are too close to the line that divides Jewish interpretative tradition from what lies beyond it.

In summary, we will follow the traditional approach, which describes the story of Yonah and the fish as miraculous. Its components may have been prepared during Creation or may have been only a small expansion of natural boundaries, which would explain why the narrative does not emphasize it. The weight of precedent and consensus, together with the testimony of early sources, lead us to reject attempts to read the incident as a prophetic vision. Rather, we should treat it a real event and interpret it accordingly.

With the question of how it could have happened out of the way, we are now ready to learn the real lessons of the fish and Yonah's sojourn inside it.

Rebirth and Repentance (Yonah 2:1–2)

> … Yonah was in the belly of the fish three days and three nights. Yonah prayed to God from the fish's belly (2:1–2).

What did Yonah do in the belly of the fish for three days?

The Midrash explains that at first, Yonah was swallowed by a male fish but he did not pray. God then commanded that fish to spit him into the mouth of another one, a pregnant female full of roe. Now Yonah was cramped in a narrow space, and that induced him to pray for salvation.

"Yonah was in the belly of the fish but did not pray. The Holy One, blessed be He, said: 'I made him a spacious place in the belly of the fish but still he did not pray. I shall prepare for him a pregnant fish carrying three hundred sixty-five thousand fry, so that he will be in distress and pray to me'" (*Midrash Yonah,* 98).[1]

This midrashic interpretation bases itself on the language of the verse. The word for fish in the first verse is *dag,* in the masculine, but changes to *dagah,* the feminine, in the second verse. At the end of the chapter it is *dag* once again. Although the word *dagah* is found in many other places as the name for all fish species (see Ezekiel 47:9), the Sages read the change in gender as a clue to meaning – that there was a male fish first and a female fish afterwards.

We may find the key to what it all means in the words of R. Bachya (on Numbers 11:5), who suggests that the word *dagah* signifies a fish that is dead. He maintains that Yonah was swallowed by a fish that subsequently died. It is of that time that the prophet speaks later on in this chapter when he describes descending to Sheol, the land of the dead, for at that moment he was literally surrounded by death in the form of a dead and rotting fish.

---

[1] Note that 365 is a significant number. "The Holy One, blessed be He, tells the angel appointed over conception: Take this drop in your palm and plant it in the field to become three hundred sixty-five parts" (*Tanchuma Pikudei* 3).

These various comments pick up on the motifs of death, pregnancy and rebirth in the story.

Yonah was in the fish's belly for three days. This number three is significant, since many important events in the Patriarchs' lives occurred on the third day (*Genesis Rabbah* 61:1). God does not allow His saints to remain in dire straits for more than three days (*ibid.* 91:9). The number three is also associated with both conception and rebirth. "He will strengthen us two days, and on the third day he will stand us up and we will live before Him" (Hoshea 6:2). In mystical thought, conception occurs within the first three days, followed by forty days for the formation of a fetus (*Otzrot Chaim,* Shaar Anach). The Torah was given after two periods of preparation: one that lasted for three days and one that lasted for more than forty (*Shabbat* 88a). Similarly, Yonah was in the belly of the fish for three days and in the booth outside Nineveh for forty days.

Not only was the belly of the pregnant fish the place of Yonah's rebirth – so was the sea itself. "As the bath is sometimes open and sometimes closed, so the gates of prayer are sometimes closed and sometimes open. Yet as the sea is always open, so the gates of repentance are always open" (*Lamentations Rabbah* 3:43).

The image of the water of the sea as a place of rebirth is particularly striking. "The Holy One, blessed be He, fashions a baby in the womb of its mother in the midst of waters, and he pronounces: There is no sculptor like our God" (*Tanchuma Tazria* 2).

The midrashic comments point us to the realization that the author of Yonah, writing under Divine inspiration, makes a connection between repentance and rebirth. Yonah was reborn within the belly – or, we might say, within the womb of the great fish, in the life-giving waters of the ocean. During those three days, a seed of repentance was planted within him, ultimately to grow and blossom into full return to God.

This makes an important point: complete repentance is not a one-time event. The Ninevites left their wicked ways, but did not change them permanently. They quickly relapsed, since this kind of repentance is doomed to failure. A seed of true and lasting change must be nurtured and maintained, first for forty days of development, then for nine months of growth, then for a lifetime. The psalm that Yonah sang while in the belly of the fish was only the beginning of his process of return.

Hemmed in on all sides by the fish's three hundred sixty-five thousand offspring, Yonah began to think about God's guiding hand in his own life and burst into song. Although this was not a complete resolution of all the issues that still separated him from God, it was the turning point. Likewise, repentance is not only an act or series of actions but also a process of growth and rebirth. The Jewish calendar institutionalizes its inherent process of growth. During the forty-day period from the first of Elul until Yom Kippur, the traditional period for repentance and self-examination, we prepare for the lessons of the Book of Yonah, which will be read in the synagogue on Yom Kippur.

The Liberation

We left the previous chapter with the image of Yonah confined in the belly of the pregnant fish, enveloped in roe packs, in discomfort and distress but poised for a spiritual leap. Now let us pause for a moment. The picture of a person inside a fish demands elaboration. Instinctively we sense that it contains special power and significance, but we may find them difficult to grasp. What the ancients could perceive immediately is difficult for us because as modern people, we are far removed from our emotive/symbolic heritage and from the world of Biblical imagery and archetype. The image of a man inside a fish does not speak to us. It only bewilders and confuses us. When they arrive at this point in the story, many readers ask: "What is all this about?"

We will attempt to show its significance by invoking a parallel and perhaps more accessible passage, as well as the symbolism and sensibility of the Jewish mystical tradition. I must caution the reader that the point of the ensuing discussion is not the esoteric teachings themselves but their contribution to clarifying the meaning of Yonah's encounter with the fish.

There is another story in the Bible of a man imprisoned inside an animal. In this story, too, he praises God and is then restored to his previous position. The man is Nebuchadnezzar, the king of Babylonia.

> I, Nebuchadnezzar, was at rest in my house, and flourishing in my palace. I saw a dream which made me afraid; and imaginings upon my bed and the visions of my head affrighted me....

> "...it is the decree of the Most High, which is come upon my lord the king, that you shall be driven from human beings, and your dwelling shall be with the beasts of the field, and you shall be made to eat grass as oxen do, and shall be wet with the dew of heaven, and seven times shall pass over you; until thou know that the Most High rules in the kingdom of human beings, and gives it to whomever He wishes." All this came upon the king Nebuchadnezzar. In that same hour, the prediction was fulfilled upon Nebuchadnezzar. He was driven from human beings and ate grass as oxen do. His body was

wet with the dew of heaven until his hair grew out like eagles' feathers and his nails like birds' claws.

At the end of that time, I, Nebuchadnezzar, lifted up my eyes to heaven, and my understanding returned to me, and I blessed the Most High, and I praised and honored Him who lives forever....At the same time my understanding returned unto me; and for the glory of my kingdom, my majesty and my splendor returned to me; and my ministers and my lords sought me; and I was established in my kingdom, and surpassing greatness was added to me. Now I, Nebuchadnezzar, praise and extol and honor the King of heaven; for all His works are truth, and His ways justice; and He can abase those that walk in pride. (Daniel, chapter 4)

The parallels to Yonah and the fish are clear. Both Yonah and Nebuchadnezzar were forced to dwell within an animal and both burst into song from inside it.

Now let us consult the esoteric writings.

The tale of a great soul held captive within an animal body calls to mind the concept of the transmigration of the soul. The teaching that some souls are given an opportunity to return in order to complete their earthly task is not our primary focus now. Some authorities argued that this concept is not a necessary part of Jewish belief, while other equally great ones upheld it. Similarly, some sages accepted that a soul may reside only in a human body, while others believed that certain sins demand purification through sojourns within various animals or even inanimate objects. This is not the place to discuss this concept. Rather, we would like to focus on how well it explains the image of a man within the fish.

The Sefer Haredim[2] says:

The Holy One, blessed be He, wished to demonstrate to humanity the possibility of transmigration into the body of an animal through the greatest of kings, the wicked Nebuchadnezzar. While he was alive, God brought him down from his throne and threw him into a field. He walked on all fours like an animal and appeared like an animal, for he had permitted his tongue to go too far in speaking against the High One. After that, when the appointed period of Divine anger has ended, God brought him back and showed him that He is all-powerful.

---

[2] Quoted in the work *Nishmat Chaim* by R. Menashe ben Israel, 4:13.

The image of Yonah within the fish parallels that of a soul within its host. Once the soul is purified, it is ready to ascend. Once Yonah began to repent, he was ready to engage in prayer.

Fish occupy the highest spiritual place in the animal kingdom. While the kosher slaughter of cattle requires transecting of both the esophagus and windpipe and fowl require at least the windpipe, fish may be eaten without any special method of slaughter. They are completely spared the pain of the slaughterer's knife. For this reason, the souls of the righteous who need to remedy a minor fault are sent into fish rather than into other animals (*Ohr ha-hayyim* on Genesis 1:26; *Maor va-shemesh*, notes to Chullin). This is also the reason why there is a custom to eat fish on Friday nights (see sources in *Zemirot Divrei Yoel*).

The image of Yonah within the belly of the fish, like that of Nevuchadnezzar eating grass in the field and living like a beast, is that of a holy soul imprisoned within the physical realm. Though there may seem to be no escape from the material world, these passages teach us that there is a way out: recognizing the Creator and expressing His praise. This recognition liberates our souls from the pull of the material world, freeing us for our spiritual journey.

> Then Jonah prayed unto the Lord his God from the fish's belly. He said: From my affliction I called out to God and He answered me; out of the belly of the netherworld I cried, and You heard my voice.
>
> You cast me into the depths, into the heart of the seas. The flood was round about me; all Your waves and Your billows passed over me. I said: "I am cast out from before Your eyes"; yet I will look again toward Your holy temple.
>
> The waters compassed me about to my very soul; the deep was round about me; the weeds were wrapped about my head. I went down to the bottoms of the mountains; the earth with her bars closed upon me for ever; yet You have brought up my life from the pit, O Lord my God. When my soul fainted within me, I remembered the Lord. My prayer came before You, into Your holy temple. Those who regard false vanities forsake their own mercy. But I will sacrifice to You with the voice of thanksgiving; I will pay what I have vowed. Salvation is of God. God spoke to the fish, and it vomited Jonah out upon the dry land.

Structure and Meaning

The study of structure in Biblical writings has become increasingly prominent in modern times, together with the shift from a focus on the meaning of Scripture to an emphasis on its language, historical and archeological background and milieu. One might say that the world has gone from trying to understand and apply timeless lessons of the Bible to attempting to particularize and restrict them to a specific bygone time and place in order not to have them trouble humanity. Structural investigation originated with the schools of thought that wished to demonstrate that the Bible is merely a cacophony of conflicting and arguing voices that we can enjoy, discuss and compare at our pleasure, but that do not obligate us to anything.

Nevertheless, the renewed focus on structure has had some beneficial results. We have learned to understand the interplay of form and function and how compositional structure communicates the Author's intent. These methods are now in wide use among all who seriously study God's word.

The second chapter of the Book of Yonah is especially suited to structural investigation, for it is all about contrasts and oppositions. Not all contrast is structural; the language and idiom also go from one extreme to another. The prophet switches between I and Thou, third person and second person, depths and heights, exhilaration and despair. We will delve more into these patterns as we go forward. For now, let us look at the overall structure of Yonah's song.

We will begin with a brief introduction and definition of terms. A chiastic pattern is one in which the beginning mirrors the ending and the middle parts are set in opposition to one another. In order to understand this pattern's role, we must recall that the ancient reader did not necessarily read as we do. Whereas we read for the plot, they read for meaning. Western readers, who are deluged with information and weaned on the classic Western novel, read forward. The ancient reader, on the other hand, read both forward and backward, frequently returning to earlier passages and sentences in order to reread them in the light of the later ones.

For an example of a chiastic structure, look at verse 9 of the Book of Jonah: "Those who care for lying vanities their own mercy forsake." It follows the A-B-B-A pattern. The word "vanities" contrasts with "mercy," while the word "care" plays off "forsake." The overall purpose of a chiastic arrangement is to turn our attention to the middle of the chiasm, where the key to meaning lies. In this case, the contrast between vanity and mercy lies at the center of the verse.

Another pattern present in this chapter is A-B-C-A'-B'. Unlike the A-B-C-B'-A' pattern that draws our attention to the central C segment, the A-B-C-A'-B' pattern is a model for progression and development. We see something from one perspective and then see it again from another. The key to this pattern is repetition of specific key words, which emphasize the relationship between sentences. Let us read the following passage together, carefully noting the repetitions and the parallelisms. I have italicized some of the words in order to make the task easier.

A. You cast me into the *depth, in the heart of the seas, and the flood was round* about me. All Your waves and Your billows passed over me.

B. I said: "I am cast out from before Your eyes"; yet I will look again *toward Your holy temple.*

C. The waters compassed me about, even to my soul; the deep was round about me; the weeds were wrapped about my head.

A'. I went down to the *bottoms of the mountains; the earth with its bars* closed upon me for ever; yet You have brought up my life from the pit, O Lord my God.

B'. When my soul fainted within me, I remembered the Lord. My prayer came before You, *into Your holy temple.*

The chiastic structure pertains to the entire chapter as well. The overall chiastic symmetry of the chapter as a whole is striking, since the first sentence – "Yonah prayed to the Lord his God out of the fish's belly" – corresponds to the last one – "God spoke unto the fish, and it vomited out Jonah upon the dry land." Thus in overall structure the first sentence serves as prologue and the last as an afterword. The second sentence is the introduction: "He said: I called out of my affliction to God and He answered me. From the belly of the netherworld I cried, and You heard my voice." The penultimate sentence is a summary that responds to the second sentence: "Those who regard lying vanities forsake their own mercy. But I will sacrifice to You with the voice of thanksgiving; that which I have vowed I will pay. Salvation is of God." This chiasmic pattern continues throughout the section, drawing us to the middle sentences and showing us that we must seek the chapter's meaning there.

The overall effect is to center our attention on the A-B-C-A'-B' sentences and what they mean. This structural device moves us along a process of development and growth as the A-B transforms into A'-B', apparently similar but actually very different. The next lesson will address how and why this is accomplished.

Foolish Hearts: The First Lesson of Spiritual Life

We considered the structure of the psalm that constitutes the second chapter of the book of Yonah. Let us now review briefly.

The chapter follows a chiastic structure that draws our attention to the center, where its meaning resides. It follows the pattern that we called A-B-C-B'-A', as follows:

Prologue: God prepared a great fish to swallow Yonah. Yonah was in the belly of the fish for three days and three nights.

A. Then Yonah prayed to the Lord his God from the fish's belly. He said: From my affliction I called out to the Lord and He answered me. Out of the belly of the netherworld I cried, and You heard my voice.

B. You cast me into the depth, in the heart of the seas. The flood was round about me; all Your waves and Your billows passed over me. I said: "I am cast out from before Your eyes"; yet I will look again toward Your holy temple.

C. The waters compassed me about, even to the soul; the deep was round about me; the weeds were wrapped about my head.

B'. I went down to the bottoms of the mountains. The earth with its bars closed upon me forever, yet You have raised my life from the pit, O Lord my God. When my soul fainted within me, I remembered the Lord. My prayer came before You, into Your holy temple.

A'. They that regard lying vanities forsake their own mercy. But I will sacrifice to You with the voice of thanksgiving. I will pay my vows. Salvation is of God.

Epilogue: God spoke to the fish, and it vomited out Jonah upon the dry land.

Compare B and B'.

B. For You cast me into the depths, into the heart of the seas, and the flood was round about me; all Your waves and Your billows passed over me. I said: "I am cast out from before Your eyes"; yet I will look again toward Your holy temple.

B'. I went down to the bottoms of the mountains; the earth with its bars closed upon me forever; yet You have raised my life from the pit, O Lord my God. When my soul fainted within me, I remembered the Lord; and my prayer came before You, into Your holy temple.

In the first B sentence, Yonah displays a curious forgetfulness. He seems not to remember that it was not God who cast him into the depths, but rather he himself who had told the sailors to throw him overboard. Instead he blames God, not recalling that he is the one who fled from God.

When Yonah first went down into the sea, he exemplified the all-too-common victim mentality. All of us have met people whose character flaws have caused them immense suffering, yet they direct their anger toward God and human beings rather than taking responsibility. A person who is wrapped in this "victim mentality" is incapable of repentance or change. Their anger, blame, and lack of insight surround and imprison them. When they see God's waves of misfortune blocking them, they say: "It is God's fault. He does not deserve my surrender to His willful injustice and abuse. I will stay where I am, showing Him that I am more faithful and righteous than He. Despite Him, I will look toward his holy Temple."

In the second B' sentence, Yonah has grown. Under threat of death, his emotional barriers have fallen and he is ready to look at his situation objectively. He no longer blames God for his misfortunes; they simply are. On the other hand, his redemption comes from God.

Once we take responsibility for our actions, we can see God as He truly is – our Savior and the giver of life. "I went down to the mountains [which was my own fault]; You have raised my life from the pit, O Lord my God…. Salvation is of God."

A Talmudic passage powerfully expresses this concept.

> R. Yochanan found the child of Resh Lakish who was sitting and repeating: The foolishness of man makes crooked his way, but his heart rages against God (Proverbs 19:3). R. Yochanan sat down and wondered: Is there something that is enunciated in the Writings that is not found in the Pentateuch? The child said to him: What, is it not alluded to? Is it not written in Genesis 42, 28: "… and Joseph's brothers trembled to each other and they said: What is this that God is doing to us?" (BT *Taanit* 9a).

Such is the nature of our self-delusion. We so often blame others for what is our own fault and are angry with the One who can save us.

We cannot grow if we do not realize this characteristic of the human psyche. The second chapter of Yonah teaches us how to overcome barriers to self-knowledge and go forward.

Touch and Go… Back (Conclusion of Chapter 2)

Yonah's prayer is full of contrasts. From the heights to the depths, from despair to exultation and from speaking directly to God to describing Him in the third person, it is a remarkable record of the back and forth of inner change. It is interesting that while most of the psalm is in the second person, we can find sentences that move fluidly from the third person to the second or from the second person to the third. These sentences follow.

> 3. He said: Out of my affliction I called out to God and He answered me. Out of the belly of the netherworld I cried, and You heard my voice.

> 8. When my soul fainted within me, I remembered God, and my prayer came before You, into Your holy temple.

> 10. I will sacrifice to You with the voice of thanksgiving; I will pay my vows. Salvation is of God.

This alternation between the second and third person is not restricted to the second chapter of Yonah. It is a feature of Jewish prayer. Although our blessings usually begin directed to God in the second person – "Blessed are You" – they immediately switch to the third person – "Who brings bread from the earth." The same is true of prayer. Students of Jewish liturgy often find this free interchange of the second and third person as one of the most challenging components of Jewish worship. Can something in this peculiar mode of expression help us to understand Yonah?

One of the earliest thinkers to take up this question was Rabbi Solomon ben Aderet, the Rashba (d. 1310 C.E.). He writes in one of his letters:

> You have learned already that there are two foundations and everything is built on them. The first one is that God's existence is necessary and non-contingent, of which there can be no doubt. The second is that the full truth of His existence cannot be known by anyone other than Himself. Although he may appear as if existing in revealed reality, in truth His essence is hidden and unattainable to anyone. In order to impress upon us these two cornerstones of religion, they [the rabbis] established the text of blessings to express both the revealed and the hidden. We begin with "Blessed are You," like one who is talking to someone else who is right in front of him. We then switch to "Who has sanctified us with His commandments..." – for the essence of his being is hidden and unattainable (Responsa 5:52; see also Ramban on Exodus 16:26).

The Rashba's theme here is pedagogical rather than devotional. It remained for the kabbalistic masters to reveal how this liturgical phenomenon is relevant to individual worship (*Tanya* 1:50; *Tzidkat ha-tzadik*, 4). They drew upon the description of the angels' service in Yehezkel 1:14 and 22, rendering it in terms of touching a profound reality and then immediately withdrawing from it.

14. The Chayot ran and returned as the appearance of a flash of lightning.... 22. Over the heads of the Chayot was the likeness of a firmament, like the color of the terrible ice, stretched forth over their heads above.

Yehezkel describes a certain boundary above which God's Presence may be glimpsed. High angels, called Chayot, are capable of extending their heads above the barrier for a moment in order to glimpse something of this Presence. Awed and overwhelmed by what they see, they immediately withdraw. The entire process is as quick as a flash of lightning.

The use of lightning imagery is significant because it shows us the concept of spiritual insight as a brief but intense illumination that we can tolerate only for a moment. The power and brightness of this flash ensures that we cannot hold on to it for long. However, armed with the memory of this glimpse, we can return to the darkness of everyday life and illuminate the path upon which we must walk (Rambam, Introduction to the *Guide*).

I believe that the relevance of the alternating second- and third-person mode of address to Yonah is the same. The prophet began his prayer alienated from his God, for he had run away from Him. Once the flow of prayer brings Yonah to the realization of his predicament, he can lift his eyes to God in prayer. Yet his bitterness is not fully gone and soon enough the alienation creeps back in. Yonah finds that when he attempts to talk to God, he can only speak about Him. Still, this is a great improvement over his previous sullen silence. The seeds of repentance are beginning to germinate and sprout. Although Yonah ends his prayer in the third person, he accedes to God's will. The door is now open, and eventually he will make his complaint directly to God.

We are about to proceed to the second part of the book of Yonah. We can understand much of what we are about to read only after reading chapter 2, in which Yonah oscillates between obedience and rebellion, reaching and retreating, realization and rejection.

It is difficult for any human being to break through the limitations of denial and self-delusion, and Yonah was no exception. Although He knew that salvation comes from God, he could not ask Him for it directly. Instead, he ended his prayer in the third person: "Salvation is from the Lord."

We often encounter people who seem to be aware of their faults and appear determined to overcome them, but fail in their efforts time and again. As we fall and rise again, realizing and forgetting the insights we gained with so much effort, life – as R. Nachman of Breslov teaches – is not a circle but a spiral. We rise and fall, then rise again to find ourselves at the same point, only this time on a higher plane. Each of us has our own "tests of destiny," which do not change as we progress spiritually. The challenge of ordinary people may be their appetite for food. Once they become spiritually great, they may become greedy for knowledge and wisdom. A desire that an ordinary person considers righteous may constitute self-indulgence and a shortcoming for a greater one. Our fate is to face the same challenges repeatedly, and our goal is to elevate the level of life's challenges as high as we possibly can.

PART III

The Beginnigs of Return (Yonah 3:1–2)

> God's word came to Yonah the second time: Arise and go to
> Nineveh, that great city, and call out to it the message that I
> tell you. Yonah arose and went to Nineveh according to the
> word of the Lord…. (3:1–2)

As THE THIRD CHAPTER of Yonah opens, we find ourselves back at the
beginning. Once more Yonah receives a call to go to Nineveh, only this time
he complies. Interestingly, the message appears to be the same one that he
had received previously. Yet now, after everything that happened to him, he
can receive it properly and understand it. Compare the two verses:

> 3:1 The word of God came to Yonah the second time, saying:
> "Arise, go to Nineveh, that great city, and proclaim to it…."

> 1:1 Now the word of God came unto Yonah the son of Amittai,
> saying: "Arise, go to Nineveh, that great city, and proclaim against
> it…." (JPS translation)

The impression that we are again at the beginning is strengthened by the
structural parallels between the first two and the last two chapters. Both start
with an almost identical command and tell of gentiles who readily accede to
God's word. In both, Yonah resists, although in the later chapters he no
longer runs away, but instead carries out his mission sullenly, under duress.
The first time, he turns to God after three days in the belly of the fish. The
second time, he contemplates His ways for forty days in an outdoor booth.
Many expressions recur, impressing themselves once again upon our
attention.

I think that we can explain the real meaning of the parallelism here by
using, once more, the metaphor of a spiral. Yonah now finds himself a turn
of the spiral that is at a higher twist, but still at the same plane. He has been
given a second chance. Since he has grown in the interim, the playing field is
much larger this time. No longer a passenger on a small boat with a crew of
perhaps a dozen, Yonah now speaks to the entire city of Nineveh which, as
we are later told, consists of one hundred twenty thousand souls. As his
spiritual stature grows, his influence grows correspondingly.

Yonah is now is much more aware of his deficiencies in relation to God's attribute of Mercy, and he already knows that "salvation is from God." This illustrates that God gives us many opportunities to correct our faults. Unfortunately, since Yonah is still not ready to speak directly to God, he remains in some measure in flight from Him. You might say that his mind has surrendered, but his heart continues to resist.

How do we reach the heart? How do we internalize and retain what we know in our minds so that it remains an integral part of our souls?

The chapters that we now read are no longer as concerned with flight and denial as they are with the nature of repentance and with how one completes the process. The people of Nineveh are the mirror through which the book contemplates and reflects upon human sincerity and self-delusion. The reader knows (and the sages point out) that the Ninevites' repentance was far from complete or sincere, for only a few years later, the prophet Nachum describes Nineveh as a bloodthirsty and oppressive Mistress of the Nations (Nachum 2:12–3:5). Facing Nineveh stands Yonah, who is himself struggling with the last and most difficult step in the process of repentance.

We never learn in this book whether he achieved success in his quest, but as we follow him, perhaps we can learn something about our own.

What's the Difference? (Yonah 3:2–4)

We would expect that after all that has happened to him, Yonah would set out for Nineveh without delay, but he does nothing of the sort. Even after reaching dry land, Yonah does not acknowledge the Divine command, nor does he set off on his mission. God speaks to Yonah again… but why was that necessary? After having humbled himself in the belly of the fish, should Yonah not have complied? Was it because the first command had lapsed, or was it because the command had changed?

An examination and comparison of the two commands will reveal significant differences between them.

1. Chapters 1, 2

> Arise and go to Nineveh, that great city, and cry out against it, for their evil has reached me.

2. Chapter 3:2

> Arise and go to Nineveh, that great city, and cry to it the call that I tell you.

The later version does not mention the wickedness of the people of Nineveh. Neither is the prophet told to cry out against the city, but rather to tell it something that he already knows.

Granted, "evil" may not refer to the city's sins but rather to the evil that God has planned to bring upon it (see Ibn Ezra). Some commentators have argued this on the basis of a similar phrase in Exodus 32:14 ("God repented of the evil that He had spoken against His people") or even in the book of Yonah itself (1:7 – 'let us cast lots that we may know on whose account this evil has come upon us" and 3:10 – "God repented of evil that He had decided to do to them"). However, I tend to side with the interpreters, such as Malbim and Metsudot, who understood the word "evil" as referring to the wickedness of Nineveh's inhabitants.

It seems to me that this interpretation is strongly supported by the implied reference to another great ancient city that occurs several times during our story – the city of Sodom (see Genesis 20:21–22). The comparison makes sense. Both of them were great metropolises that deserved to be destroyed. When we discuss the sins of Nineveh, we will return to this point.

What changed? Where did the wickedness go? God no longer seems as antagonistic to this city as He was at first. He no longer plans to destroy it; instead, He calls it to repentance.

This question led some commentators, such as Abarbanel, to conclude that during the delay occasioned by Yonah's flight, God changed His mind. For some reason He became more favorably disposed to Nineveh, offering it another chance and no longer seeking its destruction. If this is true, it is a fine example of divine irony, for Yonah's escape only succeeded in bringing closer the very thing (the salvation of Nineveh and eventul destruction of Jerusalem) that he sought to prevent. In this view, the second version of the command was necessary because the first no longer applied.

One might suggest a different explanation. Perhaps the original command contained two different imperatives. While it allowed for the possibility of repentance, its focus was on the stern message of approaching annihilation. The same is true of the second prophecy, only here the focus is on repentance, as Rashi on 3:4 points out.

> Yonah began to go one day's walk into the city. He called out, saying: "Forty days more and Nineveh will be overturned."
>
> Rashi: "Overturned" means "destroyed." He did not say "destroyed" because "overturned" has two meanings, one good and one evil. If they do not repent, they will be destroyed. If they do repent, the city

will be overturned, for the people of Nineveh will turn from evil ways to good ones.

As we noted above (see Malbim and Abarbanel on 1:2 and Responsa Radvaz 2:842), Yonah did not fully understand the depth and content of the original prophecy. Its full meaning eluded him because he was committed to Justice over Compassion. His spiritual point of view was such that he heard only the message of destruction. The concepts of repentance and forgiveness – which constituted the other side of the prophecy – were not, as it were, in his lexicon.

Nevertheless, his pain, suffering, and brush with death led to a process of growth that awakened some empathy within him for Nineveh's inhabitants. Only now could he begin to hear the other side of God's message.

The rest of the book of Yonah is about the growth of this realization and Yonah's struggle to reconcile it with his previous world view. In short, it is about Yonah's engagement with divine mercy as the underlying element of divine justice.

Walking the Nineveh Beat (Yonah 3:3–4)

> Yonah arose and went to Nineveh according to the word of God. Nineveh was a great city to the Lord, a walk of three days. Yonah began to go into the city (alternate translation: waited to go into the city) one day's walk, and he cried: "Forty days more and Nineveh will be overturned." (3:3–4)

What shall we make of this description? The city appears to have been quite large, for one day's walk is approximately forty kilometers (BT *Pesahim* 94b), giving us a diameter through the city of something like one hundred twenty kilometers. This contradicts archaeological evidence that the walls of the city were twelve kilometers and its maximum width five kilometers. Of course, it is quite possible that by that time, the city's population had outgrown the walled city proper and that the city's true measurement included surrounding suburbs and settlements. Likewise, Scripture may only be describing the length of time that it would take to cover all the major thoroughfares.

Still, it is difficult to visualize what took place. Did Yonah ensure that his message would be widely heard and distributed, and if so, how? Why did he not go around the city but merely into it? Why was his message so brief? Did he repeat his message many times along his path or did he only call it out once, as it appears from the text?

The Ibn Ezra suggests that the circumference of the city is three days' walk; thus, it would take one day to walk along its diameter from one end to another. Presumably, Yonah recited his message continuously as he traversed the city.

The Malbim offers a different interpretation. He suggests that Yonah spent one day getting deeply into the city because he wanted to make sure that the waiting period of forty days would apply equally to all neighborhoods and inhabitants of the city. It was only on the second day, as he reached its center, that he proclaimed his message. R. Bachya understands the verses as saying that God did not reveal the message that Yonah was to proclaim until the prophet had reached the city's center. This made the delivery of the message much more effective and ensured that it quickly reached the ears of the king and his court. The Yalkut Shimoni solves the practical issues in yet another manner: "As Yonah proclaimed in the market, his voice carried forty days' distance and every single house heard his voice. At that time the matter reached the palace of the King."

Why does the text tell us these specific details of Yonah's mission in this way? There must be some meaning that is inherent in this particular choice of details. What could it be?

Scripture appears to indicate that Yonah performed his mission reluctantly. This is evident not only in his delaying until God commands him a second time but also from the fact that he barely enters the city, getting just one third of the distance into it, before he delivers his message. After only one day's walk, who will hear him – peasants in the market? Passers-by rushing to the center to conduct their business? Should Yonah not have gone directly to the king, to the seat of power? Does not God's word deserve that much exposure?

Moreover, Yonah leaves the city as soon as he proclaims his message. Is it not a prophet's obligation to remain with the city that has been stood on its head with the news of its imminent destruction? Yonah should have stayed and led its frightened and bewildered inhabitants. He should have taught them, comforted them and advised them on how to avert the decree. It was his duty to lead them out of the demoralization and confusion that he himself had created. They obviously trusted him; he should have used that trust to help them. What leader frightens his charges and then leaves them?

Compassion is the defining feature of prophets. The Midrash points out: "All the prophets acted through the Quality of Mercy, for Israel and for the nations, for thus Isaiah spoke of Moab: 'Therefore my insides will cry like a harp for Moab' (Ch. 15). Ezekiel said: 'Son of man, raise a dirge over Tyre' (Ch. 16). But the prophets of the nations of the world acted with cruelty.

One [Bilaam] arose to uproot an entire people for nothing" (*Tanchuma,* Balak 1).

The verses then select precisely those details that reinforce the impression that Yonah failed the people of Nineveh to whom he had delivered a shocking message and who thus became his responsibility. The narrator wants us to see this behavior as lack of compassion, not merely as dereliction of duty or avoidance of responsibility, in order to teach us a future lesson about Divine compassion.

The King and I (Yonah 3:3–5)

> The people of Nineveh believed God. They proclaimed a fast and put on sackcloth, from the greatest of them to the least of them. When the tidings reached the king of Nineveh, he arose from his throne, took off his robe, covered himself with sackcloth, and sat in ashes. (3:5–6)

As we proceed through the next several verses, we encounter some problems. The reason why these verses are so puzzling is that they deal with the very crux of the spiritual quest: how can we, frail and limited human beings, make spiritual progress? This is the central question of the Book of Yonah, presented in this chapter through the contrast between the incomplete repentance of the people of Nineveh and the more honest but slower inner growth of the prophet himself. The importance of the subject demands a slow and deliberate development. I ask readers to bear with me as we analyze the background and develop the subject over several chapters. A careful consideration and correlation with other related passages throughout the Bible and their rabbinic interpretations will assist us in unraveling the layers of meaning in the coming verses.

As the first step, let us focus on the following question. What was Nineveh's sin? It is noteworthy that it is never stated explicitly either in God's command to Nineveh nor in Yonah's message to its inhabitants. This is surprising because it does not agree with the pattern of other Biblical books. Of course, there is ample precedent for the destruction of a sinful society by God: the Flood, the Tower of Babel, and the city of Sodom. The story of Nineveh contains many linguistic and situational parallels and allusions to these earlier examples. However, the text identifies the sin of each of these. Here, it does not. Why not?

One may speculate that this reticence is simply an expression of the moral sensitivity expressed in the following Talmudic statement: "Never say to a sincere penitent: 'Remember your original behavior?'" (*Bava Metzia* 58a).

Since the Ninevites repented, Scripture did not want to reveal their sin. However, I suspect that it goes beyond that. The focus in the Book of Yonah is on repentance, not on sin. Not everyone is revolted by sin. Perhaps the inhabitants' sin was of a kind that the reading audience might not find abhorrent. Prophetic morality is not the same as common morality. What the one considers repugnant, the other may consider commonplace or natural, if regrettable. Naming this sin might have perplexed readers, who simply would not understand the Divine reaction to an act that they felt was insignificant. At the same time, an open-hearted reader can find enough allusions to draw the correct conclusions and understand what was wrong with Nineveh.

Perhaps Nineveh's sins were political: greed, imperialism, domination and oppression of others, and a cruel foreign policy. For thousands of years, human beings believed that anything and everything was acceptable in international relations, because the state and its welfare take precedence over individual morality. People could accept that rebellion against God or interpersonal violence and injustice might condemn a society to destruction. However, until very recently, only the prophetic voices maintained that the same is true regarding the way that nations treat one another – and the people of Israel. To my knowledge, no classical thinker of antiquityy ever made an accusation as eloquent or unselfconscious as Amos's (2:1): "Thus says the Lord, for three sins of Moab and for four I will not overlook: for their burning the bones of the King of Edom with caustic lye." In God's eyes, what Moab did to Edom was evil. Moab had violated a universal standard of behavior among nations by desecrating the corpse of an enemy.

This understanding of Nineveh's sin is explicit in the words of prophet Nachum, who calls Nineveh "the harlot of nations," "for they seduced the heart of the rulers of [various] lands to join them. At the end they would overcome them and place them under their own dominion" (Rashi on 3:4). Nineveh, then, was the source from which sorcery, degeneracy and amorality, in the guise of culture and civilization, reached the entire world. "From the amount of whoring of Nineveh, fair and charming, a mistress of enchantment, who sells nations through her whoring and clans through her sorcery" (3:4, my translation). In other words, nations are seduced into gathering in Nineveh because of its abundant wealth and commerce. Entire families of nations become so enchanted by Nineveh that, blind to their own interests, they become subservient to it (Malbim) – an excellent description of cultural imperialism.

Woe to the bloody city! It is all full of lies and rapine; the prey departs not…. Because of the multitude of the harlotries of the well-favored harlot, the mistress of witchcrafts, that sells nations through her harlotries, and families through her witchcrafts. Behold, I am against you, says the Lord of Hosts, and I will uncover your skirts to your face. I will show the nations your nakedness, and the kingdoms your shame. (Nachum 3:2–5)

See also Zefaniah 2:13–15 and Isaiah 37:22–29, which describe Nineveh's egotism and arrogance.

It is in this light that we might understand why the King of Nineveh put on sackcloth. It is he who redirected the inhabitants' spontaneous individual repentance into a form of national penance. There is no more potent symbol of contrition and self-abasement than a King wearing sackcloth (See I Kings 21:27, II Kings 6:30 and 19:1).

True, Nineveh was entirely corrupt. It citizens cheated, robbed and oppressed each other. However, these actions were not the root of their problem but rather its symptom. The society's internal dissolution mirrored its external lack of national purpose, which was nothing but the pursuit of power, aggression and desire to dominate and control. Nineveh's repentance could not even begin to engage the real sin of its political culture until the pride and symbol of the haughty Assyrian state, its ruler, accepted responsibility and humbled himself.

Does this sound familiar? In our own time and place, issues of national morality have once again become a prominent issue in international politics. This is as it should be, because the prophets of Israel taught us that nations must make sure that they meet the demands of universal morality. If they do not, then God will.

Human and Beast (Yonah 3:7–9)

He [the King] had the word cried through Nineveh: "By decree of the king and his nobles: Every man and beast – of flock or herd – shall not taste anything. They shall not graze, and shall not drink water. Let them be covered with sackcloth – man and beast – and call mightily to God" (3:7–9)

This public penance that joined together man and animal is extraordinary, for "if human beings sinned, how did animals sin?" (*Yoma* 22b). We do not usually think of animals as sentient beings who can sin or repent. Yet this is not an isolated instance. Animals' participation in the drama of sin, punishment and repentance recurs in God's final answer to Yonah:

> God said: "You had pity on the gourd, for which you did not labor and which you did not raise, which came up in a night, and perished in a night. Should I not have pity on Nineveh, that great city, which contains more than sixscore thousand human beings who do not know their right hand from their left, and also much cattle?" (4:10–11)

What is the significance of animals and humans sharing the stage?

The inclusion of both human being and animal in the divine decree of destruction has parallels elsewhere in Scripture. For example, we find that "all flesh had become corrupt upon the earth" (Genesis 6:12); accordingly, "I shall wipe humanity, which I created, from the face of the earth, from human beings to beasts to crawling creatures to the birds of heaven" (ibid. 6:7). Similarly, both human beings and animals were saved in Noah's ark: "God remembered Noah and all the beasts and all the cattle that were with him in the ark" (ibid. 8:1).

This reflects the fact that when a natural disaster strikes, humans and animals share the same fate (Hosea 4:3). When a conqueror ravages a country, both its human and non-human inhabitants suffer (Yirmiah 27:6). The bellowing of animals is a kind of prayer; hence, "the beast of the field cries out to you, watercress is dried out" (Yoel 1:20). We may interpret the covering of animals with sackcloth similarly.

Nevertheless, this act contained a degree of Assyrian cruelty, for the truth is that it is wrong to cause animals undeserved suffering. Instead of turning away entirely from their abusive ways, the people of Nineveh intensified their oppression of others – in this case, their dependent cattle and beasts of burden. The Sages said: "The repentance of Ninevites was fraudulent. What did they do? They put calves on the inside and their mothers outside; foals on the inside and their mothers outside. These bellowed from the inside and the others from outside. They said: If You do not have mercy upon us, we will not have mercy on them" (JT *Ta'anit* 2:1). Like cruel children, they threatened God with the prospect of hurting His other creatures if He dared to refuse them.

A different perspective may be derived from the following verse and its rabbinic interpretation: "Save human and beast, O Lord" (Psalms 36:7). These are human beings who, although they possess intelligence, behave like animals (*Chullin* 5b).

I recently read the comments of Mordechai Beck, an artist who illustrated the Book of Yonah (the exhibition of "Maftir Yonah" was mounted at Yeshiva University in 1993–1994). One should never dismiss the words of artists because their sight, which comes from their hearts, sometimes goes deeper than ours. Beck, who has applied himself assiduously to understanding the Book of Yonah, wrote:

> Apart from its size, Nineveh is characterized by its moral waywardness. Its half-animal, half-human inhabitants are both highly civilized yet simultaneously alienated from their psychic sources. They have, under the influence of Jonah, turned to God. But just as easily they could have turned to a stranger advocating some political ideology. These people lack a basic sense of direction, "knowing neither left from right." … The parallels between the Jonah story and our contemporary dilemmas are so strong that during the three years I worked on this project I came to sense that, to a generation which is searching for both independence and meaning, the Book of Jonah is as relevant as was the Book of Job to the generation that passed, in reality or vicariously, through the traumas of the Holocaust. … We, the viewers, have become Jonah. We can flee or we can stay. Emerging from the belly of the fish into the light of day, we are forced to realize that the land of Tarshish is reached – if ever – only through the gates of Nineveh.

Heart of Darkness (Yonah 3:8–10)

> Who knows – God may change His mind and turn back from His wrath so that we do not perish (3:9).

The King had called to his people: "Let each man turn away from his evil ways and from the injustice which is in his hand" (3:8). He now expresses a hope that God will accept Nineveh's repentance and save its people from destruction. This reading of the verse as expressing doubt and hope is found in Radak and Ibn Ezra and it is supported by a similar sentiment that the sailors express during the storm in 1:6: "Perhaps God will take thought of us, that we not perish." (We find an almost identical verse, which is supported by the cantillation notation, in Yoel 2:14.[1])

---

[1] Our verse in Yonah itself is quite ambiguous in the original Hebrew, since it can also be read as: "He who knows will repent, and God will change His mind and turn back from His wrath…." This statement is much more emphatic than the previous reading, for it assumes with certainty that forgiveness must always follow repentance. This understanding, which is shared by Targum, Rashi, Ibn Ezra and Mahari Kara is supported in the verse in Yonah by its cantillation marks, which place a separating stop,

The apparent lack of certainty that God will accept sincere repentance contrasts remarkably with the assurance expressed in many other Scriptural sources. Compare it, for example, with King David's trust that God will accept his repentance in Psalm 51.

The king's attitude contradicts one of Judaism's most basic tenets: that God always accepts sincere repentance. Radak notes this in his commentary on Yoel 2:14: "Even though we said that it is one of the attributes of God, Blessed be He, that He repents of evil and this is beyond doubt, still, if the sins are great, He may not repent until minor punishment is meted out...."

The insecurity expressed by the sailors, the inhabitants of Nineveh and even in the Book of Yoel may be a reflection of the distance from God that they felt. Those who hardly think of God under ordinary circumstances suffer profound alienation and dislocation when suddenly thrust into His presence. The sailors and the Ninevites were shaken from their complacency, their numb acceptance of injustice and callousness as the normal order of things. Even the Israelites, in the midst of the plague of locusts, felt far from God's grace and forgiveness. They suddenly saw themselves and their lives as God did, when they heard the prophet Yoel. Suddenly, they were no longer paragons of virtue or the pinnacle of civilization. Now, as they stood in judgment before the Most High, they saw themselves as insignificant and lacking, bare of merits, empty of value.

This abrupt reversal in self-perception, which is a part of the conversion experience, has been known to psychological literature since William James. The total reversal plunges the self into utter darkness that can only be relieved by surrender of what were, until now, the most precious, basic and ingrained components of one's personality, a sacrifice of self in order to save the self. Human beings do surrender before the overwhelming might of God, offering up parts of themselves in a shaky hope for salvation and survival. There is little security, love or elevation in this kind of experience, although it may first bring relief. Surely it is better than nothing, yet it is full of darkness and very tempting for darkness to come in.

Most Jewish thinkers see this sort of repentance as suspect. On the deepest level, it demands a form of self-annihilation – the renunciation of a part of one's personality, past history and nature. It is often accompanied by feelings of deep regret and loss, grief and depression or, in an attempt to deny that loss, by hostility directed outwards in the form of religious

---

a kind of a comma, after "repent" and not after "knows," so that it reads, "He who knows will repent, and God will change His mind..." rather than, "Who knows? God may repent and change His mind...."

intolerance and fanaticism. Sometimes penitents, unable to bear the loss, quickly revert to their former lives. At other times, they remain profoundly conflicted. Instead of a life-affirming and uplifting religious experience, the process of conversion/repentance leaves the individual in a place of darkness and loss.

Even if the change is stable, the real work of inner change only begins in the conversion experience. (See more on this in the beginning of *Orot ha-teshuva* by Abraham Isaac Kook). One has to change one's ways, not only one's actions.

The rabbis were suspicious of Nineveh's repentance. To my mind, the book of Yonah appears to set up a contrast between Yonah and the Ninevites. Yonah did not repent all at once, but resisted throughout. Yet as he surrendered one cherished personal belief after another, he changed inside in ways that were far more meaningful and lasting than if he had undergone a sudden conversion. The book contrasts Yonah's long process of inner change with the quick and unexpected change of heart of the sailors in Chapter 1 and that of the Ninevites in Chapter 3.

The King of Nineveh understood that repentance is more than a conversion experience. He asked his people to return the "injustice" in their hands and he also called them "to turn each man from his evil way." Significantly, they complied only in regard to "God saw their deeds, that they turned away from their wicked ways…." It does not appear that they "left the injustice in their hands" behind at all. The rabbis debate the meaning of this omission.

The next chapter will take up the disagreement between the Babylonian and the Jerusalem Talmud in this regard and the two different understandings of repentance that underlie their positions.

Fear and Love

All repentance is motivated by something. The repentance of the men of Nineveh was caused by fear. The narrative makes this quite clear, saying: "The men feared the Lord greatly. They offered sacrifices to the Lord and made vows" (1:16). The episode of the sailors' repentance parallels that of Nineveh.

However, the repentance of Nineveh, unlike that of the sailors, is characterized by a conversion experience. "The men of Nineveh believed in God. They called a fast and put on sackcloth from youngest to oldest" (3:5). The psychological link between fear and belief is highlighted in the verse, "The people feared the Lord and believed in the Lord and Moses His servant" (Exodus 14:31).

We have spoken of the essential instability of the conversion experience. Although a newly-assumed belief can be a powerful motivator to sacrifice one's deepest aspirations and principles and accept a new set of convictions, this change often does not last. It may be followed by the long, hard work of self-examination and progressive inner change, or it may end with angry rebellion and a return to the former lifestyle. Not surprisingly, most of the books of Exodus and Numbers are accounts of the frequent backsliding of the Children of Israel despite the fact that they feared and believed. This kind of repentance, which requires the renunciation of major aspects of one's personality and the forcible impoverishment of the self, is far from ideal. The rabbis called it "repentance through fear."

The sailors and men of Nineveh embody this kind of repentance: an abrupt change of course, but not necessarily of heart, before God's power. At the same time, it remains focused on the repentance of the prophet Yonah, which was qualitatively different. Yonah, who is not afraid of God, will not be bowed by His power and might. On the other hand, his heart is open to learning from the events and circumstances that befall him. Yonah struggles with one of the two great questions of moral philosophy: not why the good suffer, but why the wicked prosper. Unlike Job, whose problem was the Quality of Justice, Yonah cannot abide the Quality of Mercy. In his view, the world should be run by Justice. The sin must be cleared by the death of the sinner. There can be no second chances and there must be zero tolerance for evil. Therefore, he does not preach repentance to Nineveh willingly because he rejects the very idea of repentance.

Yet God's tolerance of his own rebellion, together with His mercy in saving him in the fish's belly, shakes Yonah's confidence in his rigid morality. He succumbs and goes to Nineveh. Yonah is now confused, but not yet fully convinced. He must witness further revelations and experience God's personal kindness once more. Eventually he learns, and what we learn stays with us forever. This kind of repentance, which is done for its own sake and which our sages termed "repentance through love," is solid and stable.

The major distinction between repentance through fear and repentance through love is that while the former fragments and impoverishes the personality, the latter is integrative. No renunciation of the past is necessary because the past led the penitent to the new knowledge. Thus the past becomes redeemed and reaffirmed.

Consider a hypothetical case of two boys who grew up in difficult circumstances. In their neighborhood, all young men joined gangs. As they rose and gained status within the gang, they realized the dangers and immorality of their lifestyles. They watched their friends die or go to prison, and finally decided to leave. One enlisted in the army, moving to a farm after his discharge. He never returned to the old neighborhood lest he revert to his previous lifestyle. He made a clean break, which is commendable.

Yet he lost so much. He renounced his parents, friends, schoolmates, upbringing, and memories. Is there any doubt that his move, while necessary and right, made him poorer and caused him deep inner injury?

His friend chose differently. Inspired by his new beliefs, he returned to his old neighborhood as, let us suppose, an addiction counselor. He built a social service organization, using his intimate knowledge of criminal culture, its distribution networks and patterns of association in order to work for communal renewal. By doing so, he turned his negative past into an inspiring future, for it was precisely his past that enabled him to accomplish all this. Rather than renouncing his past, he made it the foundation for new gains.

Repentance through love turns sins into assets because if not for the sins, there would be no assets.

> Resh Lakish said: Great is repentance, for to a penitent, deliberate sins become as if they were unintentional ones, as it is written: "Return, Israel, to your God, for you have stumbled in your crime" (Hosea 14). "Crime" refers to deliberate sin and yet it is called "stumbling." Is this really so? Did not Resh Lakish say, "Great is repentance, for it turns sins into *merits,* as it says, 'When the wicked turns away from his sin… he shall live [in the sense of "prosper"] (Ezekiel 33). There is no problem, since one statement is about repentance motivated by love while the other is about repentance that is motivated by fear. (BT *Yoma* 86b)

This specifically Jewish understanding of repentance determined how the Jerusalem Talmud (but not the Babylonian Talmud) understood Nineveh's repentance. (We will soon address the actual texts.) Some faiths teach that repentance means painful sacrifice and that utter rejection of the past is an inevitable part of the universal battle against evil. One who sinned must reject and disavow the sin.

This dualistic vision of good and evil is foreign to classic Jewish belief. As a faith that teaches the absolute unity of God, Judaism advocates the integration and unification of all disparate phenomena of the physical and spiritual world. All multiplicity ultimately stems from the One; on some high level, even evil comes from Him. This is not to justify evil, but to point out that according to this system evil, too, serves the purposes of the good. In Jewish thought, sin may be redeemed, integrated and harnessed toward good. We may surmise that the Jerusalem Talmud's attribution of this perception of repentance to Yonah and the alternate understanding of repentance as denial, rejection and renunciation to the Gentile inhabitants of Nineveh stems from this view.

The Two Talmuds

We now have enough background to examine the fact that the Babylonian and Jerusalem Talmuds disagree about whether the repentance of Nineveh was genuine or superficial and self-serving. Let us read the relevant passages together after looking at a few points of methodology.

The Talmudic text rarely fleshes out its understanding of Scripture. Instead, it usually expresses it as pithy comments upon specific verses, and the full picture must be extracted from these comments. We should also remember that the Talmud reports many ancient traditions and that divergent interpretations of these traditions may arise over time. As a result, we may encounter language that is mostly similar, but may differ in a slight change of words or emphasis. As we will see, the verses on which these comments are based lend equal support to multiple interpretations, which is also a general feature of Biblical writing.

As with other rabbinic statements, it takes great care and thought to interpret our sages' words. To start, let us look at one comment.[2]

The Mishna in *Ta'anit* 16a seems to support the premise that Nineveh's repentance was genuine because it cites it as an example for others. In describing the procedure that was followed during public fasts for rain, the Mishna notes: "We take the Ark out to the thoroughfare…. The elder among them speaks words that induce humility. 'Brothers, it says not regarding the men of Nineveh that God saw their sackcloth and their fasting but that He saw their actions, that they turned away from evil.'" The Babylonian Talmud adds a note: "From the violence that was in their hands – Samuel said, 'Even if they stole a beam and built it into a palace, they tore down the palace and returned the beam to its rightful owner.'" Here the repentance is complete, sparing no expense.

In fact, Yalkut Shimoni says that the King of Nineveh tore down his own palace because every brick in it had been stolen from someone else. Samuel appears to have understood the expression "in their hands" as referring to their property, meaning real estate, a common idiomatic usage.

---

[2] I will focus on only one because of space limitations. However, a detailed comparison of two others can be found in A. Rivlin's work, *Yonah: Prophecy and Rebuke,* Yeshivat Kerem b'Yavne: 1979.

By so doing, the people of Nineveh went beyond what Jewish law required, for the Sages had instituted a special law called "for the benefit of penitents." They realized that sometimes restitution is too much of a burden. The effort to restore a situation to its previous state may place an inordinate burden on those who wish to make restitution, keeping them away from complete repentance. The Sages therefore outlawed the demolition of a building in order to return a brick, requiring monetary compensation instead (BT *Gittin* 55a).

According to the Babylonian Talmud, the repentance of Nineveh was complete and exemplary.

This is not at all what we find in the Jerusalem Talmud on the very same mishna in Ta'anit. Instead, we find the following: "R. Yochanan [a generation before Samuel] said: What was in the palm of their hand they returned, but what was packed away in a chest, closet and safe, they did not return." He takes the expression "in their hands" literally, as referring only to what they held in their hands at that moment.

When we think about these two approaches, the former seems more reasonable at first. After all, since Nineveh was not destroyed, its inhabitants' repentance must have been genuine. However, we must realize that the author of the Book of Yonah scattered discordant notes throughout the narrative, waiting for astute readers such as Rabbi Yochanan or more contemporary readers, such as ourselves, to discover them.

Among these textual dissonances is the fact that of the six verses that describe Nineveh's repentance (3:5–10), three are an account of the king's command: "Let all the people turn back from their evil ways and from the violence that is in their hands." Although Biblical text would usually say something like, "The people of Nineveh did as the king commanded," we find nothing of the sort. We are not told that the king's command was obeyed, nor is there any mention of inner change. Clearly the Ninevites believed Yonah, but what were the results? They called to God, fasted and put on sackcloth – all out of fear. Were they remorseful? Apparently, they were not.

The king commands that the people turn back from "evil ways and from violence which is in their hands." That seems to have happened only halfway: "God saw that they turned away from their evil ways." There is no mention of their refraining from violence.

Finally, as we had mentioned previously, there is no echo of a repentant Nineveh anywhere else in Scripture. On the contrary, the books of Yoel, Zefaniah and Isaiah tell us is that it was a bloodthirsty, greedy, imperialistic and aggressive "harlot of the nations." This description is hardly consistent with total and sincere repentance. If such repentance in fact took place, it quickly passed.

The Jerusalem Talmud can also be read in a deeper vein. The treasure in the Ninevites' storage places that they refused to return may allude to their past experiences, opinions and thinking habits. The Ninevites were quite willing to restrain themselves from that point onward. They gave back what was in their hands but not what was deep inside their psyches.

As we discussed above, this kind of repentance sees as its goal the negation and rejection of evil, not its redemption and transformation into good. The beam that was built into a structure is a symbol of the evil that lies buried deep within. One may thing that it must be uprooted and returned to its original pure state. In reality, it is better to leave it in place and instead redeem the entire building.

Repentance in its purest form requires the sometimes painful process of owning up to personal failings and examining and restructuring the inner self in humility and strong faith. Anything else is self-delusion and will not last. The unredeemed self will fight, undermine the walls that may be erected around it, eventually reassert itself and demand a return to the status quo. The result is either angry backsliding, complacent hypocrisy or self-delusion.

R. Yochanan, who lived in Palestine in the fourth century C.E. – a time of great religious ferment and sectarian strife – was certainly familiar with the forms of repentance preached there by the newly ascendant Gnostic movements of all kinds. They taught the rejection of evil but not the rebuilding of the self, which was identified with the evil outside and believed to be beyond redemption. They taught that evil cannot be redeemed and that rejection and constant affliction of the self and unremitting struggle with the body was the only path to salvation. R. Yochanan felt that this belief was fundamentally not Jewish, and he saw the Ninevites' repentance as flawed – motivated by fear rather than by love, rejecting rather than redemptive, fragmenting instead of integrative. Therefore, it was destined to fail.

The Path of Sin: Who Is Right?

Nineveh's repentance was a complicated affair. The understanding that it was faulty and incomplete comes from Nineveh's general image in Scripture, many textual clues and the sense that a distant and foreign nation could not gain access to the vision of repentance that the Israelite prophets taught. At best, it would repent as many nations do, by negating and rejecting the past rather than redeeming and transforming it.

The Jerusalem Talmud's opinion, which is well-founded, rests on strong textual and theological evidence. However, one clue suggests that Nineveh's repentance was of the highest caliber, as the Babylonian Talmud teaches. This clue is the description of Nineveh's repentance as "turning people away from their evil path." To understand that, we must consider what turning away from a path of evil generally means in Scripture.

Scripture seems to present two different ways to repent. Sometimes, repentance is described as consisting primarily of confession and regret. These two basic elements combine with others such as prayer, making restitution, bringing oneself to weep and feel shame over the misdeed, fasting and wearing sackcloth, but the essence of repentance remains these two elements.

On other occasions, however, the penitent may change his entire way of life, making the other manifestations of repentance appear less important. The classic medieval work on repentance, *Shaarei teshuva* by R. Yonah of Gerona, explains that there are two different kinds of repentance.[3] Since the passage is too lengthy to reproduce here, I will paraphrase it (though, regrettably, without its magnificent Scriptural references).

According to R. Yonah, sometimes, an individual of good character may be overcome by a sudden desire, become vulnerable or simply be unprepared to contend with the unexpected attack of the evil impulse. The way back for such people is relatively simple. After acknowledging and confessing their misdeed, they must direct all their being to spiritual growth so that they will never again be tempted in the same way.

Those who are habituated to sin, whose inner being and personality are bound up with evil, require a different process. Those whose character is built upon greed, envy, cruelty, and disregard for others cannot take time for acknowledgment and confession. They must leave the path of sin at once, with the rest of the inner work to follow.

If they do not do so, to what may this be compared? To one who immerses in a purifying bath while clutching the carcass of a rodent – a thing that renders anyone who touches it ritually impure (Taanit 16a). It does no good to immerse in a cleansing bath while clinging to a source of impurity. First, the bather must discard the carcass, and only then is the purification complete. Yet for one who has been steeped in sin for a long time, throwing away the source of impurity is only the start of the process.

In this light, the fact that each inhabitant of Nineveh "left his evil ways" becomes significant. It indicates that their repentance was not only genuine but also sophisticated. The Babylonian Talmud understands from this phrase

---

[3] In 1:13.

that Nineveh's repentance was sincere, genuine and accomplished in the correct manner.

At this point, one may now ask: How can the views of the Jerusalem Talmud and of the Babylonian Talmud both be correct? Even though the text supports both views, is it not a fact that only one can be historically factual while the other is in error?

To the rescue comes the concept of multi-valence in Biblical literature. This approach to reading sacred text argues that our Western habit of reading literature developed from our encounter with the classical works of antiquity. The habit is an artificial one, since it demands the imposition of a coherent story onto a human reality that is anything but straightforward and coherent. From the earliest grades in school, we are taught to ignore dissonant details and inconvenient patterns in favor of an easily-understood, consistent narrative.

Biblical writing is different. It tells a story that is rich, detailed and overwhelmingly complex. Scripture is not a collection of pious writings but a Divinely-inspired record of the interaction between human beings and God. It seeks not to be consistent but rather to be accurate, wise and real. It knows that human beings can be pious and devoted yet wicked and cruel at the same time. It knows that a city that embraces faith wholeheartedly may also be full of deceit and hypocrisy. By telling us both sides of the story, Scripture teaches us about the complexity of spiritual life.

Conclusion of Chapter 3 and Introduction to Chapter 4

As we read the Book of Yonah, we saw that it is organized according to certain literary and symbolic principles. It is this sophisticated construction that enables it to evoke and inspire so strongly.

The book contains five major elements: the story of God's call, the prophet's avoidance of it or incomplete response to it, the Gentile sailors' repentance, Yonah's inner growth, and finally his response to God's command. We might map the book as follows: ABCDE ABCDE – F, with F being a direct quotation from God Himself.

The first five basic elements repeat twice, the correlation supported by the same turns of phrase and situational positioning in case we miss the point. The first set is the story of Yonah and the sailors, while the second one is that of Yonah and the city of Nineveh. Let us look at some of the elements.

Part 1. Yonah and the sailors

 A. The injunction and its violation: "The word of God came to Yonah" (1:1)

 B. The sailors' repentance: "Perhaps God will take thought for us and we will not perish" (1:6)

 C. The sailors repent: "The men feared God greatly" (1:16)

 D. Yonah's rebirth in the belly of the fish (2:1)

 E. Yonah speaks to God (Ch. 2)

Part 2. Yonah and Nineveh

 A. The injunction: "The word of God came to Yonah a second time" (3:1)

 B. Nineveh's repentance: "Who knows? Perhaps God will change his mind… and we will not perish" (3:9)

 C. Nineveh repents: "The people of Nineveh believed in God" (3:5)

 D. Yonah's lesson in the booth (4:5)

 E. Yonah speaks to God (4:1)

Closing

 F. God's reply to Yonah

Underlying this sequence is the recounting of Yonah's journey against the background of his ill-fated trip to Tarshish, his sojourn in the belly of the fish, his foray into Nineveh and finally his forty-day confinement in the booth. All this movement indicates inner change as the reluctant prophet slowly comes to accept the concept that God has mercy upon His creatures, including upon the undeserving, and that this is good. The concept that inner change is slow and additive and that it occurs in response to trials and tribulation of life, guided by the Divine Teacher's loving hand, is perhaps the major point of this work. The underlying concept is that spiritual growth is a spiral on which one ascends and descends, facing the same issues but, it may be hoped, always on a higher level.

 At the heart of Yonah's final experience is his forty-day confinement in the booth. The number forty is significant, since the Bible uses it to indicate a period of preparation and elevation.[4] Moses spends forty days on Mount Sinai and Eliyahu spends forty days in the desert. Just as the three days in the

---

[4] An interesting work devoted solely to the significance of the number forty in Jewish religious literature is *Tov nenoraich* by N.A. Auerbach, published by David Ringer, Jerusalem: 5760.

belly of the fish signify conception, the forty days evoke the forty days required for the formation of a fetus (Rashi, Genesis 6:4). In this manner we follow Yonah's evolution from sullen anger to the point where, when God speaks to him, he can hear and understand His words. Finally Yonah can complain to God, and the book ends with God's response.

We never find out whether Yonah allowed himself to be persuaded and what he did with God's answer. As all spiritual quests, his did not end when the book did. However, since Scripture did not want to suggest a final and conclusive ending, it leaves his response to our imagination. Perhaps this is because there is no single, conclusive response to the Divine call. There is no limit to how high Yonah – and we ourselves – can climb in the spiritual quest. This is perhaps the final lesson of the Book of Yonah.

PART IV

Yonah's Problem

AS WE ENTER the fourth chapter, the story's direction becomes clearer. Until now we encountered several characters, including the sailors, the inhabitants of Nineveh and their king. Had this book been solely about repentance it should have ended at the conclusion of third chapter, with Nineveh's repentance. The fact that the story continues indicates that it is about something other than repentance alone.

In Chapter Four, Yonah himself comes into focus. In fact, the chapter contains only three actors – Yonah, God, and the *kikayon,* the ricinus plant. It therefore appears that we must seek the key to the book's message among them.

The book wastes no time getting to the point.

"Yonah felt very badly and became angry" (4:1).

The construction used here is unique. The closest parallel usually denotes causing damage, as in II Samuel 20:6 or Psalms 106:32. Only in Nehemiah 2:10 do we find it signifying "displeased" ("When Sanballat... heard it, it displeased them greatly that someone has come intending to improve the Israelites' situation"). As we discussed above, since the Hebrew used in the Book of Yonah shares certain features with late Biblical style, this expression probably means the same thing here that it means in the Book of Nehemiah.

What upset Yonah so? The prophet's complaint in verse 2 is direct. This is intentional because, as several commentators point out, it would be chronologically inappropriate to be told so at this point in the narrative, since it could not have happened until the forty days allotted to Nineveh had expired. Recall that in verse 5 Yonah built himself a booth in which he waited "to see what would happen in the city." Thus, verse 5 chronologically precedes verse 2. However, this is not how the events were presented. The complaint comes before the events because we need to experience the power of Yonah's protest right now, at this juncture.

> He prayed to God, saying, "Please, O Lord! Was not this my word when I was still in my own land? This is why I hastened to flee to Tarshish: I knew that You are a compassionate and gracious God, slow to anger, abounding in goodness, repenting of evil. Now, O Lord, please take my life, for I would rather die than live" (2–4).

This emotional outburst appears to have called forth a temporizing response from God, such as one would expect from a parent who is trying to deal with a child in the midst of a tantrum. Like the patient father of an angry child, God plays for time. The interaction is framed in a way that emphasizes God's patience and kindness. Although God's response validates the reality of Yonah's emotion, it does not answer him.

The Lord replied, "Are you really angry?"

Now when seen objectively, the characteristics of compassion, graciousness, slowness to anger, abundant goodness and repenting of evil are excellent ones. So why is Yonah complaining? What about these qualities provokes such frustration and disappointment in Yonah that he would rather die than live? Was he perhaps expecting a God who does not abound in goodness? The complaint is almost irrational. In fact, we almost feel irritated with this bothersome and obstinate prophet. God should have lost all patience with him long ago. By any reasonable standard, a servant who repeatedly disobeys his master deserves punishment. Yonah is no ordinary servant. He is a prophet and should know better. Why, then, is he saved, protected and given chance after chance instead of the punishment that he appears to deserve?

Yonah knew what he was talking about!

It is important to realize that the other side of forbearance and graciousness is delayed justice. Absolute justice demands immediate, fair, and complete compensation for evil as well as for good. While "slow to justice and abounding in goodness" sounds good in the abstract, it allows wickedness and injustice to flourish. A victim of evil acts by human beings experiences Divine forbearance as indifference and lack of compassion, as an affront that permitted his or her suffering. Such a victim pines for justice, not kindness. This pain is not assuaged by pious platitudes but only by immediate recompense. When one is suffering such terrible pain, little can justify Divine dawdling. The only thing that can reconcile a victim is the realization that he or she not only loses by God's inaction and delay but also benefit from His immeasurable, direct and personal kindness. Accepting God's tolerance requires a realization that it benefits every single individual to an infinitely greater extent than would strict application of blind justice.

Thus, in Lamentations:

> He filled me with bitterness and sated me with wormwood. He also broke my teeth with gravel stones and made me to wallow in ashes. My soul is removed far off from peace; I have forgotten prosperity. I said: 'My strength is perished, together with my expectation from

God.' Remember my affliction and anguish, the wormwood and gall. My soul remembers them still and is bowed down within me.

This I recall to my mind, therefore have I hope. Surely God's mercies are not ended, surely His compassions fail not. They are new every morning; great is Thy faithfulness. "God is my portion," says my soul. "Therefore will I hope in Him." God is good to those who wait for Him, to the soul that seeks Him. (Lamentations 3:15–26)

R. Yehoshua Ben Levi said: "Why were they called Men of the Great Assembly? Because they restored the ancient glory. Moses came and said, "Great God, mighty and awesome" (Deuteronomy 10:17). Jeremiah came and said: Foreigners croak in his palace – where is his awesomeness? He did not say "awesome" (Jeremiah 32:18), but rather "Great and mighty is God; the Lord of Hosts is His name." Daniel came and said: "Foreigners enslave His children. Where is His strength?" (Daniel 9:4)…. They [the men of the Great Assembly] came and said: "On the contrary, this is His strength – that He conquers His desire and gives the wicked a great deal of time…." As for the prophets, how could they do so and change the formula that Moses had enacted? Because they knew that God was Truth. They did not speak falsely of Him (BT *Yoma* 69b).

As Nineveh's might increased, so did its crimes. Its rulers oppressed, exiled and murdered innocent people. Because of the depth of its sin, Yonah did not believe that its repentance would last. As he saw matters, Nineveh deserved immediate, unsparing justice rather than a reprieve, lest it continue doing what it had always done. He protested bitterly, refusing to accept Divine Mercy until the incident with the *kikayon* showed him in a direct, personal way that kindness is preferable.

The problem with mercy goes much deeper. The attribute of mercy makes the world as we know it, with free choice, possible. If every evil act were to be punished immediately, would anyone willingly do evil? It is precisely the delay in the administration of justice that allows us to form the impression that we may do wrong without suffering the consequences. The attribute of mercy is responsible for the problem of theodicy, the old and difficult question of how a kind and loving God can allow suffering. To complicate the problem even more, we can say that it is the attribute of mercy itself that indirectly produces evil.

In this light, Yonah's feelings become appropriate for a man of his spiritual level. He did not understand mercy until God removed the *kikayon*, allowing the heat of the sun to beat down upon him. Only then did Yonah understand.

Scripture does not offer philosophical answers to tragedy, suffering and pain. Moreover, words do not convince those who are suffering. Instead, at the end of the book we realize that an answer can only arise from a personal experience of Divine mercy. "From my flesh I will see God" (Job 19:26).

Intertextuality

The concept of intertextuality has made its way from the study of literature to the field of Biblical interpretation and midrash studies. Jewish interpreters have made much use of it in recent years. In this work, we also use it to compare similar prophetic passages. Before we contrast Yonah's formulation of Divine mercy with those of other prophets, it is appropriate that we discuss the legitimacy and applicability of this method for those who uphold the traditional understanding of Scripture as Divine revelation.

In my opinion, intertextuality as defined in literary criticism should not be applied to sacred texts. Once you get past the jargon, what it means in literary criticism is that all texts are unconsciously in dialogue and conversation with earlier texts. In other words, all that writers have ever read affect how they formulate the aims of their writing, the expressions and devices that they use, and how they shape their materials into a coherent and meaningful narrative. This definition is clearly unacceptable to a believing Jew, since prophecy comes only from God and is a conscious and supernaturally endowed endeavor from beginning to end.

Nevertheless, is it legitimate to suppose that prophets may have had some influence on how they delivered the message that had been revealed to them? Is it conceivable that they deliberately invoked previous prophecies in order to increase the effect of their own message? Could God Himself have done this? If so, intertextuality can be admitted as a conscious prophetic technique, though in a limited and monitored form. If not, it is an alien technique that we should leave outside the boundaries of traditional Jewish exegesis.

I argue the former. The Talmud in *Sanhedrin* 89a says: "R. Yitzhak said: Although the formulation comes to multiple prophets, no two prophets prophesy in the same language. Obadia (1:3) said: 'The evil of your heart lifted you.' Yirmiah said: 'It will frighten you; the evil of your heart will lift you'" (49:16). According to this passage, the prophets shape the message that they deliver. This goes back to the fact that prophets other than Moses received their prophecy in the form of a vision accompanied by its interpretation. While this set narrow parameters of sentences and paragraphs, it allowes some latitude as to word choice and arrangement (see Maimonides, *Laws of Yesodei ha-Torah* 7:6). It seems that intertextuality, when properly defined and used, may indeed turn out to be a legitimate technique. Let us see how we can use it to our advantage.

Yonah mentions only mercy: "… for I knew that You are a compassionate and gracious God, slow to anger, abounding in kindness, repenting of evil." This choice of Divine attributes is identical to that found in Joel 2:13–14: "He is gracious and compassionate, slow to anger, abounding in kindness, and renouncing punishment. Who knows but that He may repent and leave a blessing behind?"

This contrasts with the prayer of Moses in Exodus 34:6–7 and Numbers 14:18, where mercy and justice are mentioned together. As in Yonah, outside the Pentateuch, prayer appears to invoke only the attributes of mercy (see Psalms 86:15; 103:8; 145:8; and Nechemia 9:17). The sole exception is Nachum 1:3, where attributes of justice predominate but there it is in the context of the God of vengeance, when He is described as overturning the might of Assyria.

Yonah's allusion to Joel and Psalms is probably deliberate. His listing of only the attributes of mercy emphasized his discomfort with mercy as the operating principle in world affairs. When he says "I knew," how did he know? He knew from his own life and those of the prophets before him. His personal awareness is now supported by a long-standing prophetic tradition and connected with an established record of revelation. Thus, Yonah's argument takes on the power and strength not only of his individual experience but also of the combined authority of the entire prophetic community.

Where Yonah Was and Where He Was Going (Yonah 4:2–4)

> But it displeased Jonah exceedingly and he was angry. He prayed to God, saying: "Please, O God – was this not what I said when I was still in my own country? Therefore I fled to Tarshish, for I knew that You art a gracious and compassionate God, long-suffering and abundant in mercy, repenting of evil. Therefore, O God, I beseech You now: take my life from me, for it is better for me to die than to live." (4:2–4)

This is the third time that Yonah utters a death wish. At the very beginning of the story, he went to sleep as the storm raged around him. Then he told the sailors to throw him overboard. Now he asks God to grant him death.

However, he is not the only one who has asked God to take his life. Moshe also did so when it appeared that his mission had failed.

> Moses said to God: "Why have You treated Your servant so badly? Why have I not found favor in Your sight, that You lay the burden of all this people upon me? Did I conceive all this people? Did I give birth to them, that You should tell me: Carry them in your bosom as a father carries the suckling child, to the land which You swore to their ancestors? Where am I to get food to give this whole nation? They trouble me with their weeping, saying: Give us food to eat. I cannot bear this whole nation on my own because it is too much for me. If You treat me this way, then kill me, I ask You, out of hand, if I have found favor in Your sight, and let me not look upon my wretchedness" (Numbers 11:11–15).

The parallels with Eliyahu are even more remarkable. There we also find a flight into the desert, sitting down under a tree, and some of the same turns of phrase and even the same words that Yonah uses.

> He went a day's journey into the wilderness and sat down under a broom-tree. He requested for himself that he might die, saying: "It is enough. Now, O God, take away my life; for I am no better than my forebears." He lay down and slept under a broom-tree…. (1 Kings 19:4–5).

These parallels gain further significance when we consider that Yonah was not only a student of Eliyahu and of his students but also that he was literally infused with Eliyahu's spirit. The following is a description of how Eliyahu revived the dead child, who was Yonah.

> He said to her: "Give me your son." He took him out of her bosom and carried him into the upper chamber, where he stayed, and laid him upon his own bed. And he cried unto God, and said: "O Lord my God, shall You also bring evil upon the widow with whom I am staying by slaying her son?" He stretched himself upon the child three times, and cried unto God, saying: 'O Lord my God, I ask you, let this child's soul come back to him.' God heeded Eliyahu. The soul of the child came back to him, and he revived." (I Kings 14, 19–22)

> He went in therefore, and shut the door upon them twain, and prayed to God. He went upstairs and lay upon the child, putting his mouth upon his mouth, his eyes upon his eyes, and his hands upon his hands; and he stretched himself upon him; and the flesh of the

child grew warm. When he returned and walked in the house once to and fro; and went up and stretched himself upon him; and the child sneezed seven times and opened his eyes. (II Kings 4:33–35, a similar event with Elisha)

These prophets breathed their own essence into the lifeless body of the boy before them. In Eliyahu's case, the boy whom he revived is traditionally believed to have been Yonah.

Yonah was of the same measure as Eliyahu. Elisha anointed him (*Mishnat R. Eliezer,* quoted in introduction to the Artscroll edition of the Book of Yonah).

The son of the widow of Zarfat (described in I Kings 17 above) was Yonah (*Midrash Shocher Tov* 26:7).

Was it therefore surprising that Yonah carried out his charge in the same way that Eliyahu had done before him? Zealous, unbending and uncompromising in his mission, Yonah was "ben Amitai," which in Hebrew means "son of truth." He maintained his commitment to truth even against God's own truth. When principles confronted reality, he saw only one solution: "Therefore, O God, I beseech You now: take my life from me, for it is better for me to die than to live."

Eliyahu achieved the pinnacle of success, successfully leading a grassroots revolt against the idolatry of Baal and his servants, convincing even Ahab himself and running before the king's chariot in a celebration of God's triumph. Yet his success was reversed in the blink of an eye. When Jezebel sought to kill Eliyahu as she had killed so many other prophets, not one of his ecstatic followers or enthusiastic converts rose to defend him. Eliyahu asked for death because he knew that he and they had failed. Although God did not grant Eliyahu's request literally, he fulfilled it symbolically, taking the prophet "to Heaven while still alive" (II Kings 2).

Yonah thought that he had failed, but he had actually succeeded. Since it remained for God to demonstrate his success, He did not grant Yonah's wish. Moshe also thought that he had failed but in reality was on the brink of success. Since he needed to be made aware of this, God told him: "Now you shall see whether My word shall come true for you or not."

Yonah needed to be taught that truth and mercy are not mutually exclusive and that mercy sustains life. The rest of the chapter is about the completion of Yonah's education.

In the Booth of Lovingkindness (Yonah 4:5)

> Then Yonah left the city. He sat to the east of the city and made a booth there. He sat under it in the shade so that he could see what would happen in the city (4:5).

Although Yonah knows or at least suspects that Nineveh will not be destroyed, he refuses to resign himself to it. Why should he? Had he not upheld his principles against all odds in the past and attempted to argue with God's purpose before? He fashions himself a booth and stubbornly waits "to see what will happen in the city."

What is this mysterious booth? We would naturally assume that Yonah had some sort of shelter. Why, then, is this detail of the desert environment supplied while so many others are not? More surprisingly, the booth seems to disappear in the very next verse and a plant takes its place-"The Lord God appointed a ricinus plant which grew above Yonah to provide shade over his head...." What happened to the booth that provided the shade before?

Some commentators suggest that it must have withered in the hot sun during Yonah's forty days of waiting. Nevertheless, this does not explain why the booth was mentioned at all.

We may begin to understand the meaning of this enigmatic booth by reading the passage using structural analysis.

As noted above, the book of Yonah is designed like two facing pages of text with particulars of the second column mirroring the contents of the first. When seen in this way, Yonah's booth corresponds to the fish's belly. Yonah's three days inside the fish signify the three days of conception, while his forty days in the booth evoke the forty days of the formation of a fetus. Together these periods of time represent the stages of Yonah's maturation and inner growth towards acceptance of God's sovereignty and, above all, his mercy. A booth symbolizes this openness to the Divine. As Samson Raphael Hirsch pointed out in his well-known explanation of the commandment to build *sukkot,* a booth contains walls against the outside world, but its top is open to Heaven.[1]

When the prophet leaves the belly of the fish, he is ready to open his mouth and sing God's praise, but he is not yet ready to hear God speak to him. In fact, he speaks so much in order not to hear. The first level of denial has been breached but deeper layers remain in place. Complying reluctantly with his mission, Yonah goes to Nineveh, but refuses to accept God's forgiveness of the city and exiles himself to an area east of it. The east is

---

[1] *Collected Writings,* Vol. 8, Feldheim, 120–124

where the unrepentant go – for example, Adam, Cain, the builders of the Tower of Babel, and Lot, Abraham's nephew (Genesis 3:24, 4:16, 11:2, 13:11).

After Yonah complains to God that He is too merciful, God answers, "Are you so very angry?" (4:4). The plain reading is that this line represents a response. However, the Mesorah, the traditional guide to the punctuation and parsing of verses, indicates that there is a line (*setuma*) between Yonah's complaint and God's response. This signifies that verse 4 begins a new paragraph and is not the conclusion of the previous one. If so, it is not an answer to Yonah's current complaint but the beginning of a new chapter and should be translated as follows: "God said: 'Have you been sufficiently troubled?'" God initiates the conversation. This promises trouble, and trouble follows.

The rest of the story is about Yonah's troubles. He sits brooding in his booth east of Nineveh, grimly determined not to give in to God. Never will he accept that the world is ruled by Mercy. He wants Justice and the complete destruction of the wicked. Yet even as he obstinately refuses to accept it, a realization grows and takes shape within him that he himself, as a limited and weak human being subject to weakness and illness, must rely on Divine mercy for his very survival.

The booth disappears from our view and overnight Yonah's final spurt of inner growth, as sudden and unexpected as the sprouting of the ricinus plant, takes its place. Meanwhile, God waits patiently. When the time is right, He speaks to his prophet once more, completing the education of Yonah.

In the Desert

Yonah sat in his booth east of Nineveh for forty days, waiting "to see what would become of the city." As it appears from the description shortly thereafter, the place in which he found himself was dry and extremely hot. In Scripture, the east is generally associated with desolation and rebellion against God, since that is where the rebels eventually go. The mountains of Judah were flanked on the west by lush and fertile coastal land, but on the east by the Judean desert and the Dead Sea. The imagery of desert in Scripture, particularly in Psalms, often represents spiritual isolation.[2]

These bleak surroundings reflect the inner aridity that the prophet experiences during this part of his flight from God's redeeming kindness.

---

[2] It is interesting that in Kabbalah, on the other hand, the east represents kindness (chesed) or beauty (tiferet). See Zohar Lech Lecha 7; Noach 101 and 163, and *Midrash Talpiyos,* Kinuy ha-middot.

Just as the storm in Chapter 1 served as a metaphor of inner torment and turmoil, the desert brings the reader into the parched inner sanctum of the prophet, who sits bereft of and in rebellion against God's kindness. As in the earlier chapter, God intervenes to save his prophet in an unexpected way. Notice the parallel:

> God cast a great wind upon the sea…. The Lord appointed a great fish to swallow Yonah…. (1:4; 2:1).

> The Lord God appointed a ricinus plant…. God appointed a worm at dawn… which attacked the plant and it withered. (4:6–7)

Once more, God saves Yonah, and once more, Yonah does not appreciate God's kindness. Is it because of the terrible heat and dryness that surrounds him, or is it because of the desolation within?

There was another prophet who, in parallel circumstances, conducted himself similarly. As we mentioned previously, Yonah was the child of the Zarephite woman, a child whom Eliyahu brought back from the dead. Thus, he was a product of his master's holy breath and replayed his teacher's conduct almost to the letter. However, what God tolerated in Eliyahu was not acceptable in Yonah, and this fact contains an important lesson for us.

Are we destined to repeat the errors of the past or can we, with God's guidance, move beyond our own limitations? It is so hard to grasp truth when our constitution, upbringing and habits of thought obscure it from our sight. An appeal to precedent is not always helpful. The leaders of previous generations taught the truth as it was appropriate for that generation. We must follow the leaders of our own times in how they interpret the Torah in the circumstances of our own day – "You have only the sage in your own day" (*Sifri* Tavo 23:6). Although Yonah learned his master's teaching well, he did not draw the necessary conclusions from Eliyahu's life.

I Kings 14 tells us how Eliyahu brought a drought upon the land for the sins of Achav and the people of Israel. God commanded him to hide inside a stream, where ravens brought him bread and meat. When the stream dried up, God sent Eliyahu to a widow in the town of Zarephath. It was her child, Yonah ben Amitai, whom Eliyahu brought back from the dead. Despite the fact that he had caused the famine, Eliyahu still engaged in kind acts.

When the false prophets of Baal are miraculously subdued, the prophet flees "to the desert from fear of Jezebel," who has ordered him killed. As he lies near death, God miraculously sustains him with food and drink. However, the prophet can no longer tolerate his nation's sins. He walks forty days toward the sea but completes his quest at Mount Horeb – literally, the mountain of dryness. There he complains about the Israelites: "I have been jealous on behalf of the Lord of Hosts, for the Children of Israel have abandoned Your covenant. They have destroyed Your altars and killed Your prophets. I alone remained a prophet and they sought to take my life" (I Kings 19:14). Even though God still appears to Eliyahu, He does not respond to this, for it is not what He wanted to hear. Is it then surprising that at this point, Eliyahu's prophetic career is essentially over? He ties up a few loose ends, appoints Elisha as prophet in his stead and is taken in a fire to heaven.

The parallels between Yonah and Eliyahu are striking. Both are in the desert, unable to perceive that God is sustaining them with His kindness or to thank Him for it, and neither perceives that what the Holy One, blessed be He, really wants from them is an impassioned appeal for His mercy.

The Plan

> The Lord God [Hashem Elokim] appointed a ricinus plant that rose above Yonah to save him from [the sun's] evil. (4:6)

This is truly miraculous. A plant rises over Yonah's head, protecting him from the heat of the sun. Moreover, it grows to enormous size overnight (verse 10) without Yonah seemingly taking note. As described, the imagery is that of Yonah sitting in the desert, and suddenly a large and bushy leaved plant rises directly above him. Surprisingly, Yonah remains oblivious to the implications of this marvelous event.

What is the evil from which Yonah was saved? Although classic commentators understood it to be the heat of the sun, a suggestion has been made that it is the same 'evil' described in verse 1; in other words, the distress and frustration that seized Yonah when he realized that Nineveh would be saved after all (A. Rivlin, *Yonah: Nevuah ve-tochacha,* p. 168).

This is the only time in the Book of Yonah that the Hebrew text refers to God using the Tetragrammaton followed by the name Elokim. Most often, it employs the term Elokim, which is often translated as God. Among the few deviations from this pattern is when He appointed the fish to save Yonah (2:1); He was then referred to by the Tetragrammaton. We may well ask why the text uses the names YKVK Elokim here.

A comment by Rashi on Genesis 1:1 may enlighten us. He takes note that while the text uses the name Elokim in Chapter 1 of Genesis in order to describe the creation of the universe, it uses the name YKVK Elokim in Chapter 2. Rashi writes: "In the beginning Elokim made heaven and earth" – at first, God thought to create the world with the quality of Justice. He saw that if He did so, the world would not be able to survive, so He placed the quality of mercy before justice and made them partners. This is what Scripture means by "On the day that YKVK Elokim made heaven and earth" (Ch. 2). Thus the name Elokim stands for justice while the Tetragrammaton stands for mercy.

Yonah also found himself in the classic situation in which justice and mercy were intertwined, and in which mercy preceded justice.

> YKVK Elokim (the Lord God) appointed a ricinus plant that rose above Yonah to save him from its evil…. (4:6).

> God [Elokim] appointed an east wind and the sun beat down on Yonah's head (4:8).

Throughout his story, Yonah struggled against mercy as God's guiding principle for running the world. He wanted God to direct the world by justice, since he found the success of the wicked more intolerable than the suffering of the righteous. Yet he did not realize that the world is not run by either justice or mercy exclusively, but by both together. Therefore, it is no wonder that he did not understand the message that the ricinus plant's miraculous growth represented. At that point it was neither justice nor mercy, for when the plant grew over Yonah's head, he had not yet begun to suffer. God sent the cure before the illness (*Megillah* 13b), but Yonah could not see that.

Often, when events and situations occur whose significance we do not understand, we are being prepared for what is yet to come. As we have seen in past chapters, mercy requires that God's hand in history and in our own lives be hidden. If it were visible and open, we would have no freedom to choose good or evil and the attribute of pure, uncompromising justice would dominate the world.

Nevertheless, mercy waits to become manifest. We might say that the power of incipient evil is always countered by what already exists and by what has already been set in motion. Mercy always precedes justice and is already in place to meet and mitigate it.

Every human being has experienced events that appear to be disastrous when they happen, but are later found to carry the seeds of salvation. We have all known times when mercy preceded justice, but like Yonah we could not see that. People of faith find consolation in the idea that mercy precedes justice, which enables them to cling to God despite life's trials. By the very nature of existence, they have every reason to expect deliverance to sprout from the seeds that were planted and trust in God's salvation, which will surely come.

To Give Is To Love

> God appointed a ricinus plant that grew above Yonah to provide shade over his head. Yonah felt great joy about the plant. (4:6)

Why was Yonah so happy about the plant?

Imagine the prophet as he sat in the desert outside Nineveh, isolated and angry. Even God had told him that He was not happy with him. He had no hope that things would ever be better. Then, suddenly, a plant grew over his head.

Prisoners who have been in solitary confinement recall that their greatest suffering did not stem from the incarceration itself but rather from the lack of living companionship. In this state of complete isolation, many prisoners were saved from despair by the appearance of some living thing such as a mouse or even an insect. Perhaps now we can understand why the plant made Yonah so happy. It showed him that God still cared for him and was reaching out to him. But then, the hope that had begun to sprout within Yonah was crushed when the plant suddenly withered. At the loss of the plant and all that it represented, Yonah plunged to such a depth of sorrow that he wished for death.

While this explanation makes Yonah's joy understandable, it does not explain how the plant and the prophet's reaction to it become the crux of God's lesson about His Mercy.

> You had pity upon the plant, for which you did not labor, nor did you grow it…. Should I then not care about Nineveh, that great city, in which there are more than twelve myriads of people who do not know their right hand from their left, and much livestock? (4:10–11).

In order to understand the meaning of this rebuke, let us focus for a moment on the nature of attachment and love. R.E. Dressler explains in his work *Michtav me-Eliyahu*[3] that human nature is such that we love others when we invest in them something of ourselves. It is the giving of ourselves or, at the very least, a perception of ourselves being present in others that creates attachment and ultimately love. This is why we love our children, our neighbors and our communities, and why it is so difficult for us to love a stranger.

[3] Vol. 1, 35–37.

While R. Dessler does not mean to exhaust all there is to say about the nature of love, this is an important component in how we grow to recognize and love others, as it is written, "You shall love your neighbor as yourself."[4]

Yonah did not relate to the people of Nineveh. They were evildoers, cruel enemies of the Israelites, and foreigners. The lesson of the plant was precisely this: that lack of empathy stems from alienation and from seeing those outside ourselves as the "other." God was telling Yonah: "Even though you did not work for this plant, you loved it because you identified with it. It is only when we see others as ourselves that we can grow to love them as ourselves."

The Alshich comments that the first verse of the fourth chapter can be read as follows: "Yonah was angry, and that hurt him." Yonah was troubled by his inability to grieve for Nineveh's fate and by the inner barrenness that made him unable to accept God's mercy for the wicked city. Where were his generosity and graciousness? Did not other prophets mourn the destruction even of enemy nations? Had he lost all ability to care because of his own suffering and pain? The sprouting of the plant reassured Yonah that he was still capable of human feeling, still redeemable. When the plant dried up, Yonah felt as if his joy had not been sufficient or authentic enough to sustain it. Surrounded by desert and empty within, Yonah preferred death to life without love or feeling.

God's message to Yonah was simple and direct. "You loved the ricinus plant because your hopes were invested in it. You did not love Nineveh because you had given it nothing of yourself. You must give in order to love or feel pity. Shall I not have mercy upon the great city of Nineveh which I planted and sustained and in which I invested?"

> The Glory of God shall be forever. God shall rejoice over what he has made. (Psalms 104:31)

> Yonah felt great joy over the ricinus plant....

One has to give in order to rejoice and see oneself in others in order to love.

The Almighty Planter

As we work to understand the meaning of the ricinus plant's miraculous growth and death, we must stop for a moment to consider why its meaning is so hard for us to grasp. Some metaphors in Scripture speak to us directly,

---

[4] See a discussion in my book *With All Your Heart: The Shema in Jewish Worship, Practice and Life.* Jerusalem: Targum/Feldheim, 2002, 68–70.

while others remain obscure no matter how hard we try to decipher them. The problem may be our remoteness from the time, place, culture and language in which the Bible was written, or our distance from the world of prophecy and divine inspiration from which the text stemmed. When we are faced with such a difficulty, we must often turn to parallel passages in order to grasp the metaphor.

The perception in Scripture of God as Planter relates to three levels: the individual, the national, and Israel.

1. Individual

God's providence and patronage of individual is often expressed by Biblical writers in terms of planting a sapling or watering, pruning or uprooting a tree.

> He shall be like a tree planted by streams of water, that brings forth its fruit in its season and whose leaves do not wither, and whatever he does shall prosper. (Psalms 1:3)

> Is a tree of the field a human being, that you should lay siege to it? (Deuteronomy 20:19)

> Blessed is the man who trusts in God and whose trust God is. For he shall be as a tree planted by the water, that spreads out its roots by the river, which does not see when heat comes, but its foliage shall be luxuriant. It is not anxious in the year of drought and never ceases from yielding fruit (Jeremiah 17:7–8).

2. National

God plants and uproots peoples. The rise and fall of nations is in His hand and according to His will. Prophets cite this idea a great deal, and Jeremiah repeats it eight times. Here is one example.

> Then God stretched out His hand and touched my mouth, and God told me: Look, I have put My words in your mouth. See, this day I have set you over the nations and over the kingdoms, to root out and to pull down, and to destroy and to overthrow, to build and to plant. (Jeremiah 1:9–10)

3. Israel

Finally, the House of Israel, God's special inheritance, "the stock which Your right hand has planted, and the branch that You made strong for Yourself" (Psalms 80:16).

> Then the nations that are left round about you shall know that I, God, have built up the ruined places and planted that which was desolate. I, God, have spoken it, and I will do it. (Ezekiel 36:36)

> I will appoint a place for My people Israel, and will plant them, that they may dwell in their own place and be disquieted no more. The children of wickedness shall no longer afflict them as at first (II Samuel 7:10).

Isaiah has an entire chapter on this:

> Let me sing of my well-beloved, a song of my beloved about his vineyard. My well-beloved had a vineyard on a very fruitful hill. He dug it, cleared it of stones, and planted it with the choicest vine.... For the vineyard of the Lord of Hosts is the House of Israel, and the people of Judah the plant of His delight. (Isaiah 5:1–7).

The metaphor of the Divine Planter is somewhat foreign to the way that we think about God. However, in an agrarian society such as the Israelites once were, it must have been a basic and accessible image.

Is the ricinus plant supposed to remind Yonah of Who planted and sustains him? Does it represent Nineveh, that great nation, "the rod of My anger, which holds My indignation in its hand like a staff" (Isaiah 9:5), that God made to sprout temporarily, but whose destruction has already been determined? Could this shade-providing plant refer in some way to God's redemptive plan for His people Israel, "of whom we said: 'Under his shadow we shall live among the nations'" (Lamentations 4:20)?

It could mean any one of them, or all of them. One thing is certain: the plant is not a mere device, an opening for God's rebuke, but itself carries an important message about God's providence and about the One who lovingly plants, nourishes and maintains individuals and nations.

Yonah Breaks His Silence

Yonah's communication with God grows richer and more complex as the story unfolds. As a withdrawn child is taught first to listen, then to speak and finally to converse, Yonah's conversation with God starts with a denial, proceeds to the prophet praising God but not speaking to Him and continues with a complaint to which God responds. Although Yonah ignores God's answer, he is finally drawn into a true conversation with Him. To demonstrate the progression, each of these four instances of attempted communication repeats and expands the language of the previous one. The device of verbal restating and repetition focuses us on the stepwise progression of the conversation.

In 4:1, Yonah's prayer to God is described with the same words as in Chapter 2.

> This was a great evil to Yonah, and he prayed to the Lord…. (4:2)

This is an allusion to:

> Yonah prayed to the Lord from the belly of the fish. (2:2)

God responded to Yonah, but Yonah did not answer.

> The Lord replied, "Are you that deeply troubled?" (4:4)

This is exactly where the conversation picks up again next time.

> God said to Yonah, "Are you deeply troubled about the plant?" (4:9)

This time, however, Yonah answers,

> "Yes, to the point of death" (4:10)

Finally, Yonah is willing to listen, opening himself to the possibility of rebuke. No longer does he dismiss his opponent with silence. He is now engaged in a conversation, open to the unexpected, and there is no greater sign of growth than that. Finally, God can get through to Yonah, and He immediately tries to do so.

The most amazing things about the entire process of God's bringing Yonah to the stage where he is ready to hear are His patience and persistence. He pursues His prophet, sending one messenger after another, hoping and waiting for a response.

> And God made a great wind…. The Lord appointed a great fish…. The Lord God appointed a ricin plant…. God appointed a worm…. God appointed the east wind….

Finally, Yonah answers. When he does, the curtain is ready to fall, and Yonah's story will soon be completed. Although we are not prophets, we can also hear God's call "today, if you would hearken to His voice" (Psalms 95:7). Does this still apply even though the events of our lives are nowhere near as miraculous as those in the Book of Yonah and we never merit a direct revelation of God? Do we deserve such a revelation if we cannot make use of it? It took Yonah, who was an experienced prophet and an exceptional servant of God, a long time and several close brushes with death before his mind and heart were sufficiently open. Do we believe that we could do any better? Is it any wonder that prophecy has ceased?

However, even if we are not prophets, we are still "descendants of prophets" (BT *Pesahim* 66a). God speaks to us also in the language of everyday trials and tests. He gives us messages that He thinks we are capable of perceiving. It is for us to open our hearts, listen for the message and then respond appropriately – to kindness with gratitude, sincere prayer and increased Divine service and to misfortune, God forbid, with repentance and soul-searching.

Conversations with God are a funny thing: they require a great deal of preparation before they can even begin.

Justifying God's Ways (Yonah 4:10–11)

> God said: "You had had pity on the gourd, for which you did not labor and which you did not grow, which came up overnight and perished overnight. Should not I then have pity upon Nineveh, that great city, which contains more than one hundred twenty thousand souls who do not know their right hand from their left, and also much cattle?" (4:10–11)

Finally, God has an opening to make His case to Yonah. He reminds him about how he had felt about this short-lived plant, which He then relates to Divine Providence over Nineveh. One might expect God to be able to offer a convincing intellectual argument, but He does not. The argument is intentionally obscure, and its second part is a non-sequitur. This is not so uncommon in Scripture in general. In order to understand it, we will need a brief discussion of Biblical rhetoric and its use of parable.

Even a cursory reader of the Hebrew Bible will soon realize that it speaks directly to the heart. God speaks in order to motivate, not only in order to convince. The skillful use of narrative, poetic expression and grandeur of expression and sentiment characterize Biblical verse. This does not mean that Scripture does not employ logic. However, the goal is to make an impression, not to argue a case. The Bible's intent is not to lay out a logical or philosophic basis for religion. Its aim is to draw us into the inspired world of prophets, sages and mystics so that we may make it our own.

At first glance, God's argument is a logical one, what Hebrew calls *kal va-chomer* and Latin *a fortiori*. The essence of this type of proof is the demonstration that if a feature or characteristic applies to a less strict case, it should certainly apply also to a stricter one or vice versa. *Genesis Rabbah* 92:7 lists ten examples of this argument in Tanach, four in Pentateuch and six in the rest of Scripture. R. Ishmael's thirteen principles of interpretation[5] illustrate this first of his principles with the example of Miriam. "God said to Moses: 'If her father were to spit in her face, would she not be ashamed for seven days?'" – a fortiori for Divine. "Let her be isolated for seven days and readmitted afterwards" (Numbers 12:14).

The argument is that had Miriam been rebuked by her father, she would have placed herself outside the camp for seven days. Surely she should do at least that much after a Divine reprimand – a true *kal va-homer*. What is strange about this Midrashic passage is that it does not document many more apparently "a fortiori" arguments in Scripture.[6] Our passage in Yonah is one such example that is not listed in *Genesis Rabbah.*

I suggest that although, like the others not listed in *Genesis Rabbah,* our passage takes the form of a logical argument, it is in essence a parable, not a logical proof. That is why such passages are not listed.[7] A parable gives us access to a teaching that otherwise might be difficult for us to understand, forcing us to transpose elements of meaning from the parable to the passage that it seeks to elucidate. A parable must also set up tension between its apparent meaning and the one that it proposes. It must draw the audience into the process of reconciling the parable to its moral and stimulate interpretative solutions.

God's argument to Yonah does not make sense right away because it is a parable. Yonah's case and that of Nineveh do not match perfectly. Yonah loved the plant for the benefit that it gave him, while God spared Nineveh because its inhabitants "do not know their right hand from their left" or because they were so numerous. Certainly Yonah could have pointed out the dissimilarity between the two cases. However, God wanted to allow Yonah to justify His ways rather than bow down to His superior logic.

God wanted Yonah to take His place, even if only for a moment, and think about the world from His perspective. Yonah's ability to identify with God in the end and change his point of view demonstrates how much he has grown over the course of the story. It serves as an example for us and gives us hope.

---

5 Introduction to *Torat Kohanim.*
6 See *The Collected Writings of R. Matisyahu Strashun: Kal va-chomer.*
7 Alternatively, it is not uncommon in mishna and midrash to list a numerically significant number of examples, usually three, seven or ten, and to leave others out so as to preserve the significant number. This is called "*tanna ve-shiar.*"

Are We All the Same?

> Then God said: You cared about the plant which you neither worked for nor grew, which appeared overnight and perished overnight. Should I then not care about Nineveh, that great city, in which there are more than twelve times ten thousand people who do not know their right hand from their left, and much cattle? (4:11)

These words conclude the Book of Yonah. Yonah falls silent and does not respond. What, then, is the significance of these words and what lesson do they hold for us?

God's response to Yonah includes a great deal of mercy, which Yonah recognizes and which renders him speechless. He does not answer because the revelation of the extent to which God cares for His creatures contains the solution to his existential dilemma and, more importantly, the key to his soul.

The success of evildoers gave Yonah no rest. How could the prosperity of Nineveh – mistress of nations, oppressor of the world, the epitome of human degradation and man's inhumanity to man – be justified? How could God's partiality be defended? Although wicked Assyria dominated Israel, God's own inheritance, He refused to intervene. Moreover, He sustained Nineveh and showed it enormous patience.

Is there no justice before God? Does the Judge of the earth not deal impartially? Yonah was so convinced that Nineveh was the object of unjustified favoritism that he refused to listen because, as a man of integrity, he could not accept what he felt would be mere excuses.

As if that were not enough, God criticized Israel even as he showed favoritism to Nineveh. Therefore, Yonah challenged: Why are the wicked not held to the same standard as the righteous? When God gave him the answer with the power of simple truth, Yonah was speechless. God said: "… people who do not know their right hand from their left, and many beasts."

Who are the people who do not know their right hand from their left, and who are the beasts?

Some commentators assumed that the first clause refers exclusively to children and minor youths, who do not deserve to die together with the adults because they do not yet know right from wrong (Rashi, Rashbam to Numbers 23:9, Ibn Ezra, Radak). Rashi suggests that "many beasts" should be translated as "mature [rather than "many"] animals" and that the second part of the phrase refers to adults.

Nineveh was populated by children and adults who were little better than beasts, possessed no monotheistic religion and had never been taught to distinguish between good and evil. During the twentieth century, we encountered ideologies that called evil good and vice versa and, in this confusion of values, encouraged the commission of terrible crimes. Whole countries were filled with human beings who resembled beasts in their actions and willful ignorance. "The soul of a wicked person is called the animal soul because, like an animal, it is attracted [only] to physical desire, as it is written: 'and many beasts'" (*Shaarei Teshuva* 2:19, see also *Chullin* 5b).

What kind of Justice applies to those who suffer from ignorance? Medieval philosophers suggest that such people are not subject to individual providence. Instead, they are governed under the rules that pertain to animal species – group rather than individual justice (see *Guide* 3:17–18, 22–23, and Ramban's commentary on Genesis 18:19; Leviticus 26:11; Deuteronomy 11:13 and Job 36:7).

How should we view such primitive human beings? Do we feel envy and resentment over their success? We would if we were to think of them as being exactly like ourselves. But this is not correct because those who seek God and those who do not are not in the same league. "Do not lust after wicked persons. Do not be jealous of evildoers.... The wicked shall be cut off, but those who long for God shall inherit the earth" (Psalms 37).

Simply put, we and they could be considered as two different species. We live and function in different moral universes and are subject to different rules. Can we say that the Chofetz Chaim and Adolph Hitler belonged to the same species? Just as we take no offense when a dog barks at us, we need not be upset when such base people criticize us. Although we must pray to God for deliverance, we should not take personal offense at being held to a higher standard.

Let us look more closely at Psalm 37, which compares evildoers not even to animals, but to plants.

"Like grass they will quickly be cut down, and like herb of the field they will dry out. [Nevertheless,] trust in God and do good, dwell in the land and cherish faith." Although the wicked may prosper for a time, they will eventually be defeated. Their temporary success should not concern us. Good people must continue to do good and pay no heed to the temporary dominion of the wicked or their petty annoyances.

There will always be evildoers on earth. They are part of the human landscape. Sometimes God lets them linger, while at other times He quickly allows their deeds to bring on their own consequences. In either case, He has His reasons. We must bear in mind that we are not in the same category as they, and their success should not offend us.

Does this mean that good people should not care what happens to the wicked? Scripture does not teach this. Just as God has mercy upon all His creatures, we should also try to approach all human beings with love and kindness (when it is safe to do so) and teach them His ways of compassion, mercy, morality and goodness. Even wicked human beings are created in God's image and therefore have the potential to become good and great.[8]

At the same time, we must remember that the wicked are not like us in many important ways. We must not be tempted to keep company with them. Although good people and wicked people inhabit the same physical world, in the spiritual dimension they are far apart.

Although it is difficult to maintain a balance between caring with healthy emotional distance, such are the imperatives of religious life. The last sentences of the Book of Yonah tell us how to relate to those "who do not know their right hand from their left" and even to "great beasts."

Conclusion

The ending of the Book of Yonah makes us uncomfortable. What other Biblical book ends so abruptly and ambiguously, with so many unanswered questions? Did Yonah finally give in to God or did he persist in his rebellion? Where did he go, and what eventually happened to him? Above all, what does the book seek to teach us?

Besides being one of the briefest books in Scripture, Yonah is also one of the most mysterious and difficult. Although it is ostensibly a prophecy and was therefore placed among the Twelve Prophets, it reads like more a story. Although it appears to be about a man running away from God, it ends with God's finding that man and justifying Himself to him. It is the only Biblical tale that takes place entirely outside of the Land of Israel, with Gentiles playing all the supporting roles. It resists simple characterization and simplistic sermonizing.

Many scholars and commentators have attempted to explain this book and unravel its mysteries. We, too, have taken our place among those seekers and studied the book sincerely, with the strong desire to understand its message. Nevertheless, we have barely begun to penetrate its complexities and depth. We have taken the low-hanging fruit and been nourished, and now we are ready to go forth, strengthened and inspired.

---

[8] See a discussion in *Likkutei Torah* by the Alter Rebbe, at the beginning of Ekev.

To echo the *Hadran* formula recited at the conclusion of study of a book or tractate: "May we return to you, Book of Yonah, and may you come back to us. We shall not stop thinking about you, Book of Yonah, and do not stop thinking of us – neither in this world nor in the World to Come." May the insights we have gained remain with us, guiding us safely along our journey in this world and in the paths of Torah and wisdom as we continue to learn and study God's gift of the Torah.

While Yonah portrays a Jewish prophet who struggles with the world outside Israel, the Book of Ruth is built around the figure of a young Moabite woman who attaches herself to the Jewish people, finds meaning and purpose in her new nation, and becomes the progenitor of the Davidic line. The Book of Yonah deals with the relationship between God and humanity, while the Book of Ruth teaches us about the interactions between human beings. Its focus is the connection between the individual and society, between woman and man (and woman and woman), the role of idealism and faith vis-à-vis family, relatives and strangers, belonging and exclusion, and the role of kindness in cementing human relationships.

Yonah speaks of faith, trust in God and personal destiny that God imposes on the solitary human being; Ruth tells about redemptive power of kindness and benevolence and how one person gives to another. It teaches us how to live by our faith even among people who test it sorely. It helps us to understand the roots of the fascinating and mysterious figure of King David. Our ultimate hope is that it will show us how to achieve the balance between the private life of the spirit and its intense preoccupation with a personal God, and living within a community of other people and sharing their hopes, aspirations, and misfortunes.

While the Book of Ruth is about God and the human being in community, the Book of Yonah is about the individual and God alone together. Both books are about Redemption, for even as all human beings are alone in the world, we are also inextricably connected to one another and to God. There is no individual salvation within Judaism that is not ultimately also a redemption of community and the entire world. The Books of Ruth and Yonah complement one another in what they teach and the manner in which they do so.

"We shall return to you, Books of Ruth and Yonah, and you shall return to us. We shall not forget you, Books of Ruth and Yonah, and may you never forget us, neither in this world nor in the World to Come."

ABOUT THE AUTHOR

MEIR LEVIN is a physician, Torah scholar, and teacher who lives in Monsey, NY. A former pulpit rabbi and a popular lecturer, he is an author of *Novarodok: The Movement that Lived in Struggle and its Unique Approach to the Problem of Man* (Jason-Aronson, NJ, 1996), *With All Your Heart: The Shema in Jewish Worship, Practice and Life* (Targum/Feldheim, 2002), and *The Rabbis' Advocate: Chacham David Nieto and the Second Kuzari* (Yashar Books, 2006). Many of the essays in this book had been presented as a series on torah.org.